IMPRESSIONISM

IMPRESSIONISM

Phoebe Pool

BOOK CLUB ASSOCIATES · LONDON

*I am extremely grateful to Sir Anthony Blunt
for reading and criticizing the first chapter, and would also like to thank
Dr Robert Ratcliffe, Mr Alan Bowness and Mr Bruce Laughton,
all of the Courtauld Institute, for their helpful suggestions.*

THIS EDITION PUBLISHED 1975 BY
BOOK CLUB ASSOCIATES BY ARRANGEMENT
WITH THAMES AND HUDSON LTD

© 1967 THAMES AND HUDSON LTD LONDON
PRINTED IN GREAT BRITAIN BY JARROLD AND SONS LTD NORWICH

Contents

CHAPTER ONE
The roots of Impressionism 7

CHAPTER TWO
Pissarro, Renoir and Sisley up to 1869 37

CHAPTER THREE
Monet and Bazille up to 1869 61

CHAPTER FOUR
Events leading to the Impressionist exhibition of 1874 88

CHAPTER FIVE
The relationship of Manet and Degas to the Impressionists 118

CHAPTER SIX
The period of High Impressionism: 1874–c. 1880 151

CHAPTER SEVEN
Impressionism in the art of Cézanne, Gauguin and Van Gogh 179

CHAPTER EIGHT
The later works of Monet, Renoir and Pissarro 216

CHAPTER NINE
Impressionism outside France. Conclusions 251

Selected Bibliography 270

List of Illustrations 272

Index 282

CHAPTER ONE

The roots of Impressionism

The history of Impressionism is now so well known that we rarely pause to wonder why a group of friends, men of different temperaments and with widely dissimilar early experiences, should so rapidly have come to share so many assumptions about the nature of painting. Why did so many great painters commit themselves to an immediate and faithful rendering of some passing scene, actually before their eyes? Why did Monet, Pissarro and their friends paint mainly landscapes or city scenes, and only rarely human figures dominating their backgrounds? And why did they disdain the religious and historical subjects which in the 1860s and later were still the most admired and respected choice of more conventional and academic painters? Why did they all insist on painting in the open air, and on the use of bright prismatic colours? Why did they consider light and the exchange of coloured reflections as the unifying elements of a picture, instead of relying on the traditional method of construction based on drawing, outline or sharp contrasts of light and shade? Why do their canvases often display visible, choppy strokes of paint applied with a hog's-hair brush, rather than the smoother surface achieved by Delacroix and Corot, whose work they admired? How were they able to ignore or bridge the gulf which even a forward-looking critic like Baudelaire considered to exist between a spontaneous preparatory sketch and the finished work?

These are interlocking questions which we can answer no more dogmatically than Monet, Renoir and Pissarro themselves did. At no time did they enunciate a set of principles, nor were they inclined to produce manifestoes, as Courbet and Signac did. In common with many thinkers and writers of the 1860s and 1870s (such as Flaubert, Sainte-Beuve and the Goncourts), the Impressionist painters distrusted intellectual generalities. They created Impressionism in the

7

act of painting, and the evolution of their styles was undoubtedly influenced to some degree by obscure instincts, which they themselves could not identify or analyze. And unfortunately for the historian, there are no records of the many conversations they are known to have had on the meaning of painting.

Yet some clues to their development can be found in the impact of particular experiences and friendships on leading members of the group, and in their letters and notebooks. Also worth consideration is the cultural, social and political climate of the mid-nineteenth century, which affected painters in various new ways: for example, through easier communications, café life, and the sophisticated attempts of their literary friends and enemies to interpret them.

Before the French Revolution the artist had been considered, in the social scale, as someone in the order of a higher domestic or a lower civil servant. Several self-portraits emphasize the artists' hardworking respectability (for example, those of Chardin). But the Romantic generation, as portrayed by themselves, look proud, intransigent and totally unemployable. The first half of the nineteenth century, a period of social conflict and change, favoured the artists in their desire for status; as Malcolm Easton has pointed out, the *nouveaux riches* were in no position to disdain them. In spite of some eccentricities of dress in the more bohemian cafés, it was usual for painters to be sprucely and conventionally attired, as in Fantin-Latour's *Homage to Delacroix* (*Ill. 67*) and the picture of Bazille's friends in his studio (*Ill. 69*). Further evidence that the Salon artists, at least, were considered socially respectable is furnished by the attitude of the Superintendent of the Gare St-Lazare towards Monet, whom he mistook for a man of some substance (see p. 164).

It is well to remember that many of the ideas and practices fused together and transformed by the Impressionists were already nascent in the early years of the century. Even such neo-classical painters as Claude Michallon and Pierre-Henri de Valenciennes, who inspired Corot, made careful oil studies out-of-doors. Indeed, Valenciennes (*Ill. 1*) wrote a treatise on perspective which Pissarro recommended to his son. A more direct and concrete inheritance (acknowledged by the Impressionists in their maturity) was transmitted to the group

8

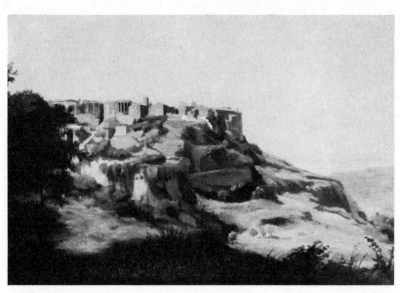

1 Valenciennes *Tivoli*

by admired forerunners and advisers, particularly Constable, Delacroix, the Dutch landscape painters, Corot, the artists working near Barbizon, Boudin and Jongkind, Courbet and Manet.

Various attitudes shared by the young Impressionists were derived from Romanticism – that complex and enduring change in European thought and feeling. Their distaste for painting that was too formal or overworked (what E.H.Gombrich calls 'the fault of faultless-ness') had its origins in Romanticism; and this was also true of their notion of the independent artist as a man always at war with accepted opinion and continually exploring the new and unknown. Their feelings about nature were certainly conditioned by one of the central features of Romantic ideology.

Jean-Jacques Rousseau's cult of the spiritual refreshment to be found in country solitude had permanently deepened and altered man's response to 'nature'. In the 1860s, which was the formative decade for Monet and his friends, there was a reaction against the Romantic self-projection and pathetic fallacies which had been fashionable in the two decades before 1850. Nevertheless, when

Pissarro wrote, 'Salvation resides in nature', or Monet, the arch-Impressionist, spoke of his 'constant commerce with the outside world' and declared that his only wish was to be fused with nature, they were using this concept in a sense that would have been impossible in the previous century. To Dr Johnson, Sir Joshua Reynolds or Diderot, the word 'nature' still meant common sense or a common standard ('What is pleasing to those in whom human nature is most highly developed'). On the other hand, the Impressionists were using it to signify the outside world, and particularly the country as opposed to the town. This use of the word sometimes implied that there was some link or interplay between the outside world and the soul of man, a notion expressed by Coleridge, Wordsworth and other writers of the nineteenth century. This feeling was reinforced by the dramatic and disagreeable industrialization of the period. When towns became too big, many people felt a sense of relief and recovery in escaping from them, especially poor young painters or poets from the country who found the new mammoth cities fascinating but also harsh.

The landscapes and city-scapes of the Impressionsts were inspired not only by this semi-religious emotion, but also by their observation of the ordinary habits of their day. By the time of the Second Empire a more hedonistic and informal attitude towards outdoor life had developed. The world of picnics and boating parties depicted by Renoir and Monet was not a daydream, an idealized *fête champêtre* in the Watteau manner; it was part of everyday life in France, as described in the fiction of Maupassant and the Goncourts.

The painters' bond with nature was often founded upon a genuine scientific curiosity and the desire for accuracy which prompted Degas (who was not, properly speaking, an Impressionist, as we shall see) to execute studies of different kinds of smoke and makes of bread. Constable had believed that painting should be a legitimate scientific pursuit, and during his stay in Hampstead he had made many accurate studies of the sky (*Ill. 4*), marking them with the exact time of day and direction of the wind. The same quasi-scientific attempt at accuracy can be seen in many of Théodore Rousseau's paintings: the *Marshy Landscape* (*Ill. 3*), for example, and the *Valley of Tiffauge,*

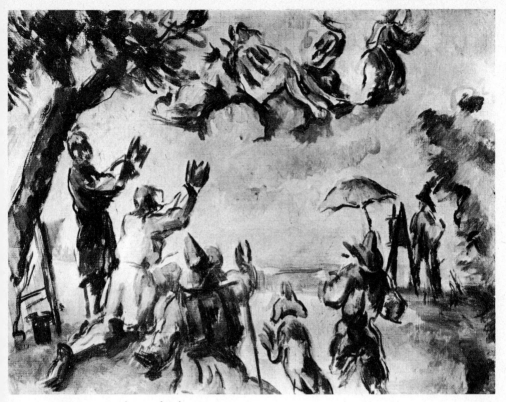

2 Cézanne *Apotheosis of Delacroix* c. 1894

a detailed rendering of rocks and marshy growths, which was criticized as being too pedestrian and was derisively nicknamed 'the soup of weeds'. Ruskin, in *Modern Painters*, analyzes sky and earth in an equally detailed manner, and Turner, though less of a naturalist and more of a picture-maker, had himself strapped to the mast of a tossing ship in order to observe the dynamics of a tempest. (Incidentally, although it has often been asserted that the high key of Turner's painting influenced the Impressionists, there is no evidence that his work was known in France early enough to have had this decisive effect. Monet, but only in some of his later works, may, however, have been indebted to Turner.)

In France, from the middle of the century onwards, there was a growing fascination with science. When Gautier assumed editorship of the *Revue de Paris* in 1851, his original programme was purely literary and aesthetic, but public demand soon forced him to include scientific topics. Even the new detective stories of Gaboriau contained pseudo-scientific vocabulary and clues. It is noticeable how often basically unscientific men such as Delacroix and Baudelaire refer to scientific discoveries and terms.

It is equally apparent that, for painters and writers alike, 'the true' was replacing 'the beautiful' as a word of praise. This change was epitomized by Sainte-Beuve, Manet's friend and one of Degas' favourite authors: 'The beautiful, the true, the good is a fine slogan and yet it is specious. If I had a slogan it would be the true, the true alone. And let the beautiful and the good get along as well as they can.'

Comte, the founder of the humanitarian philosophy of Positivism, had distrusted *a priori* principles, assigning prime importance to what was factual or the product of direct observation – a distinct parallel with Impressionist aims, as opposed to the *a priori* idealization of a painter such as Ingres. Although painters before Seurat did not make a systematic attempt to adjust their art to scientific rules, some of the new scientific discoveries must have come to their notice in the many popular booklets which began to appear.

However preoccupied the Impressionists may have been with their struggle for artistic fulfilment, they would have found it difficult not to notice scientific articles in the journals which we know they read. Paul Cézanne's mother and sister were subscribing to the *Gazette des Beaux-Arts* in 1865, at a time when Charles Blanc was writing his articles on colour. Cézanne's own interest is revealed by a note about the *Gazette* scribbled on one of the drawings for his *Apotheosis of Delacroix* (*Ill. 2*). If Cézanne was aware of these articles, Pissarro, with his tougher and more analytical mind, would surely have known them too.

The impact of science upon painters was, as one would expect, chiefly in the field of optical research, especially the constitution of colours and the structure of light. Among the spectacular advances of the times were those of Bunsen and Kirchoff (*c.* 1855) in connection with the spectrum, as a result of which the spectroscope became

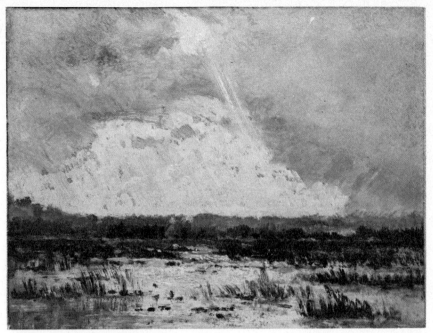

3 Rousseau *Marshy Landscape* 1842
4 Constable *Study of Sky and Trees* 1821

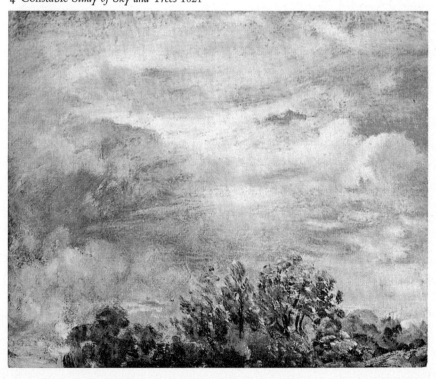

almost as important as the balance in scientific research. The fact that light is polarized by refraction had already excited an earlier generation when, in 1828, the Englishman James Nicol devised his famous prism. Between 1854 and 1862 the French physicists Arago and de Fresnel published their work on the polariscope, which included spectacular apparatus, such as revolving mirrors.

The scientist usually associated with the Impressionists' theories of colour is Eugène Chevreul, the French chemist. Chevreul began his research on colour harmonies after he had been appointed director of the dyeing department at the Gobelins tapestry factory in Paris, and his most important book, *The Principles of Harmony and Contrast of Colours, and their Application to the Arts*, was published in 1839. His principal thesis was that colours in proximity influence and modify one another. He also observed that any colour seen alone appears to be surrounded by a faint aureole of its complementary colour – that is, a red spot on a white ground will seem to tint its background green. (This phenomenon is now referred to as 'negative after-image'.) Chevreul also investigated what is known as optical mixture; in experimenting with woollen threads he found that two threads of different dye appear to have a single colour when seen together from a distance.

Writers such as Signac, in his *De Delacroix au Néo-Impressionnisme*, may have exaggerated Delacroix's systematic knowledge of the theories of Chevreul and other specialists in the study of colour. But in the latter part of his career Delacroix, whose example was important to the Impressionists, certainly observed colours and shadows in a way that would not have been possible before certain scientific conclusions about the constitution of light had been widely disseminated. In his book on Delacroix, Lee Johnson points out that a sheet in the back of one of Delacroix's North African notebooks bears a triangle, with the names of colours written against each side, and a note below it which might conceivably have been derived from Chevreul's book or from one of the popular treatises on the same subject.

As for the Impressionists, they were to be decisively influenced by Chevreul's discoveries; and there is direct evidence that Monet and

Pissarro (and, later, Seurat) had first-hand knowledge of his work. It was Chevreul's theory of optical mixture which eventually led the Impressionists to tinge shadows with colours complementary to the colour of the object casting the shadow. In addition, this theory led them to juxtapose colours on the canvas for the eye to fuse at a distance, thus producing colours more intense than could be achieved by mixing on the palette. The Impressionists also profited from the discovery that juxtaposed complementary colours, when used in large enough areas, intensify each other, whereas, when used in small quantities, they fuse into a neutral tone.

Pissarro (and, again, in due course Seurat) also studied the work of the physicists Hermann Helmholtz, James Clerk Maxwell and Ogden N. Rood. They came to realize that the brilliance of light could be rendered by allowing the spectator's eye to reconstruct it from the prismatic colours of which it was composed.

Basil Taylor has suggested that the widespread curiosity about the science of vision was responsible for the contemporary appeal of optical toys, such as the kaleidoscope and the stereoscope. What is more, optical discoveries hastened the development of the camera, which had a considerable effect on mid-nineteenth-century painting. Aaron Scharf, who has conducted extensive research into the relationship of painting and photography in that period, draws some significant conclusions. He shows that a number of photographers who habitually worked in the forest of Fontainebleau and in Arras were known to Corot and the Barbizon painters generally. He suggests that the sudden, quite radical change in Corot's style in the late 1840s was partly due to the influence of landscape photography and took place at the time of his friendship with Grandguillaume and Cuvelier, who were then feverishly engaged in photographic experiments. In early photographs taken on glass plates, a blurring, caused by moving forms, is discernible; also the strong sunlight is seen to have impinged on the structure of solid objects, eating into the shadows and, in foliage, creating the feathery appearance that is noticeable in Corot's later painting of trees. This effect, called 'halation', destroys the clarity of contour and, as in Impressionist painting, gives the sensation of movement.

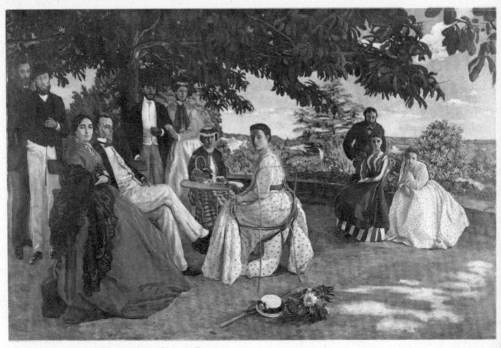

5 Bazille *Réunion de Famille* 1867

6 Monet *Boulevard des Capucines* 1873 ▶

Scharf's investigations reveal, indeed, that actual photographs were often used by the Impressionists as a basis for their compositions. Some of Frédéric Bazille's works, such as his *Réunion de Famille* (1867, *Ill. 5*) and *Terrasse de Méric*, strongly suggest that he consulted photographs. Cézanne's *Melting Snow in Fontainebleau* (*c.* 1880) was based on a photograph, as was his self-portrait (*Ill. 7*). And the representation of tiny pedestrians (much derided at the time) in Impressionist city scenes, such as Monet's *Boulevard des Capucines* (*Ill. 6*, included in the first Impressionist exhibition in 1874), duplicates exactly the effects found in contemporary photographs of similar subjects.

The influence of photography on Impressionism would be easier to assess had it not been the practice of the time to use photographs

16

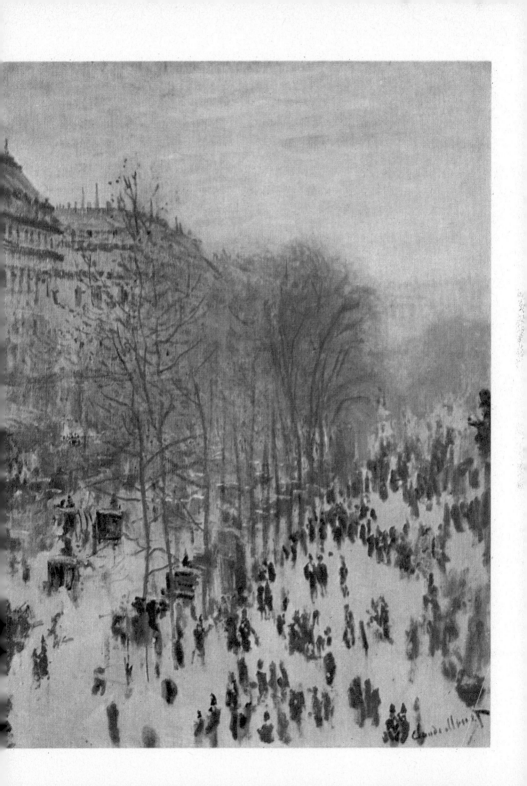

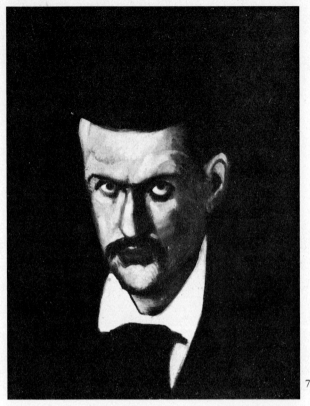

7 Cézanne
Self-portrait 1861

clandestinely. As Sickert wrote to *The Times*, in the words of a famous music-hall song, 'Some does it hopenly and some on the sly.' This secrecy was occasioned by the bitter attacks of critics, including Baudelaire, on photographic imitation as a threat to art. But photography could never rival the outstanding and original quality of Impressionist painting, which was the use of high-toned primary colours.

When the future Impressionists were first learning their *métier*, landscape painting was still regarded as being less important than the representation of supposedly more noble and elevated themes. It is

18

true that by 1817 an official award for landscape painting had already been established (by the same Valenciennes whose treatise Pissarro admired); but the very title of the award – 'for historical landscape' – hints at the barrier of prejudice which had to be surmounted before nature could be painted in its actual and haphazard state rather than in composed and imaginary forms. The traditionalists thought that nature in the raw lacked that sense of permanence and nobility which could only be imparted to it if its elements were rearranged to form an idealized whole. They also maintained that landscape should be embellished with human figures borrowed from the classical tradition. Those who held this belief controlled the Salon which, until Courbet and Manet opened private exhibitions of their own, remained the only place where a young painter could show his work. The Salon was the goal of the Barbizon painters, as it was of Corot and the early Courbet. At a later stage Manet still advised his friends, including the Impressionists, to show there, since it was the only place where they could find buyers other than the few friendly amateurs who already knew about their work. The jury of admissions and awards at the Salon was controlled by the Academy of Fine Arts, whose administrators also helped to decide which paintings should be purchased for museums as well as the award of commissions for mural decorations.

Corot, with his traditional training, almost instinctively marshalled and realigned his shapes in the manner that convention demanded. This attitude also prompted Fuseli's slighting reference in 1820 to 'that last branch of uninteresting subjects, that kind of landscape which is entirely occupied with the tame delineation of a given spot.' The same impulse was behind Baudelaire's later attack on the painters of Barbizon: 'In this silly cult of nature unpurified, unexplained by imagination, I see the evident sign of a general decline.'

The opposite of the new 'silly cult' was presumably to be found in the revival of the French Italianate tradition at the beginning of the century (Valenciennes, Hubert Robert, Victor Bertin, etc.); and still more, to go further back in time, in the great austere examples of formal landscape painting such as Poussin's heroic *Gathering of the Ashes of Phocion* (*Ill. 8*), in which horizontals and verticals are carefully balanced and the eye is led back into the distance by almost logical steps. Although Poussin could give an air of luxuriant nature to his compositions, he 'applies nature to his own purposes,' as Hazlitt says, and 'works out live images according to standards of his own thought.' This approach is utterly unlike the pure Impressionist submission to the immediate perception of the eye. In Poussin's picture the relationship between the harsh fable of Plutarch and the appropriately austere landscape is quite different from the camera-like objectivity which the Impressionists came to desire. The mood of Impressionist pictures has sometimes been compared with the cool, impersonal tone of *Madame Bovary*, and it was characteristic of the reaction in the 1860s against flamboyant and exhibitionist Romanticism to agree with Flaubert's dictum that the artist should no more appear in his pictures than God does in nature.

It is ironical that John Constable, who did so much to undermine the status of idealized landscape and whose work was one of the main influences on the emancipation of French landscape painting, should have been a great admirer of Poussin and Claude Lorrain. But although he copied their work until late in life, he did not lose his originality, nor did he abandon his stubborn reliance on observed facts. He sought for what he called 'the Chiaroscuro of nature in the

8 Poussin *Gathering of the Ashes of Phocion* 1648

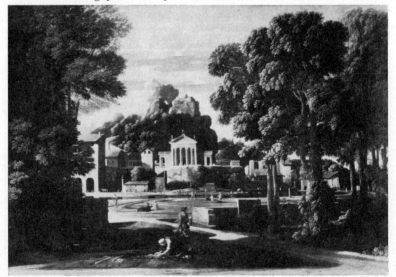

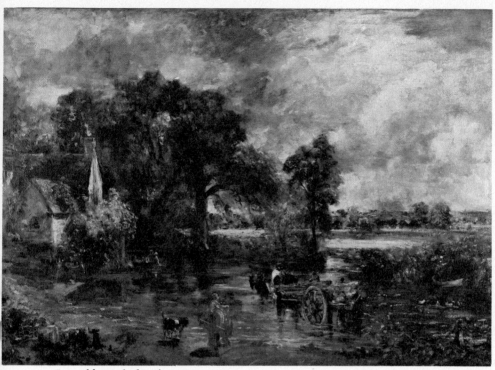

9 Constable *Study for The Haywain* 1821

dews, breezes, bloom and freshness, not one of which has yet been perfected on the canvas of any painter in the world', and he rendered them by broken touches and flecks in pure white applied with a palette knife. When his picture *The Haywain* (*Study, Ill. 9*) appeared at the Salon of 1824 it made the French realize, as the hostile critic Délécluze admitted, how 'heavy, insensitive and false was their colouring'. Chief among the new features which they found in Constable's work were the use of vivid colours divided into component elements, the depiction of homely scenes unencumbered with classical associations, and an interest in the sky as a source of light.

Frédéric Villot, who taught Delacroix the art of etching, has left an account of the effect *The Haywain* had on his pupil. Although *The Massacre at Chios* (*Ill. 10*) was almost finished, Delacroix was so struck by the brilliance and texture of Constable's picture that he gave his own an increased transparency by means of glazing and by the addition of impasto (thick pigment) for effects of light. He covered the arm of the old woman with small patches of pink, orange, yellow and pale blue, and enlivened the sand in the foreground in a similar way. About twenty years later, Delacroix recalled in his journal:

'Constable says that the superiority of the greens in his meadows is due to the fact that they are made up of a large number of different (juxtaposed not mixed) greens. What gives a lack of intensity and life to the ordinary run of landscape painters is that they do it with a uniform tint.'

Constable's work was quickly appreciated by certain French art-lovers. John Arrowsmith, a Parisian art dealer, had visited London by 1825 and bought *The Haywain* and *The Bridge on the Stour*; later

10 Delacroix *Massacre at Chios* 1824

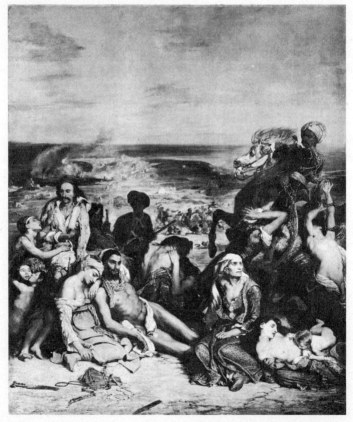

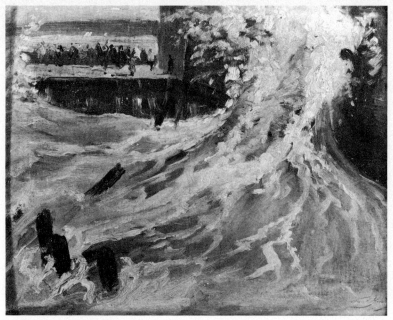

11 Huet *Stormy Sea* 1826

he bought six more pictures. A Constable sketch was bought by
Jacques Auguste Regnier, who painted historical landscapes and
admired the novels of Scott. Another dealer ordered three pictures
which he specified should be 'Hampstead views' – those in which
the sky was represented in a novel and meticulous way. Théodore
Rousseau was a friend of Arrowsmith, and he and other Barbizon
artists sold and exhibited their pictures together with Susse and
Mme Hulin, who owned Constables. Paul Huet, the friend of
Delacroix and Bonington, copied works of Constable, and this
influence can already be seen in Huet's *Stormy Sea* (1826, *Ill. 11*) and
Distant View of Rouen (1828). The broken forms and colours in
pictures by Troyon also show Constable's influence. Above all,
Daubigny's sunsets, with their free brush-strokes, recall 'the
Chiaroscuro of nature' in Constable's oil studies.

It is not surprising that the more orthodox critics became alarmed
by the vogue for Constable and begged artists not to be seduced from
their allegiance to Poussin by these formless and sketchy works. After

23

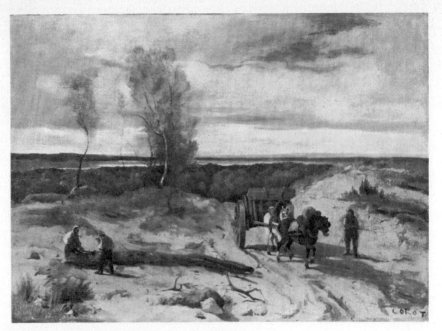

12 Corot *Fontainebleau, le charretier et les bucherons c.* 1835

13 Corot *Forest of Fontainebleau* 1846

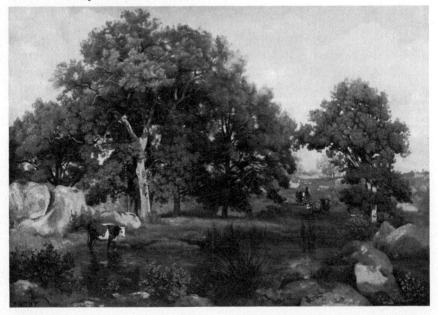

1827 Constable was less openly discussed in France, but in 1863 Théophile Thoré-Burger, a perceptive critic and friend of Théodore Rousseau, declared that Constable had been a major force in the regeneration of French landscape painting. Delacroix, as leader of the group of painters who were trying to achieve the admission of Rousseau's works to the Salon, and Thackeray, who knew Paris well as an art student, expressed the same view.

Constable, however, was not the only English painter to influence the French landscape school. It was probably as early as 1819–22 that Corot encountered the new school of realistic English landscape painting in the shape of a watercolour by Bonington. The English topographical artists were also producing travel books of a pictorial directness and fidelity that were new, since their aim was to record specific places. Girtin published at least twenty aquatints of Paris and its surroundings, and Cotman likewise produced a number. Besides travel books, English prints were bought in huge numbers during the mid-1830s, and Charles-Émile Jacque found it necessary to go to England to learn how to make them.

The East Anglian school of landscape painting had, in its turn, been deeply indebted to the Dutch masters of the seventeenth century, in particular Ruysdael, whose renderings of vast skies and shadowy plains anticipated Constable's maxim: 'Remember that light and shadow never stand still.' It is worth noting that the Dutch school of realistic landscape painting arose, like Impressionism, in a bourgeois society eager to recognize experiences and sights embodied in art, and also at a time of scientific curiosity (primarily in the fields of optics and botany). The new taste in France for English art and the desire for more direct renderings of landscape helped the French masters to appreciate these Dutch paintings, of which there were many examples in French collections. Rousseau, Daubigny and Jacque all copied Dutch pictures, and Rousseau owned four paintings attributed to Bruegel, as well as fifty prints by Ruysdael, Rembrandt and others. Corot went to the Netherlands in 1854 and kept notes of his search for animal subjects in the works of Paulus Potter, Berchem and Van der Meuler. His *Forest of Fontainebleau* (1846, *Ill. 13*), in the Boston Museum of Fine Arts, is also rooted in the Dutch tradition.

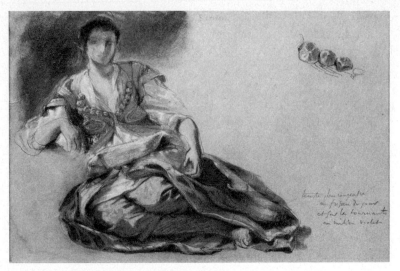

14 Delacroix *Study for Femmes d'Alger* 1833–4

The Impressionists all submitted at one time or another to the influence of Delacroix, and were themselves under no illusion as to their debt. As Lee Johnson observes in his book, which is the best guide to Delacroix as a colourist, it was only in later times that the high degree of realism in this artist's colour was overlooked in favour of its un-naturalistic subject-matter. Delacroix transmitted to the younger generation his ideas about colour, some of which he had drawn from Constable. He also checked the domination of Ingres by stressing colour rather than line and by neglecting static balance in favour of rivers of movement. By his use of light, he often avoids an over-precise arrangement of space and the neat formal outlines which had been customary – thus facilitating some of the Impressionists' experiments.

Delacroix was an even more revolutionary colourist than either Courbet or the Barbizon painters. By 1841 he believed that the most violent discords in nature could be reconciled by the unifying atmosphere and the interaction of colour reflections. His pictures are far less airless than those of his contemporaries. By banishing earth-colours and using pure, unmixed hues, Delacroix anticipated the

Impressionists. 'It is well [he wrote] if the brush-strokes are not actually fused. They fuse naturally at a certain distance by the law of sympathy that has associated them. The colour thus gains in energy and freshness.' He also noted that the addition of black sullies a colour, and does not create a half-tone. One can see the effect of these ideas in his *Femmes d'Alger* (1833–4), which shows the modifications of local colour made by daylight. Thus Delacroix notes on a pastel study for the figure at the far left that the colour of the skirt is more red at the turning of the folds, but more violet in the less illuminated parts (*Ill. 14*). In this picture he has also produced grey half-tones by blending red and green, instead of using grey.

When Antoine Guillemet refused to participate in the Impressionists' first exhibition in 1874, Corot is said to have congratulated him in these words: 'You were damned right to escape from that gang, my boy.' Yet critics hostile to Impressionism went round that first exhibition moaning, 'Oh Corot! Corot! What crimes are committed in your name!'

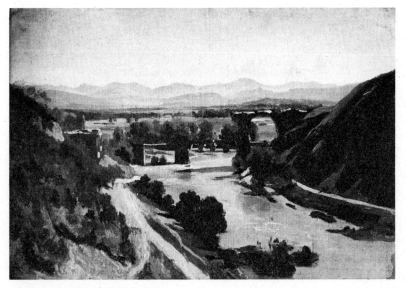

15 Corot *Le Pont de Narni* 1826

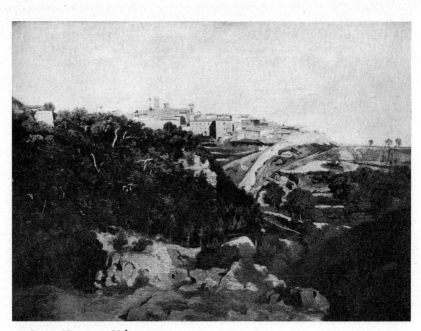

16 Corot *View near Volterra* 1834

Certainly Corot, who showed how to eliminate false shadows and artificially dark tones, creating space instead of tonality, played a part in the formulation of Impressionism. He abandoned many Renaissance devices in favour of flatter spaces and simpler, more luminous surfaces, particularly in the studies he executed between 1840 and 1863. Unlike the Impressionists, he did not break up light into its constituent colours, and he invariably arranged and simplified his shapes in order to achieve a classical pattern. But he often used brilliant white underpaint and a high tonal key, and, in general, his freshness and spontaneity were new to the official Salon.

In a sketch-book of 1856 Corot advised the student above all to submit to the first impression: 'Never abandon it, and in seeking truth and accuracy never forget to give it that "wrapping" which we have devised.' This emphasis on truth, accuracy and the first sensation is similar to the Impressionists' ideals. Corot is supposed to

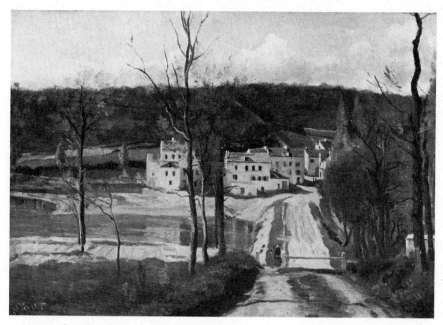

17 Corot *L'Hôtel Cabassus à Ville d'Avray* 1835–40

18 Corot *Harbour of La Rochelle* 1852 (Yale University Art Gallery)

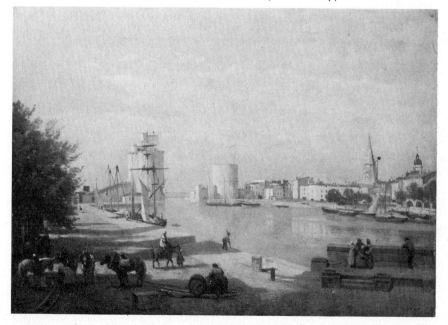

have told the Swiss painter Albert Barier that Constable's example had assisted him, since Constable 'was a man who felt as I did'. Corot himself taught the Morisot sisters and Pissarro, who always revered him. As in the case of Constable, there was at first a great stylistic gap between his little sketches and the big works intended for official exhibition. But by the late 1840s he had learned to bridge this gap, and works such as his *View near Volterra* (*Ill. 16*) and *Harbour of La Rochelle* (1852, *Ill. 18*) combine vivid immediacy with subtle composition.

Once the Barbizon school, particularly Rousseau, Daubigny and Millet, had adopted open-air painting (and Rousseau began as early as 1827), anecdotalism declined and illusionism, together with the study of light, progressed rapidly. Rousseau called light 'the secret of Prometheus' and wrote: 'Without light there is no creation, everything is chaos, death or pedantry.'

The Barbizon painters, when compared with the mature Impressionists, seem to aim at achieving an effect of permanence: their light is so much less free and changeable, so much more closely bound to the objects represented. Yet if we compare them with painting of an earlier period, their light is extremely variable, and Rousseau and Daubigny even painted what were virtually a series of the same subjects under different conditions of light and weather – thus anticipating Monet. Daubigny was often attacked for painting only 'an impression'. Gautier made this charge against him in 1861, and in the next sentence accused him in effect of being an Impressionist in the manner of Monet. 'Each object is distinguished by a real or apparent contour, but the landscapes of M. Daubigny offer little more than a juxtaposition of spots of colour.'

Thus amongst the Barbizon painters the visual approach gradually ousted the structural. Eventually artists were to become more interested in the small dabs of paint than in what they represented. But Millet, Rousseau and Daubigny did not reach that point; they still had a more Romantic interest in nature. As Rousseau said: 'I understand by composition that which is in us entering as deeply as possible into the external reality of things.'

There is no lack of evidence for the influence of the Barbizon painters on the Impressionists. The young Monet's letters to Boudin, written from Paris, are full of praise for them. Thus in 1859 he declared: 'The Troyons are superb and for me the Daubignys are really beautiful . . . there's a clever fellow for you who knows what he's about and who understands nature. . . . The Corots are absolute wonders.' And a year later he saw an exhibition of the school of 1830 which proved 'that we are not so decadent now as people think'; after mentioning 'the splendid Delacroix', he cited Millet and Corot. As early as 1856, when he had very little money, Monet bought a Daubigny.

The Barbizon painters developed in a period when a whole literature of country life came into vogue. Since 1832 George Sand had been celebrating her native Berry, which her friends Rousseau and Dupré liked to paint. Then Pierre Dupont published a novel called *Les Paysans* and a collection of lyrics, *Chants Rustiques*; and Courbet's friend Max Buchon translated German rural poetry as well as collecting the songs of the French countryside. The Barbizon group benefited from the revolution of 1848. Louis Blanc and the Fourierists had been demanding an art of actuality, and after Charles Blanc was made director of fine arts, state commissions were awarded to Millet, Rousseau, Daubigny and Dupré. But the social basis of the conflict between academic art and realistic landscape painting was underlined by Count Nieuwerkerke who, as Superintendent of Fine Arts, directed official patronage under the Second Empire; he said of the Barbizon painters: 'This is the painting of democrats, of those who don't change their linen and who want to put themselves above men of the world. This art displeases and disquiets me.'

Another painter who would have disquieted Nieuwerkerke after 1848 was Gustave Courbet, whom the public associated with Barbizon and whose style does in fact owe something to Millet and to Rousseau's paintings of the Auvergne. Courbet was more important to the Impressionists as a noisy, liberating force, a man who taught them not to fear subjects which seemed unpromising and casual, than as the exponent of any particular new technique. None of the Impressionists could have ignored his vehement statement of

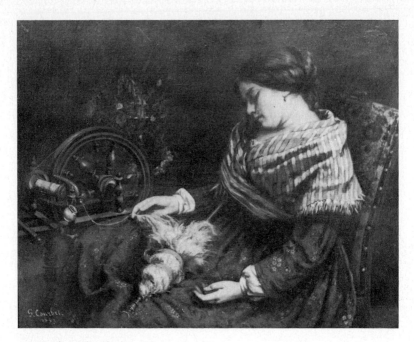

19 Courbet *The Sleeping Spinner* 1853

realistic principles in the *Courrier du Dimanche* in 1861: 'I hold that painting is essentially a concrete art and does not consist of anything but the representation of real and concrete things.' When Renoir was drawing from the antique in Gleyre's studio the master demanded: 'Can't you understand that the big toe of Germanicus has to be more majestic than the toe of the local coal-man?' Courbet's example helped to free Renoir from such thinking, and in about 1865 not only Renoir, but also Cézanne and Pissarro were trying to adopt the broad principles of Courbet's work, even imitating his use of the palette knife. A work like Renoir's *At the Inn of Mother Anthony* (1866, *Ill. 20*), executed in Fontainebleau, draws upon Courbet's factual and simple treatment, on a big scale, of everyday life, as in *After Dinner at Ornans* and *The Sleeping Spinner* (*Ill. 19*). Other works by Renoir, such as *The Painter Le Cœur in Fontainebleau Forest* (*c.* 1866), show Courbet's influence as a colourist.

32

20 Renoir *At the Inn of Mother Anthony* 1866 ▶

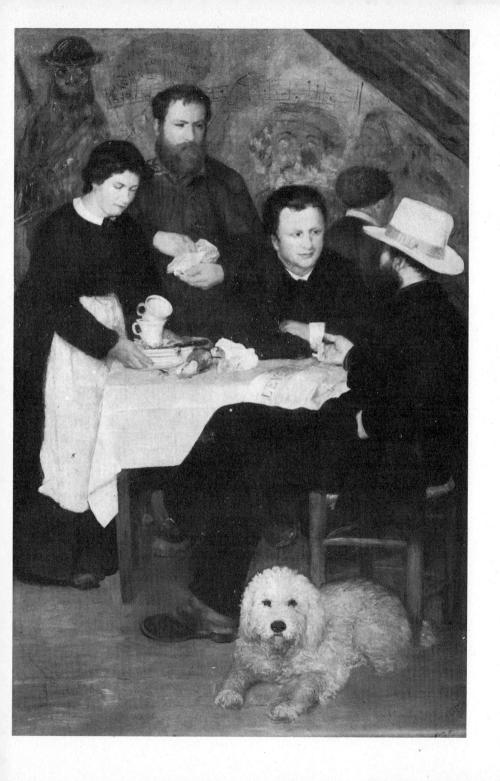

In his modest autobiography, published in *L'Artiste* in 1887, Boudin wrote: 'I may well have had some small measure of influence on the movement that led painters to study actual daylight and express the changing aspects of the sky with the utmost sincerity.' Certainly his effect upon Monet before 1863 was decisive. They met in Le Havre during 1856–7 and Boudin persuaded Monet to abandon the caricatures he had been making and to work on landscapes out of doors. 'It was as if a veil had suddenly been torn from my eyes,' wrote Monet. 'I understood. I grasped what painting was capable of being.'

Boudin influenced Monet's pictorial vision to the end of his life. The former had a gift that was almost Impressionistic for improvising on the actual canvas, and Baudelaire, who had met him in Le Havre, was particularly struck, on seeing his work in the Salon of 1859, by Boudin's direct jotting of the sea and sky as they changed according to season, time of day, and wind.

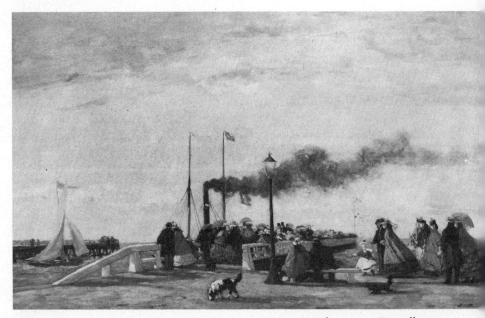

21 Boudin *Jetty at Trouville* 1865

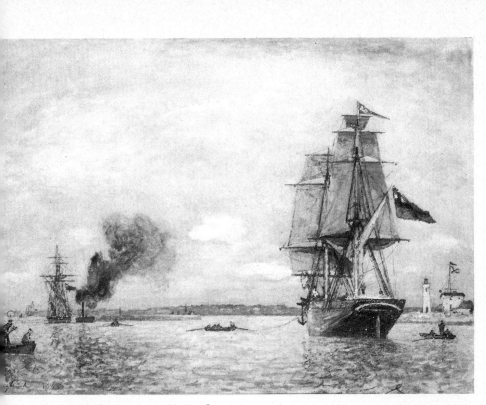

22 Jongkind *Sortie du Port de Honfleur* 1865

Monet was also affected by the work of the Dutch painter J. B. Jongkind. In 1862 Jongkind returned to the region of the lower Seine where he had previously worked with J. B. Isabey. In the interval, although he had some success at the Salon with views of Norman harbours, he had fallen into such frequent bouts of drunkenness that Monet wrote to Boudin: 'Do you know that the only good marine painter we possess, Jongkind, is dead as far as his art is concerned? He is quite mad.' By 1862, however, Jongkind had recovered, and until 1866 he spent the summers at Le Havre, Sainte-Adresse and Honfleur, working alongside Boudin (*Ill. 21*) and Monet, and producing vibrant and luminous watercolours of considerable power. He was a bolder, more stormy character than Boudin, who admitted,

'I came in by the door which he had already forced.' Monet, for his part, based his *Breakwater at Honfleur* (*Ill. 46*) on a contemporary canvas by Jongkind.

Looking at Jongkind's watercolour *The Beach at Sainte-Adresse* (1863, *Ill. 23*), one can appreciate Edmond de Goncourt's verdict of 1882: 'One thing strikes me – the influence of Jongkind. All the landscapes valued at the moment derive from him – they borrow his skies, his atmosphere, his terrain.' In 1897 Roger Marx declared: 'The élite, but only the élite, recognize him as the initiator of Impressionism.'

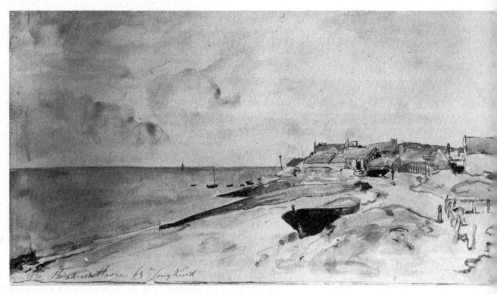

23 Jongkind *The Beach at Sainte-Adresse* 1863

CHAPTER TWO

Pissarro, Renoir and Sisley up to 1869

Camille Pissarro was the oldest, the most capable of dullness, and yet, next to Monet, the most influential of all the Impressionists. His influence was partly due to his seniority; by 1871 he was already over forty and had attained a degree of maturity and accomplishment, whereas his friend Monet, ten years younger, was not yet fully expressing his varied range. But qualities other than age made Pissarro capable of being, at different times, the mentor of Gauguin, Van Gogh and Cézanne, who said of him, 'He is a man worth consulting and something like God Himself.' Pissarro felt strongly that there was a connection between the emancipation of the artist's vision and the freedom of man, and also that any skill or knowledge acquired by the individual should belong to the whole community. An anarchist in politics, he was by temperament the least quarrelsome and intransigent of all the Impressionists, and his quiet tenacity did much to hold the movement together in its early days. He was the only one of the major Impressionists who showed works at all eight of their exhibitions.

Pissarro's art is less intense than that of his great followers Van Gogh and Cézanne. The sobriety of his pictures occasionally verges on the commonplace. His perseverance may have been responsible for some of the dull patches in his work, for he painted as a routine even when he had no compelling experience to communicate. Jerrold Lanes, in his review in the *Burlington Magazine* of a large Pissarro exhibition in New York (1965), wrote of him severely as an artist who kept returning to the same problems without solving them. He was an extremely eclectic artist, and, as Lanes says, eclecticism, to succeed, requires synthesizing powers of a higher order than Pissarro had. He found it difficult enough when young to fuse such diverse styles as those of Corot, Renoir and Millet. Later, he failed when he tried to assimilate the art of Monet or Seurat whole.

37

Pissarro had a far stronger sense of underlying structure than most of the Impressionists, perhaps because he practised drawing regularly, as Degas did, and he repeatedly urged his son Lucien to do the same. A writer in the *Burlington Magazine* in 1920, when the word 'Impressionist' was virtually a term of abuse among art critics, even expressed the doubt that Pissarro could be called an Impressionist at all, since he seemed so much more interested in earth and solid substances than in light or water. The charm of his pictures, like that of Constable's, often derives from the sense which they give the spectator of pleasurable recognition of the subject – frequently the peasants and countryside of northern France. Pissarro knew that his was a reticent talent which did not always appeal at first glance, but when he writes of his 'passivity of a Creole' we should remember that on many occasions he was capable of brave and positive action.

Born in 1830 at St Thomas in the Virgin Islands, Pissarro was the youngest son of a merchant of Spanish-Jewish descent who had married his own aunt and kept a fairly prosperous general store. Pissarro was sent to school in Paris and began to show a taste for art while he was there. In 1847 he returned to work as a clerk in his father's store, but devoted most of his time to sketching the exotic life around him. After five years he ran away to become a painter, sailing to Venezuela with Fritz Melbye, a Danish artist whom he had met in St Thomas. His parents then decided that, if he must paint, Paris would be a better place for him. Thus he arrived in Paris again, at the age of twenty-five, in time to visit the enormous World's Fair of 1855. Among the innumerable paintings on exhibition there were only six by Corot, but these were the ones which most impressed Pissarro. Indeed, he paid Corot a visit on this occasion. He also liked works by Courbet, Daubigny and Millet. After a short spell at the École des Beaux-Arts he began to attend the free classes of the Académie Suisse. He was promised help by the painter Antoine Melbye, his friend's brother, and when he sent his first picture to the Salon of 1859 he was listed as Melbye's pupil.

The earliest surviving works by Pissarro (many were destroyed by the Prussians in the war of 1870–1) are exotic views executed just before and after he went to Paris, such as *Cocotiers au Bord de la Mer,*

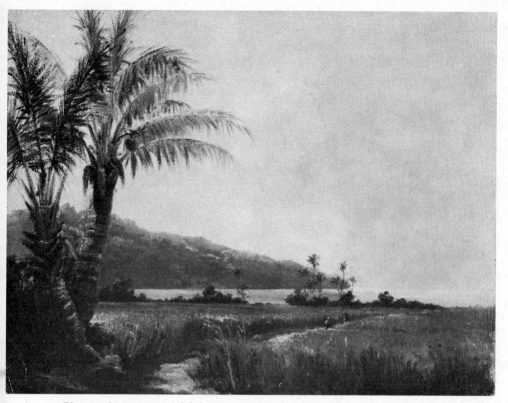

24 Pissarro *Cocotiers au Bord de la Mer, St Thomas* 1856

St Thomas (Ill. 24). This picture is rather in the style of the Orientalists Alexandre Gabriel Decamps and Eugène Fromentin, although it has clearer, lighter tones than their work. A number of scenes of the Ile-de-France, painted in 1856–7, recall works by Corot, but even this early in his career Pissarro was more interested than Corot in distant planes and the organization of space, and certain lights behind the trees are unlike anything by Corot. It is possible that Pissarro's use of high colours, which continue to appear intermittently in his works, may be attributed in the first instance to Daubigny's example. On the whole Pissarro's colours are clearer and more naturalistic than the grey-green or silvery tones of Corot; for example, where Corot would use a grey, Pissarro often used a powdery blue.

It was characteristic of Pissarro that, in spite of the romance with which his contemporaries invested 'the big city' and its new mammoth developments (best expressed in Baudelaire's *Les Fleurs du Mal*, 1857, and *Peintre de la Vie Moderne*, 1863), he soon began to make his way to the countryside outside Paris. Indeed that first picture he sent to the Salon of 1859 was a scene in Montmorency near Pontoise, an area well known for its forests.

Although Monet was working at the Atelier Gleyre, Pissarro seems to have met him at the Académie Suisse, some time before 1860. According to Monet's recollections, Pissarro 'was then tranquilly working in Corot's style. The model was excellent; I followed his example.' In 1863 Pissarro was apparently warned by the critic Jules-Antoine Castagnary against a too passive imitation of Corot.

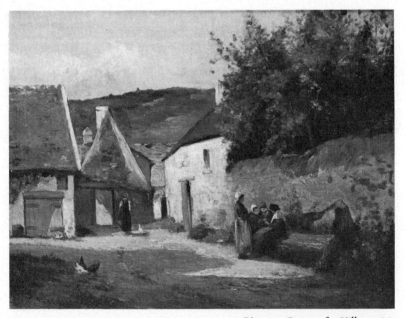

25 Pissarro *Corner of a Village* 1863

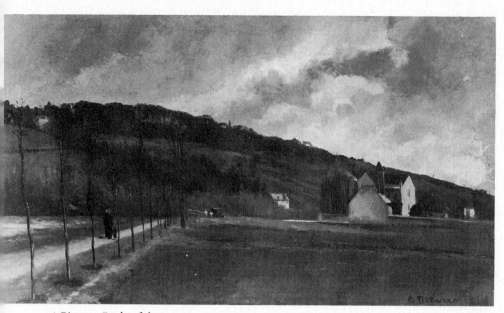

26 Pissarro *Banks of the Marne in Winter* 1866

However, there are works of about this date, such as *Corner of a Village* (*Ill. 25*), in which the motif might have been borrowed from Corot but has been transformed into Pissarro's own idiom by the lighted surface of the roofs and the spatial treatment of the houses. Another characteristic touch is the setting of the motif far back, as in *Banks of the Marne in Winter* (*Ill. 26*), exhibited at the Salon of 1866. Its solidity of construction blends very happily with a chromatic lightness. One can already see the beginnings of the influence of another master, Courbet, in the use of the palette knife, but Pissarro's colours in this picture are less dour than those that Courbet used. By 1865, Pissarro's palette was becoming noticeably lighter and he was beginning, according to Venturi, to avoid black bitumen, sienese brown and ochre. Some of his landscapes after 1866 were painted entirely out of doors, and John Rewald records that already at this time Pissarro was encouraging his friends to work directly from nature.

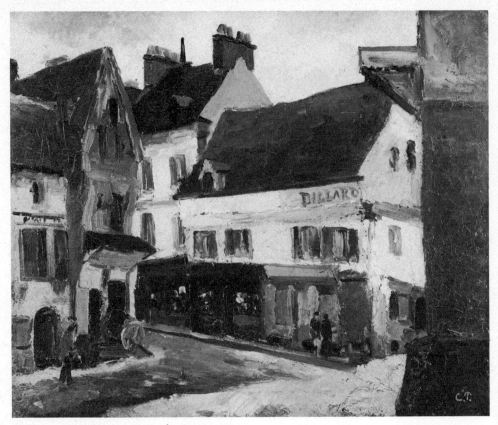

27 Pissarro *La Roche-Guyon* 1866–7

In 1864 and 1865 Pissarro exhibited at the Salon as a 'pupil of Corot', but after that there was a falling out between them. It is believed that the young painter had displeased Corot by gravitating towards the more realistic style of Courbet and, in particular, adopting increasingly Courbet's method of opposing light and dark masses in preference to Corot's more tranquil, poetic depiction of nature. The sombre brown and grey-coloured *La Roche-Guyon* (1866–7, *Ill. 27*), with its emphasis on contrasting planes, shows Pissarro, like Cézanne and Renoir, imitating the broad principles of Courbet's art.

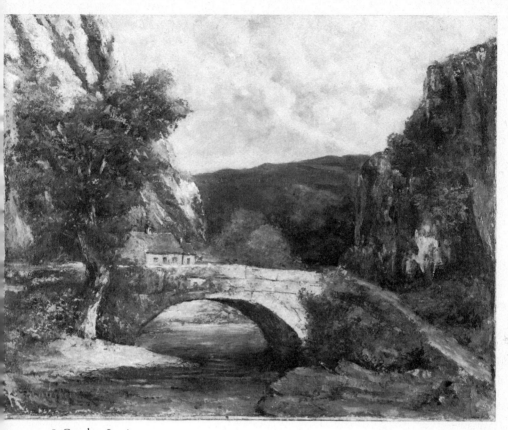

28 Courbet *Le vieux pont*

Some renderings of the landscapes around Pontoise, where
Pissarro settled in 1866, are large canvases reminiscent of Courbet's
works, but they are painted with a broad brush rather than a palette
knife, in subdued browns, greys and low greens – rarely in pure
colours. But Pissarro's early Pontoise landscapes (for example, *The
Gardens of the Hermitage, Pontoise*) are less tactile and material than
Courbet's paintings, and more airy and poetic. If Pissarro achieves
less grandeur here he has a greater lightness of touch; the leaves in
these pictures, already immersed in atmosphere, are particularly well

43

rendered. The works by Courbet which are most comparable are landscapes of the 1860s, such as *Le vieux pont* (*Ill. 28*). Pissarro was also sometimes capable of producing very dramatic contrasts of light and shade, as in the *View of Pontoise, Quai du Pothuis* (1868, *Ill. 29*).

Throughout most of his life, and especially in these early years, Pissarro was forced to spend a great deal of his energy on the struggle to support his family. For years he had an affair with his mother's maid Julie Vellay, who bore him a son in 1863 and a daughter in 1865. (He eventually married her in London in 1870.) The couple had seven children in all; five were sons, all of whom, to Mme Pissarro's despair, devoted themselves to the same hazardous career as their father. In spite of the admission of Pissarro's early work to some of the Salons, his paintings were refused in 1861 and 1863. No doubt hostility to his work increased as it became less like Corot's; besides, his subjects were considered commonplace and even vulgar. Thus the critic Jean Rousseau said that the *Banks of the Marne in*

29 Pissarro *View of Pontoise, Quai du Pothuis* 1868

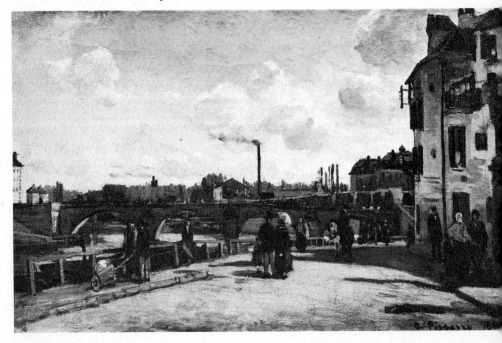

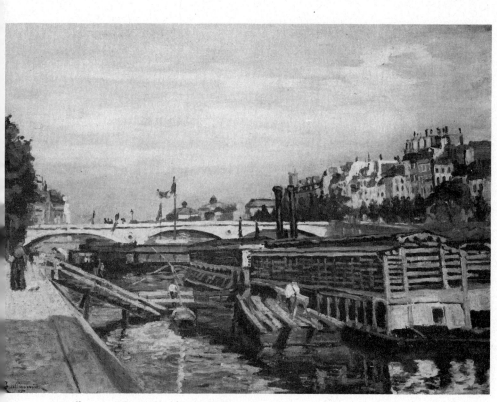

30 Guillaumin *The Bridge of Louis Philippe, Paris* 1875

Winter was 'an ugly, vulgar motif . . . the artist is employing a robust, exuberant talent to show the vulgarities of the contemporary world, perhaps with a satirical intention.' This judgment illustrates the extent to which taste was at that time conditioned to expect painters to treat overtly picturesque and sentimental subjects.

Zola's attitude, however, was different. In *Mon Salon* (1866) he wrote: 'You must realize that you won't please anyone and your pictures will be found bare, too dark. Then why the devil do you have the arrant clumsiness to paint solidly and to study nature frankly? An austere and serious kind of painting, an extreme concern for truth and accuracy. . . . You are a great blunderer, Sir, you are an artist that I like.'

Owing partly to Daubigny's support, Pissarro came to be represented in the Salon every year except 1870. And after 1868 he was no longer listed as the pupil of any artist. Nevertheless, in 1868 poverty compelled him to accept commercial work. In this he was helped by Armand Guillaumin, a peripheral figure among the Impressionists. A friend of Cézanne, Guillaumin was at first a civil servant, who gave up his post in the Compagnie d'Orléans in 1868 to devote all his time to painting (*Ill. 30*).

Auguste Renoir's development into an Impressionist was very different from Pissarro's. In the *Biographia Literaria* Coleridge declares that the distinction between the poet and the scientist is that the former has, as his immediate object, not truth but pleasure. Pleasure seems the most obvious quality of Renoir's work – the immediate, glowing pleasure which he took in painting and which we derive from his productions. As Lawrence Gowing says: 'Sternness and excess were foreign to him, the surface was his kingdom.' If he was not quite 'unclouded by thought', as Gowing suggests, he was nevertheless temperamentally incapable as a young man of fretting over the problems of style which obsessed such as Cézanne and Seurat. When his master Gleyre, who regarded painting as a severe formal exercise, said to him, 'One doesn't paint for amusement,' Renoir replied, 'But if it didn't amuse me I shouldn't paint.' He also said, as Matisse might have done, that the purpose of a picture was to decorate a wall and that this made it important for the colours to be pleasurable in themselves. In many ways he was the most traditional of the major Impressionists, the one most soaked in the work of early painters. He was always shocked by the suggestion that black should be banished from the palette, and still more, no doubt, by Pissarro's and Duranty's view that the Louvre ought to be burnt down. 'It is in the museum', he said, 'that one learns to paint.' And another time: 'I believe I have done nothing but continue what others have done better before me.'

Renoir was born in Limoges in 1841, one of the five children of a poor tailor who moved his family to Paris when Auguste was only four years old. Gounod, who was the choir-master of his school, considered him to be musically gifted. For at least four years he was apprenticed to a porcelain painter, and it has often been suggested that this early experience fostered in him a precise use of the brush, a delicate touch and an appreciation of the effect of bright colours on a smooth white ground. Renoir always retained a technical brilliance in his handling of surface and texture; moreover, dark shadows and rich impasto cannot be achieved on porcelain. He often spoke of painting as a handicraft, observing that good craftsmen are needed to do it well and that the disappearance of the old apprenticeship system was by no means an artistic gain. The introduction of printed designs on pottery drove Renoir's employer out of business in 1858.

Renoir had already visited the Louvre (where he was later to bring the reluctant Monet) and learned to love the eighteenth-century painters, who were only gradually emerging from the disrepute in which they had been held since the time of David and the Revolution. Edgar Degas, who as a very young man had seen eighteenth-century pictures in the collections of his father's friends Lacaze and Marcille, often pointed out that the eighteenth century was by no means merely frivolous. But Renoir may well have liked the period just because he did think it was frivolous. After losing his job in the porcelain works, Renoir began to paint fans for a living, copying pictures by Watteau, Lancret, Boucher and Fragonard. This phase had a considerable effect upon his mature work; indeed, he has sometimes been called the Fragonard of modern art. Though he certainly achieved Fragonard's grace and sensuous charm, Renoir's work has greater intensity and a more noble, monumental simplicity. He earned a little extra money by doing odd jobs, such as adapting heraldic designs, painting window-blinds and decorating a café. By 1862 he had managed to save enough money to enter the Atelier Gleyre, where the students included Monet, Sisley and Bazille, all of whom became his close friends.

Gleyre has been described as the most lenient and least aggressive of the art teachers in Paris at that time. His own pictures were nearly all of a historical and anecdotal character (*Ill. 31*). He feared that colour might go to his pupils' heads, and another teacher, Émile

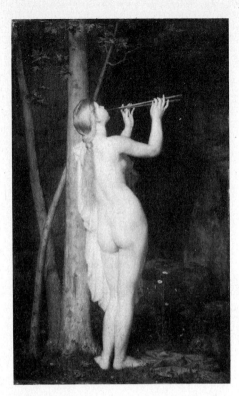

31 Gleyre *La Charmeuse* 1868

32 Renoir
La Baigneuse au Griffon 1870 ▶

Signol, 'beside himself on account of a certain red that I had used' – so Renoir later told Vollard – 'warned me, "Be careful not to become another Delacroix."' Years later, at the Salon of 1870, Renoir's *Femme d'Alger*, both in colour and subject, demonstrated his admiration for Delacroix.

When Gleyre retired in 1864 Monet took his colleagues to Chailly, in the forest of Fontainebleau, not far from where the Barbizon masters were working. At this time they were all trying to imitate Courbet's use of the palette knife, and this can be seen in Renoir's *At the Inn of Mother Anthony* (1866, *Ill. 20*) and *Diane Chasseresse* (*Ill. 33*), which was refused for the Salon exhibition of 1867. Renoir, however, was gradually to discard the use of the palette knife because, as he later told Vollard, it prevented him from retouching any part of his canvas without first scraping it. Even such a late painting as *La Baigneuse au Griffon* (1870, *Ill. 32*), however, is still under

48

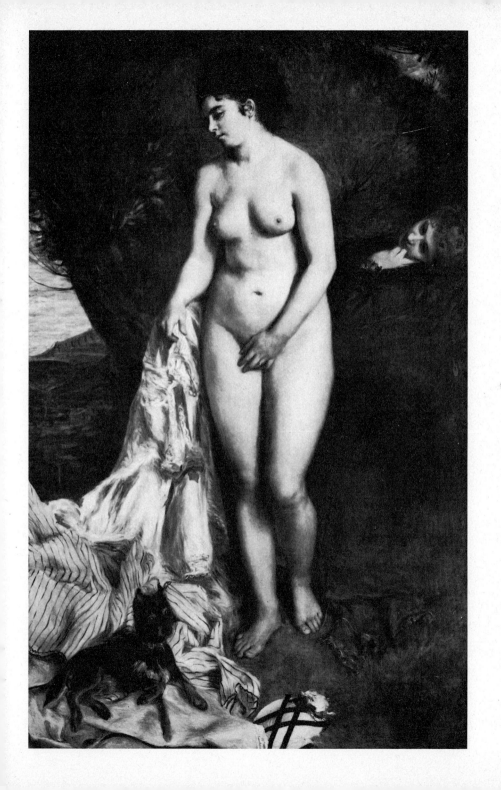

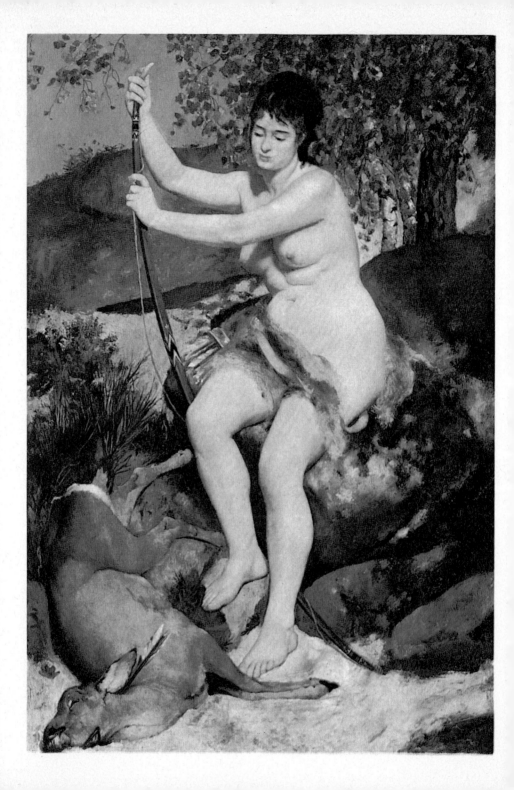

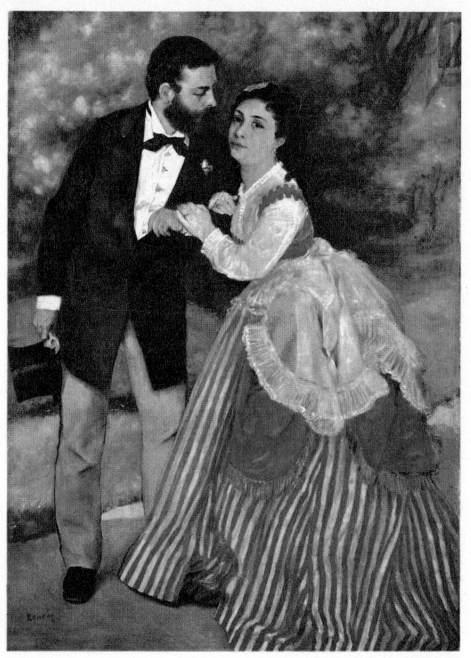

34 Renoir *Alfred Sisley and his Wife c.* 1868

◀ 33 Renoir *Diane Chasseresse* 1867

Courbet's influence, evident in the weighty, continuous modelling, the massive figure, the slightly greasy flesh-tints and in a certain indefinable relationship with Courbet's *Demoiselles au bord de la Seine*. The creamy drapery too is like that of the model in Courbet's *Atelier*.

The story that, as late as 1874, Manet tried to persuade Renoir's friends to stop him painting has now been discredited. If true, it would have been doubly ironic; in many ways Renoir was the most graceful and professional painter of the whole group and he felt the deepest possible admiration for Manet's work. The dexterous manipulation of Manet's paint and his choice of strong frontal lighting were sometimes echoed by Renoir. The *Boy with a Cat* (1868) most nearly approaches the early style of Manet, but Manet's art is generally harsher, with less sinuous grace in the flow and interlacing of the lines. The well-known portrait of *Sisley and His Wife* (1868, *Ill. 34*) is superficially like Manet's work in its boldness, but the modelling and interplay of coloured shadows are characteristic of Renoir.

In spite of Daubigny's intercession, Renoir's entries were rejected by the Salons of 1866 and 1867. He was sometimes too poor to buy paints, although he was often helped by his fellow-painter Bazille and his friend Jules Le Cœur. Le Cœur and Renoir had mistresses who were sisters, the daughters of a country postmaster called Tréhot. Renoir's affair with Lise Tréhot lasted for eight years and she can be identified as the sitter in at least fifteen of his pictures, including the well-known and rather formal Salon picture *Lise à l'Ombrelle* (1867), as well as *Diane Chasseresse* and *La Baigneuse au Griffon*.

Unlike most of his friends, who enjoyed vehement discussions about art and indulged this taste in such meeting-places as the Café Taranne or the Café Guerbois, Renoir detested all theoretical conversations. 'Don't ask me whether painting ought to be subjective or objective,' he said, 'I don't give a damn.' His only aesthetic theory was a mock defence of the irregular in art – a theory of no theory at all. He also said: 'You construct a theory – and nature knocks it down.' He declared that he had been forced to break with many of

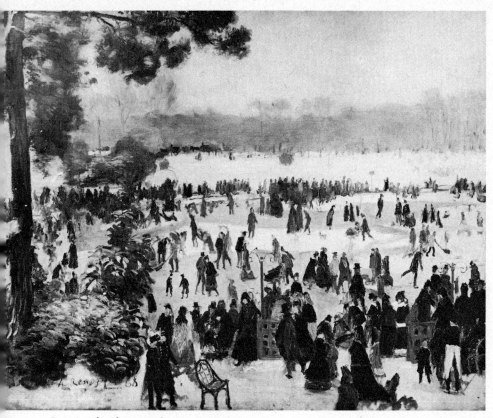

35 Renoir *The Skaters in the Bois de Boulogne* 1868

his friends who argued so late into the night that they could not get
up in time to paint the next morning.

Renoir's figure paintings in the 1860s resembled those of Courbet,
and were technically less advanced than a near-Impressionist work
like *The Skaters in the Bois de Boulogne* (1868, *Ill. 35*), which he
painted with bold, direct strokes of the brush in a manner reminiscent
of Manet. *The Skaters* reminds one of Renoir's remark that Courbet
seemed part of the tradition but Manet embodied the new generation
of painting. It is also interesting as one of Renoir's few 'snow pieces';
he later deplored Monet's taste for painting snow, which he described
as 'the leprosy of nature'.

53

In 1869, Renoir and Monet were beginning to paint the shimmering atmosphere of light and water at La Grenouillère, the bathing place at Bougival on the Seine. It was from this close partnership (the styles of the two painters were indeed barely distinguishable at this period) that Impressionism emerged, as Cubism was later to develop from the time when Picasso and Braque worked 'as if roped together on a mountain'. The critic Castagnary had already declared that 'a revolution in form and content has taken place'. Although one cannot say definitely that the Impressionist movement was launched in any particular year, since its genesis was inevitably gradual, the

36 Monet *La Grenouillère* 1869

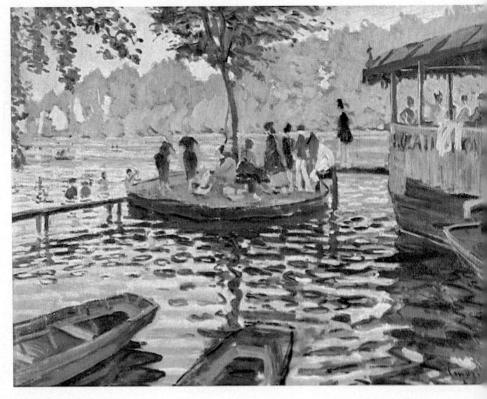

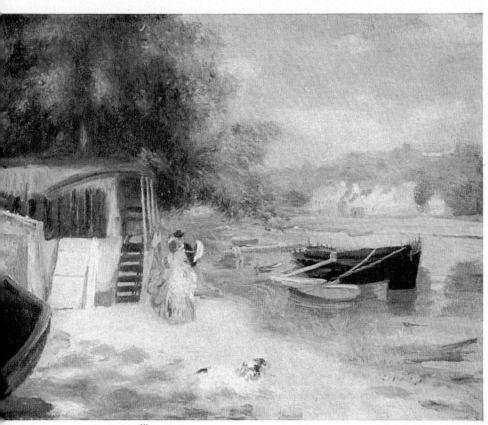

37 Renoir *La Grenouillère* 1869

year 1869, during which Renoir and Monet were painting together at La Grenouillère, may perhaps be called the most decisive. It was there that Renoir and Monet made their discovery that shadows are not brown or black but are coloured by their surroundings, and that the 'local colour' of an object is modified by the light in which it is seen, by reflections from other objects and by contrast with juxtaposed colours. They began more and more to use pure, unmixed colours, particularly the three primaries (red, yellow and blue) and their three

55

complementaries (green, violet and orange), banning blacks, browns and earth colours. In order to seize and convey a sensation of movement and quivering light they learned to handle paint more freely and loosely and did not try to hide their fragmented brush-strokes. Renoir (*Ill. 38*) employed a treatment less broad and opaque, softer and more feathery than Monet's. For both painters, as never for Courbet or Manet, light had become the great unifying factor of figure and landscape. Although five years were to pass before the first Impressionist exhibition was held and the movement acquired its name, in fact Impressionism was already born.

38 Renoir *La Grenouillère c.* 1869

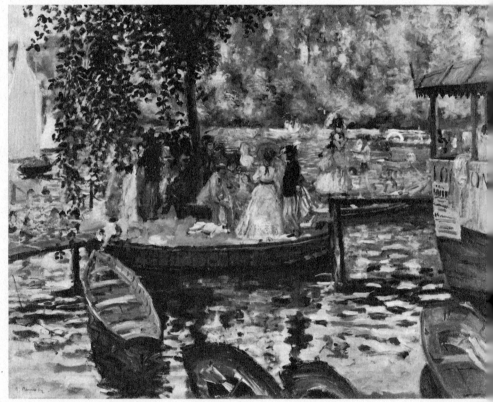

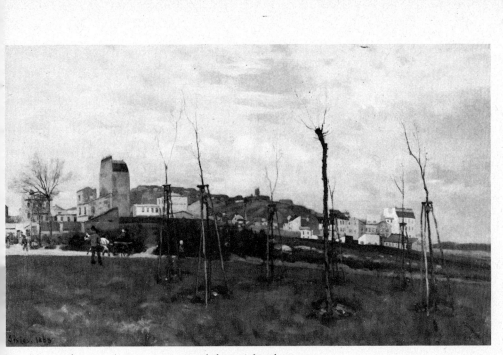

39 Sisley *Vue de Montmartre prise de la Cité des Fleurs* 1869

During this time, working quietly alongside Renoir, or sometimes Monet, was their friend Alfred Sisley, whom they had met at the Atelier Gleyre. Sisley was born in Paris in 1839 of English descent. His father was in the silk business and his mother was a cultivated Londoner with musical tastes. When he was eighteen Sisley was sent to London to prepare for a business career, but after four years he abandoned the attempt and came back to Paris, where he joined the Atelier Gleyre in 1862. Until 1870 he received money from his father, but later he was often as poor as his friends. His first landscape paintings, frequently executed at Marly or St Cloud, are sombre, with heavy browns, greens and pale blues. Like the other Impressionists, he was influenced by Corot and Courbet. The *Vue de Montmartre prise de la Cité des Fleurs* (1869, *Ill. 39*) shows his fundamental qualities – his sense of construction, love of space, and just feeling for colour-values – but it is very sharply outlined in contrast with his later works. By 1870 he was adopting a freer manner, which

57

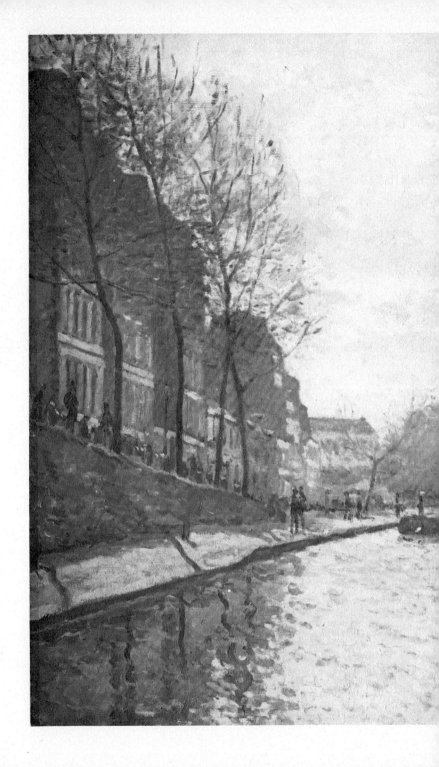

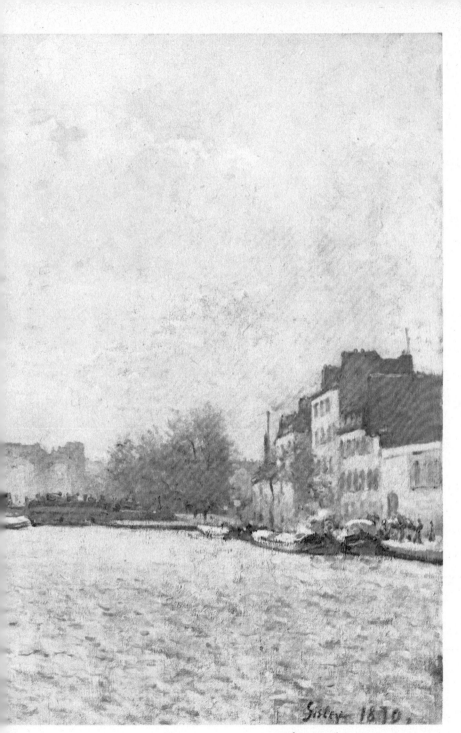

40 Sisley *Canal St Martin, Paris* 1870

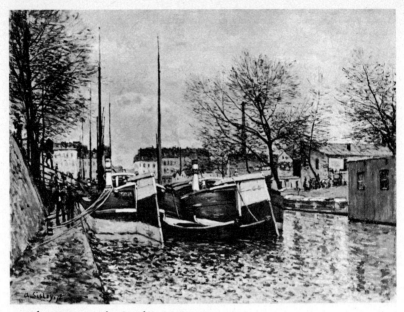

41 Sisley *Barges on the Canal St Martin* 1870

can be seen in his *Barges on the Canal St Martin* (*Ill. 41*). He now began to follow his bolder friends in using the Impressionist technique of clear colours and chromatic division.

Sisley's talent was far from negligible and he later became perhaps the purest Impressionist of them all – in the sense that he never deviated into figure painting, and that he confined himself almost entirely to characteristic Impressionist scenes: villages near Paris, and particularly the Seine. Kenneth Clark has written that he doubts whether a picture could be much truer to a visual impression, with all its implications of light and tone, than Sisley's paintings of Hampton Court – and, one might add, the delicate studies of floods at Marly (*Ill. 135*). Sisley was the only member of the group who did not ultimately find that Impressionism either failed to satisfy him or led to an impasse from which he felt compelled to escape. The fact that his later works are less successful may be only a coincidence, but it has often been taken to illustrate the argument, dear to Degas, that the use of Impressionist technique inevitably led to sketchiness and triviality.

60

CHAPTER THREE

Monet and Bazille up to 1869

Félix Fénéon, the art critic, collector and friend of Seurat, wrote in 1888 that 'the word "Impressionist" was created for Monet and it fits him better than it does anyone else.' Georges Grappe went even further in his obituary of the artist in 1926 when he pronounced him to be the *only* Impressionist. It is more usual and indeed more correct to regard Monet as the arch-Impressionist, the most searching and consistent practitioner of an idiom which he had done the most to evolve, the Impressionist who trusted most firmly in his own visual sensations. Renoir admitted that during their early struggles he would often have given up but for the tenacity of his friend. Vollard reports Cézanne as saying, 'Monet is only an eye, but my God what an eye!' This judgment is unfair, for Monet was instinctively a picture-maker as well as an 'eye'. Yet it describes that vital part of Monet's nature which he discussed with his friend Clemenceau: 'Colour is my day-long obsession, joy and torment. To such an extent indeed that one day, finding myself at the death-bed of a woman who had been and still was very dear to me, I caught myself focusing on her temples and automatically analyzing the succession of appropriately graded colours which death was imposing on her motionless face. There were blue, yellow, grey tones – tones I cannot describe. That was the point I had reached.'

Monet was particularly attracted by scenes of dissolution – ice-floes on the Seine, thaws, fog, mist (see *Rough Sea, Etretat*, 1883, *Ill. 42*). As Adrian Stokes has pointed out in a highly perceptive study, some of Monet's best paintings are of 'a frangible, crumbling world'. He had little or no perception of the separateness of objects and never used the defined foreground of the classical-picturesque tradition which closed the picture at the bottom. Those who particularly love the classical and architectural type of painting are inclined to consider Monet loose and sloppy. The strident colours, apparent

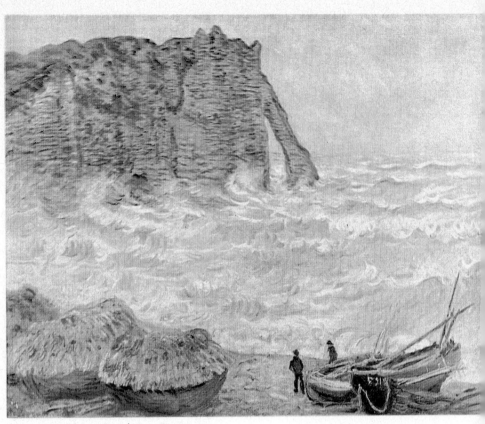

42 Monet *Rough Sea, Etretat* 1883

formlessness, the air of relaxation and the excesses of his worst pictures make one long for the disciplined purity of Seurat. These qualities caused his work to be viewed with disfavour by *avant-garde* critics in the period when Roger Fry was preaching 'significant form'. But, after years of poverty and frustration (and before Fry's doctrine became prevalent), Monet did gain considerable recognition. His success began at the time of his joint exhibition with Rodin in 1889 and increased for about thirty years. Even in the years of fashionable disfavour his greatness was conceded. The artist William Coldstream recalls that when he was a student at the Slade School of Art in London at the time of Monet's death in 1926, the principal,

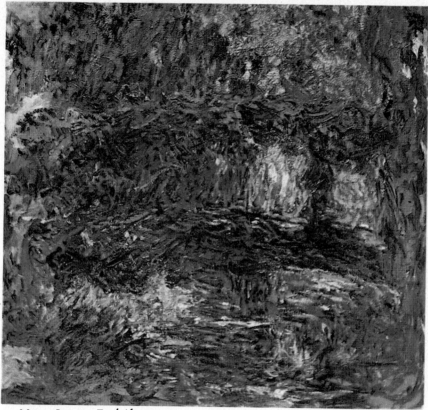

43 Monet *Japanese Footbridge* 1922

Henry Tonks, assembled the whole school and suggested that representatives should lay a wreath on a work by Monet in the Tate Gallery. Monet regained general approval after 1950 when abstract expressionist and *tachiste* painters such as Jackson Pollock and Riopelle derived inspiration from his later work and claimed him as a forerunner (*Ill. 43*).

Claude Monet was born in Paris on the same day as Rodin, 14 November 1840. He was the eldest son of a wholesale grocer and chandler who, because of financial difficulties, moved to Le Havre when Claude was five. The seashores of Normandy had a decisive effect on his sensibility, and he later wrote of the sea: 'I should like

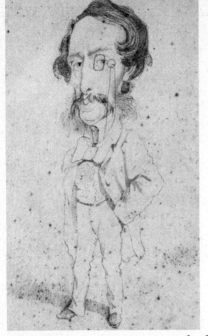

to be always near it or on it, and when I die to be buried in a buoy.'
Monet was not a religious or intellectual youth; he was strong, with
an enormous appetite, and could be both taciturn and bad-tempered.
He always retained something of his provincial roughness and directness, qualities which were advantageous compared with the delicacy
and self-mistrust of Boudin, who felt that his own touch was
constrained and that he lacked verve of execution.

Monet's touch was rarely constrained, yet there was much that
Boudin could teach him. Boudin, a sailor's son from Honfleur, was
running a stationery and picture-framing shop in Le Havre and
painting the sea, which he had been encouraged to do by his cus-
tomers Couture, Millet and Troyon. Monet had been drawing
caricatures (*Ill. 44*) which were exhibited in the same shop-window
as Boudin's work. At first Monet detested Boudin's pictures, but he
was soon won over by Boudin to paint with him in the open air, an
experience which proved a revelation to the eighteen-year-old boy.

In his notebooks Boudin expressed the revolutionary doctrine that
the effects of shimmering colour and fleeting light could best be

achieved by painting not merely the sketch but the whole picture in the open air. (It is likely that the only other painters doing this at the time were Daubigny and the group called the Macchiaioli in Florence.) Boudin was trying desperately to retain his first impression of a scene, and found that 'everything that is painted directly on the spot always has a force, a power, a vivacity of touch that cannot be re-created in the studio.' He communicated this principle to his new friend, and it has been said that 'all Monet's future is already in these timid notebooks of Boudin.' When, in March 1859, Monet's father tried in vain to obtain for him a municipal grant to study art, Boudin was named as his teacher. Soon, however, Monet was to need more powerful examples and this led him to neglect Boudin for the somewhat cruder art of Daubigny and Courbet.

To begin with, Monet's family, impressed by his precocious caricatures, were sympathetic towards his painting. This was particularly true of an aunt, Mme Lecadre, who was herself an amateur painter and in whose attic Monet is supposed to have discovered a landscape by Daubigny. His family paid for him to visit Paris in 1859 and Boudin gave him an introduction to Troyon, which Monet repaid by letters describing the pictures he saw in the Salon. He praised works by Corot, Daubigny and Troyon, of whose *Departure for the Market*, which is probably the picture now called *Le Matin* in the Louvre (*Ill. 45*), he wrote: 'There is a great deal of movement –

45 Troyon *Le Matin* 1855

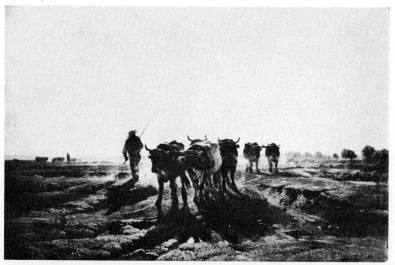

of wind in the clouds. It's superb, but above all it's very luminous. One might almost imagine oneself in the open countryside.' Other works by Troyon, however, he considered to be too dark in the shadows. When shown some of Monet's still-lifes, Troyon praised the colour but recommended that, on account of his very facility, the young painter should practise drawing and pursue a course of serious studies.

Monet proceeded to disturb his parents by staying too long in Paris, by studying not at the École des Beaux-Arts but at the Académie Suisse, and by frequenting the Brasserie des Martyrs, the meeting-place of Courbet and the other realist painters. As he himself told Courbet later, Monet led a dissipated life and wasted a great deal of his time. As a result his parents withdrew their support, and when he drew an unlucky number in the lottery for military service in 1860 his aunt refused to buy him out. His admiration for Delacroix's Algerian pictures led him to choose service in the Chasseurs d'Afrique, and he was sent to Algeria. Studying the light there was to have a beneficial effect upon his future work, just as Seurat was later to be helped by his long hours spent watching the sea on sentry duty. 'You cannot imagine how much I learned there,' Monet declared later. 'I did not realize it at first; it was not until

46 Monet *The Breakwater at Honfleur* 1864

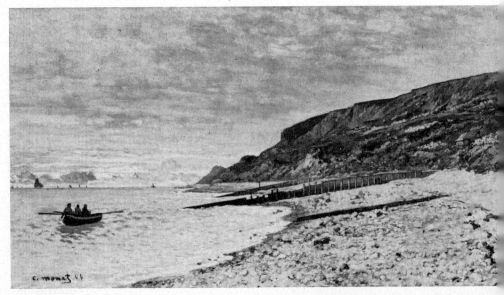

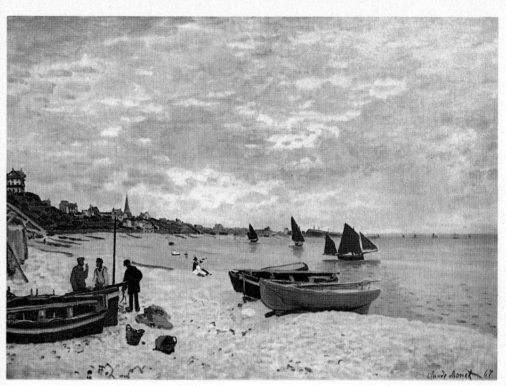

47 Monet *Beach at Sainte-Adresse* 1867

later that the impressions of colour and light which I had received
sorted themselves out; but the germ of my future research was
there.'

While in Africa Monet developed anaemia, and at the end of a
period of sick-leave his parents bought him out of the army. In the
summer of 1862 Monet met Jongkind: 'He asked to see my sketches,
invited me to come and work with him, explained to me the why
and wherefore of his manner and thereby completed the teaching I
had already received from Boudin. From that time he was my real
master; it was to him that I owe the final education of my eye.'
Jongkind spent the greater part of 1863 working at Honfleur and
returned there during the following two years. At this time
Castagnary observed that Jongkind's greatness 'lies in the impression

67

he renders', and praised the free and rapid touches of his water-colours. Unfortunately, many of Monet's early landscapes have been lost, but *The Breakwater at Honfleur* (1864, *Ill. 46*) was apparently painted directly after a picture of Jongkind's; and the somewhat later *Beach at Sainte-Adresse* (1867, *Ill. 47*) also bears traces of the Dutchman's strong luminosity.

Monet's parents were still suspicious of his friends and his ambitions. Mme Lecadre complained in a letter to the painter Armand Gautier that 'his sketches are always rough drafts, like those you have seen; but when he wants to complete a picture, they turn into dreadful daubs in front of which he swanks and finds idiots to congratulate him. He pays no attention to my remarks. I am not up to his standard, so I now keep deep silence.' This letter indicates that the Impressionist in Monet was beginning to emerge.

In November 1862 Monet was given money to return to Paris on condition that he accept the tuition of some well-known master, and he was put under the guidance of his cousin by marriage, a successful and insipid painter called Toulmouche. Toulmouche had been a pupil of Gleyre and advised Monet to enter his atelier. There Monet met Renoir and Sisley, who were working comparatively hard, but Monet himself, who later declared that he painted as a bird sings, always found tradition and discipline uninspiring. He resented Gleyre for telling him, 'Nature, my friend, is all very well as an element of study, but it offers no interest. Style, you see, style is everything.' This was the attitude expressed by the character Fagerolles in Zola's novel *L'Œuvre* when he criticized the way a student had rendered the model's thighs. 'But Sir, her thighs *are* like that.' 'If they are like that she's wrong.'

Accounts of life at Gleyre's studio (which often involved the performance of charades and obscene plays with elaborately painted scenery) were sent home to his parents by Monet's latest friend, Frédéric Bazille, who was considerably better educated than Monet and was also able to help him financially. Bazille was born in 1841 in Montpellier, the son of a prosperous wine-grower. His family was cultivated and closely linked with the collector Alfred Bruyas, who had a large collection of modern French paintings, including works

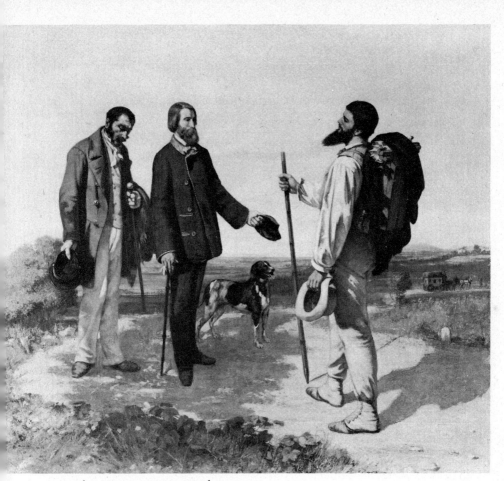

48 Courbet *Bonjour Monsieur Courbet* 1854

by Géricault, Delacroix, Corot, Millet, Diaz and Courbet. When Bazille was thirteen, Courbet's famous visit to his patron Bruyas took place – a visit commemorated by the picture *Bonjour Monsieur Courbet* (*Ill. 48*), which always remained one of Bazille's favourite works. He studied medicine in Montpellier for three years and in the winter of 1862 went to Paris, where his spells of painting at Gleyre's studio began to distract him from his medical studies.

Bazille's earliest landscapes have been lost or destroyed, but his letters suggest that at this period he was chiefly under the influence

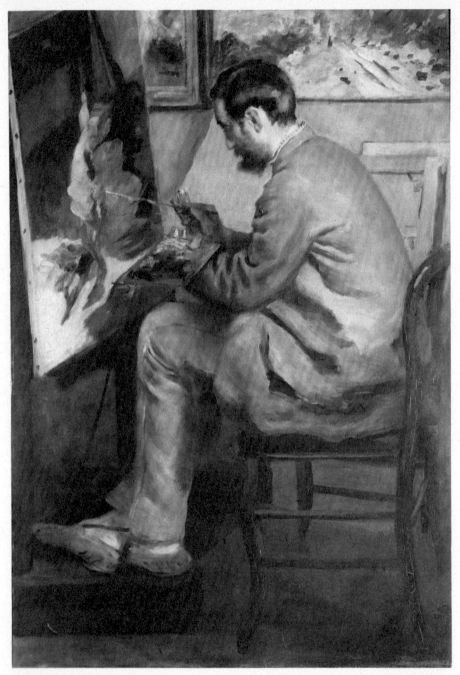
49 Renoir *Portrait of Bazille* 1867

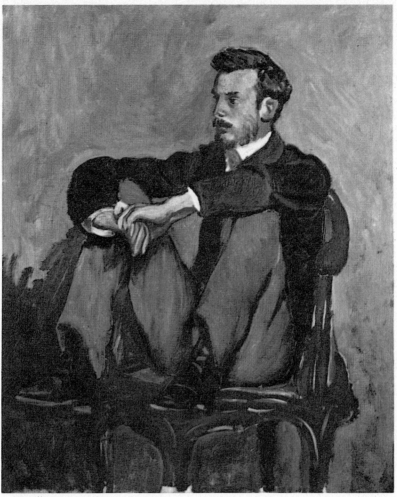

50 Bazille *Portrait of Renoir* 1867

of Monet. 'I have been with my friend Monet, who is quite good at landscapes; he has given me advice which has helped me very much.' It may be debated whether Bazille was ever a true Impressionist, partly because he died (in 1870) before the use of small, vibrant touches and the division of tone became general among the group, and partly because of his classical tendencies, which directed

71

him towards motifs which were permanent and strictly constructed rather than mobile and transitory. It is also difficult to think of any other Impressionist, except perhaps Pissarro, who would have enjoyed painting so often the massive walls of Aigues-Mortes (1867, *Ill. 82*). F. Daulte, his excellent biographer, insists that it was Bazille's southern temperament (like Cézanne's) that explains his interest in form, construction and line, whereas a northern painter, such as Monet, was largely concerned with suggesting an object. Like Degas, and unlike the Impressionists proper, Bazille used the traditional method of preparing his pictures by a series of drawings and studies from nature. Although he might simplify and order these to some extent, he still painted the final picture in the open air, as Degas did not. In view of the aim he declared in a letter of 1868 – 'I should like to restore to every subject its weight and volume, and not only paint the appearance' – there might be grounds for calling him the first Post-Impressionist, striving to develop, as Degas and Renoir later succeeded in doing, a new language to express modern life in a classical and monumental form.

Some time in 1863, before Delacroix's death in August, Monet and Bazille, looking from the window of a friend's studio in the Rue de Furstemberg (where they later lived themselves), were able to observe the master painting down below. They were greatly intrigued, and a little scandalized, to see that Delacroix started painting only after his model had gone away. It is interesting that Delacroix (who, contrary to general belief, often spoke of himself as a classical painter) had the strongest effect upon those Impressionists with the most classical bent. Monet, the northerner, expressed great admiration for him, but Delacroix was less important to his formation than Boudin, Jongkind or Courbet. For Renoir and Cézanne, however, the example of the great colourist was crucial. Bazille too was influenced by Delacroix; he had been able to see the *Femmes d'Alger* in the Salon in Montpellier in 1860, and on the way to Normandy in 1864 he had stopped at Rouen to admire *The Justice of Trajan*.

It is probable, however, that the future Impressionists were less affected by Delacroix's death than by three other events at about the same time: Manet's first exhibition at the Galerie Martinet in 1863, the establishment (also in 1863) of the Salon des Refusés in which Manet, Pissarro, Cézanne, Fantin-Latour, Boudin, Jongkind and Whistler exhibited, and the closing down of Gleyre's atelier in 1864, which occurred partly because of the master's failing eyesight and partly because his generosity over fees led to financial difficulties.

At Louis Martinet's gallery on the Boulevard des Italiens, Manet exhibited fourteen of his best works, including *Lola de Valence*, the *Spanish Dancers* and the highly original *Musique aux Tuileries* (*Ill. 51*). Baudelaire, who was Manet's constant companion at that time, appears in profile in this last picture, which is surely a direct answer to the poet's cry for a painter of modern life who could show 'how great and poetic we are in our frock-coats and patent leather boots'. The informal and crowded arrangement of this canvas and the impersonal atmosphere appear to derive from the technique of the camera, and the faces of several friends were executed from photographs. Some sketches (but certainly not much of the final picture) were painted in the open air. Monet and his friends were greatly impressed by these examples of Manet's work, and Manet's position was to be further enhanced and confirmed by his notoriety in the Salon des Refusés.

The jury for the Salon of 1863 had been particularly severe. Three-fifths of the works submitted were rejected – partly, it was believed, because of the intolerance of Signol, the master who had warned Renoir against becoming another Delacroix (see p. 48). Furious articles in the press, criticizing the Salon's attitude, eventually came to the notice of the Emperor, who liked to pose as a liberal in matters which he regarded as unimportant. Louis-Napoleon paid a surprise visit to the Salon and asked to see the works which had been rejected. Pronouncing these to be quite as good as the pictures which had been accepted, he ordered that all the rejected submissions should be exhibited in the Palais de l'Industrie near the official Salon. Pictures by Jongkind, Pissarro and Cézanne were shown in this Salon des Refusés, but the greatest publicity was given to Manet's *Déjeuner sur l'Herbe* (*Ill. 54*). Both the style and subject-matter of this painting were freely criticized. Manet's forcible, spontaneous brush-work, his

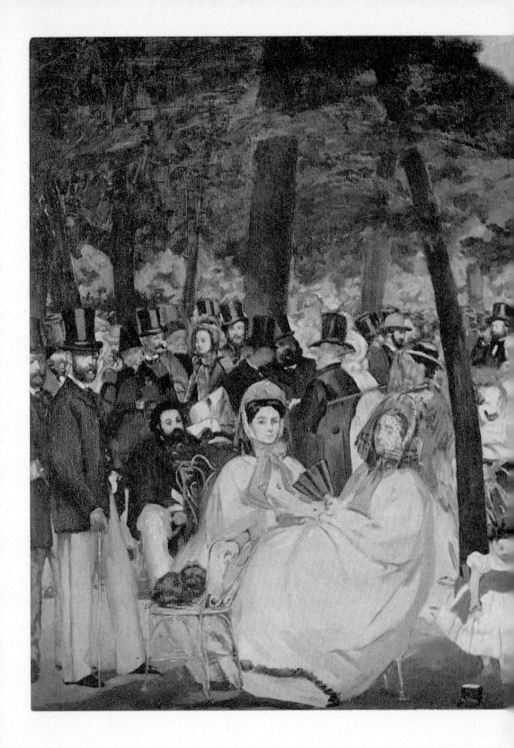

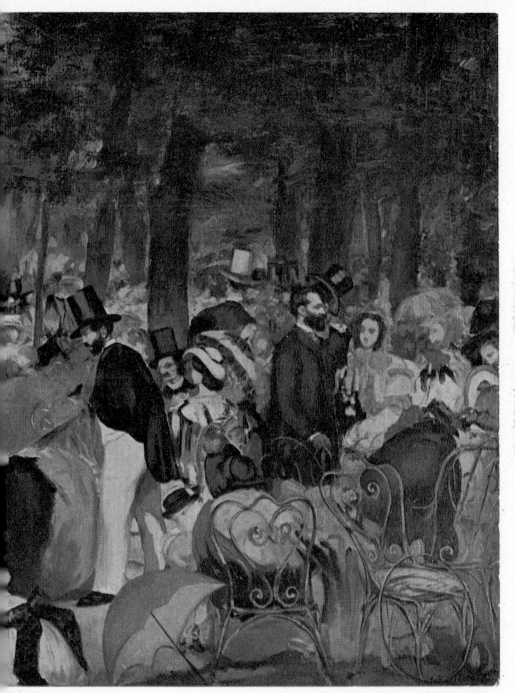

51 Manet *Musique aux Tuileries* 1862

summary indication of form without the use of lines, his disregard of smooth modelling and careful transition annoyed the critics almost as much as the naked woman and the clothed men – a subject which the Emperor declared was immodest, although it had been adapted from a work by Giorgione and an engraving by Marcantonio after Raphael, the idol of the École des Beaux-Arts. Zacharie Astruc, however, founded a temporary daily paper, *Le Salon de 1863*, to uphold the unpopular view: 'Manet! One of the greatest artistic characters of the time! . . . Brilliance, inspiration, powerful flavour, surprise.' The full impact of Manet, and particularly of the *Déjeuner*, on Monet, Bazille and their friends did not become apparent in their work until 1865, when they began to paint their large figure compositions in the open air.

Meanwhile, in the spring of 1864, the group went to Chailly, where Monet and Bazille had briefly worked the year before, and some of the paintings of this visit survive. They each bear the imprint of an older artist's influence. Thus Monet's bright, by no means Impressionist, *Road in the Forest with Wood Gatherers* is reminis-

52 Daubigny *Evening*

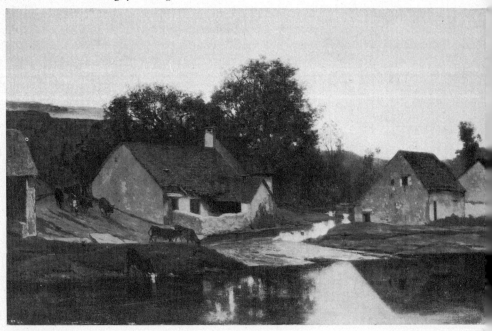

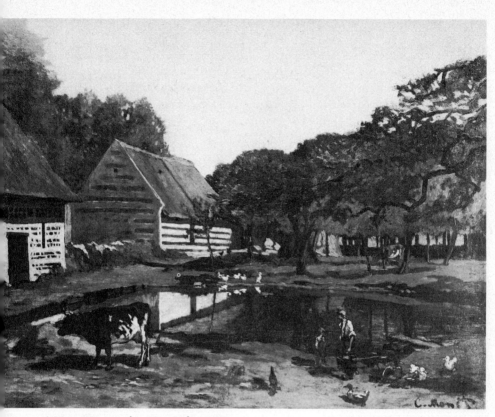

53 Monet *Farmyard in Normandy* c. 1864

cent of Millet, who often depicted peasants carrying faggots. Apparently Monet never knew Millet personally; he was afraid to approach him after being told that he was often insulting to newcomers. Sisley found Corot's style more congenial, and Renoir was greatly influenced by Courbet. By this time Monet had met Courbet, probably through Bazille, and some of Courbet's influence is discernible in his *Farmyard in Normandy* (*Ill. 53*), though this picture reminds one more of Daubigny's style in such a work as *Evening* (*Ill. 52*). Courbet's influence on Monet became more noticeable later in the snow scenes, and in such pictures as *The Evening Meal* (1869), one of the earliest Impressionist paintings of artificial light, which shows the Sisleys having dinner in the Rue de la Paix.

Monet's *Farmyard in Normandy* was probably painted in the summer of 1864, after he and Bazille had taken a boat down the Seine to Honfleur, where they lodged outside the town on the cliffs at the Ferme St-Simeon. Once again Jongkind was in Honfleur. He and Monet would argue whether the artist should be free to add to reality; Monet denied that the artist had such a right. At this time the drawings of both Jongkind and Monet were very impetuous and *mouvementé*. Like Constable, Jongkind had discovered that 'local colour' changes with the season, and he had painted two pictures of Notre-Dame from the same position but in different conditions: one in the cold morning light, the other during a warm sunset. It is likely that Monet, who derived so much from Jongkind, adopted this idea also, for he painted what appears to be the same road in Normandy on two occasions, once when it was covered with snow (1865) and again under a sullen sky (1866). This experiment was to bear fruit thirty years later, in 1894–6, in the long series showing Rouen Cathedral in different lights (*Ill. 177*).

Although Monet was developing prodigiously and was on the brink of making great discoveries for Impressionism, his family naturally could not know that this was so. After he had visited them at the end of the summer of 1864, they cut off his allowance again. In despair he wrote to Bazille, sending him three pictures which he hoped Bruyas might buy, but the collector refused to take them. Returning to Paris, he managed to survive by sharing Bazille's studio in the Rue de Furstemberg.

The admiration that Manet's pictures inspired among these young painters may have acted as a catalyst for a new stage in their stylistic development. Under Monet's lead they all began around 1865 to paint large figure compositions in the open air. Monet's *Déjeuner sur l'Herbe* (1865–6, *Ill. 55*), with its light colours, informal grouping and simplified lines, obviously originated as a tribute to Manet, but it still has something of Courbet's more solid and structural treatment. It says much for the young Monet that he was vigorous and independent enough to emancipate himself from the forceful influence of Courbet, who evidently watched some of the picture being painted and was full of scorn for Monet's decision to paint as much of the

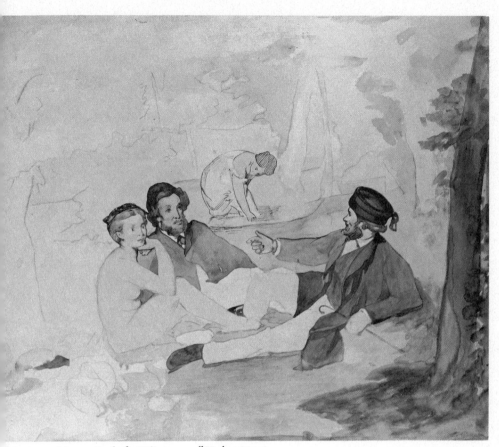

54 Manet *Study for Déjeuner sur l'Herbe* 1865–6

composition as possible in bright sunlight. In Courbet's own *Demoiselles au bord de la Seine* (1856) the figures were certainly executed indoors, and Delacroix had criticized the lack of harmony between figures and background which had resulted from this practice in another work by Courbet, the *Baigneuses*. The notion that models should pose in the open air was quite new (except perhaps in Switzerland, where in 1861 Frank Buchser had produced a picture of a young Englishwoman, painted in a wood).

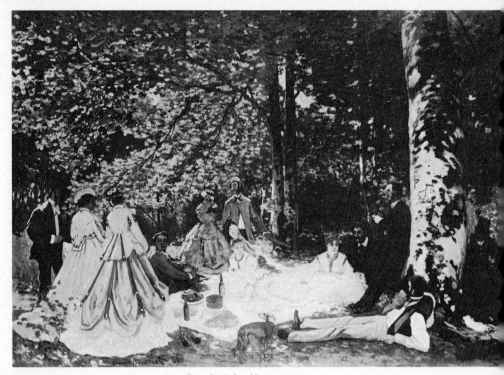

55 Monet *Déjeuner sur l'Herbe* (Sketch) 1866

Discouraged by Courbet, Monet ceased work on *Déjeuner sur l'Herbe* and left Bazille's studio, leaving his canvas behind as security for unpaid rent. When he returned several years later it had been rolled up and was mouldering. There now survive only two fragments. As far as one can judge from these and from a sketch in Moscow, it is a less successful picture than Manet's, but far more advanced technically if considered as a stage in the development of Impressionism. Whereas Manet had started by composing his figures and treating the landscape as a background arranged in planes, Monet began with landscape studies and treated his figures in a more summary way than the leaves, the trees and the dappled light, which are boldly rendered with broken brush-work. Monet also gives a more intense impression of air actually circulating throughout the scene and there is less confusion in his lighting than in Manet's, which reveals the fact that the figures had posed indoors. Figure composition, however, remained less suited to Monet's talents than to those of Bazille and Renoir. The group's new interest in this branch of painting evoked from Bazille some of his most characteristic works, such as *La Robe Rose*, and from Renoir the various pictures showing his mistress Lise.

In spite of an accident to his leg, 1865 and 1866 were good years for Monet. Two of his sea pictures were accepted for the Salon of 1865, and the life-size portrait of his mistress Camille Doncieux, painted in four days, had considerable success at the Salon of 1866. Zola praised Monet's vitality and modernity, calling him 'a man amidst this crowd of eunuchs'. (The 'eunuchs', however, included Degas, Pissarro and Renoir in 1865, and Bazille and Sisley in 1866.)

Even earlier, in 1864, the Salon had accepted two fresh and delicate landscapes by a young woman called Berthe Morisot, who was to become a member of the Impressionist group, sharing their aims and showing pictures alongside theirs in most of their exhibitions. Like Bazille and Renoir, Berthe Morisot was born in 1841. She was the daughter of a wealthy and cultivated prefect who retired in 1855 and went to live in Passy. Berthe and her sister Edma took lessons in painting and drawing from the painter J.-B. Guichard, who made them copy works by Gavarni and the great Venetian masters in the Louvre. Guichard quickly saw that Berthe's interest in painting was so great that she might well devote herself entirely to art, and he warned her mother against such a 'catastrophe'. It is an interesting illustration of the times that already in 1860 she was anxious to paint out of doors, and that Guichard disapproved.

In 1861 she was introduced to Corot, who began to visit her parents' house once a week and was a dominant influence on her development. She worked with him in Ville d'Avray and with his pupil Cudinot at Auvers, where she met Daubigny and Daumier. In spite of her interest in landscapes she often painted the simple incidents of domestic life around her: her sister beside a cradle,

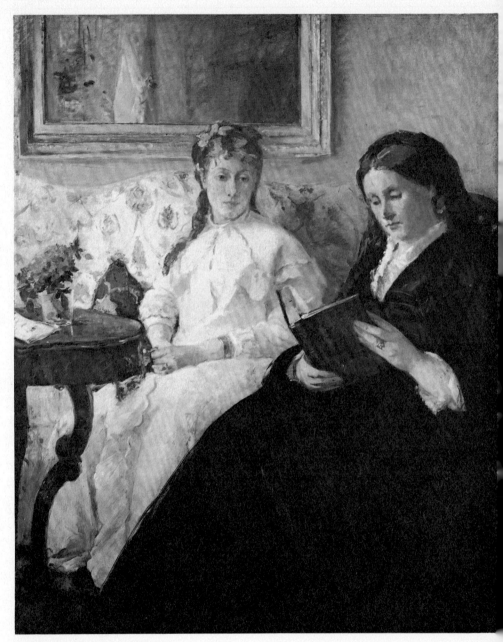

56 Morisot *La Lecture* 1869–70

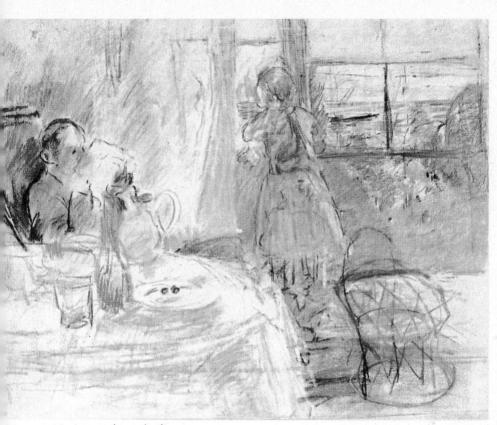

57 Morisot *Eugène and Julie Manet* 1868

women sewing or at their toilette. Even her early works show a remarkable feeling for ensemble and luminosity, which can be attributed to Corot's training.

In 1868, when she was copying a painting by Rubens in the Louvre, Fantin-Latour introduced her to Manet, with whom she formed a friendship that was to modify her whole art and life, and probably Manet's as well. From 1868 she was well launched in his circle. In the autumn of that year she posed for his *The Balcony* which, according to John Richardson, was inspired partly by the sight of an actual group of people on a balcony at Boulogne and

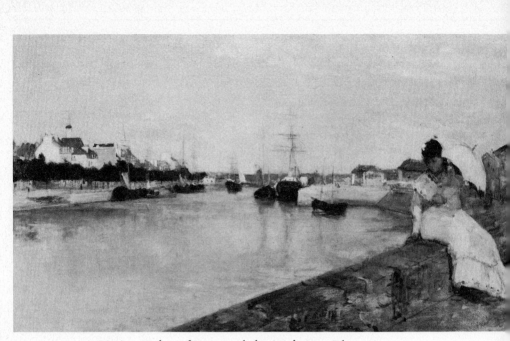

58 Morisot *Harbour of Lorient with the Artist's Sister Edma* 1869

partly by Goya's more unified *Woman on the Balcony* in the Prado. She became sufficiently dependent on Manet to be extremely irritated and disconcerted when, in 1869, he became somewhat preoccupied with his new pupil and model, the handsome Eva Gonzalès. In 1869 Berthe painted the charming *Harbour of Lorient* (*Ill. 58*), for which her sister Edma posed in the open air; Manet was so admiring of this picture that she presented it to him. The Salon of 1870 accepted both a portrait of her sister and a double portrait of Edma and their mother reading (*La Lecture, Ill. 56*), but the latter caused her considerable embarrassment; Manet had made so many alterations in it that she no longer felt justified in exhibiting it as her own. She eventually married Manet's brother Eugène in 1874. She made friends with Degas and Puvis de Chavannes, and her delightful letters to her sister give vivid descriptions of these two artists as they appeared at Alfred Stevens' frequent parties.

84

The last two or three years before the dispersal of the Impressionist group by the Franco-Prussian War were not only the crucial period during which Monet and Renoir did so much to develop Impressionist technique; they were also the years of these two painters' greatest financial hardships. In 1867 their works were rejected by the Salon, along with those of Pissarro, Sisley and Bazille. Monet's family, who had been impressed by his success of 1866, now stopped his allowance yet again and for a while succeeded in separating him from his mistress Camille, who was now pregnant. Like the young Pissarro, Monet and Renoir often could not afford to buy canvases. On one occasion Renoir had to steal bread from his mother's table so that Monet might have something to eat. There was also a period

59 Monet *Quai du Louvre, Paris* 1866–7

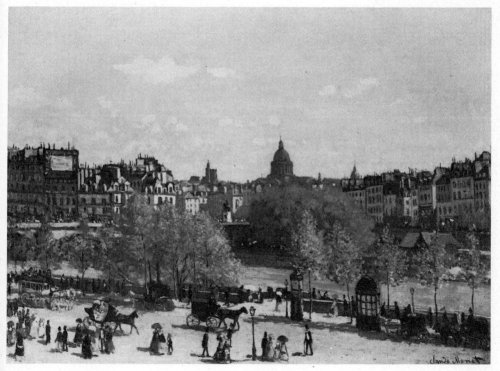

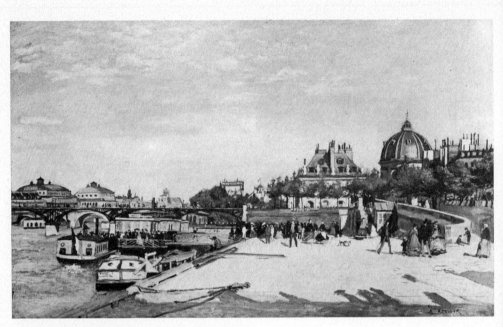

60 Renoir *Pont des Arts, Paris* 1867

when Monet had a temporary failure of eyesight, and in 1868 he wrote to Bazille that he had even attempted suicide.

The two new themes adopted by the group during the late 1860s were views of Paris and reflections in water, subjects which were to be characteristic of Impressionism at its height. Once again Monet seems to have been the initiator, with his views of the *quai* from the Louvre (*Ill. 59*) and his *Jardin de l'Infante* (1866). These solidly constructed city-scapes, reminiscent of Corot, belie the view that Monet was totally haphazard when choosing sites from which to paint. But they do suggest that at this time, like Renoir in his *Pont des Arts, Paris* (1867, *Ill. 60*), he was still representing moving figures as his mind knew them to be rather than as the blurred dots later dictated by his vision.

It has been well said by W.C. Seitz that, for the Impressionists, 'reflections became a means of shaking off the world assembled by memory in favour of a world perceived momentarily by the senses.

In reflections the artifices so important to workaday life are transformed into abstract elements in a world of pure vision.' This is particularly apparent in Monet's *Argenteuil*, or *The River* (1868, *Ill. 61*), in which the figures are subordinated to the sunlit atmosphere and the water, whose reflections make the woman look flatter. The picture as a whole reproduces the effect of a momentary glance; that is why some details are indicated in a cursory way. The boats and human figures seen across the river are scarcely identifiable as such, being represented simply by spots of colour.

61 Monet *The River* 1868

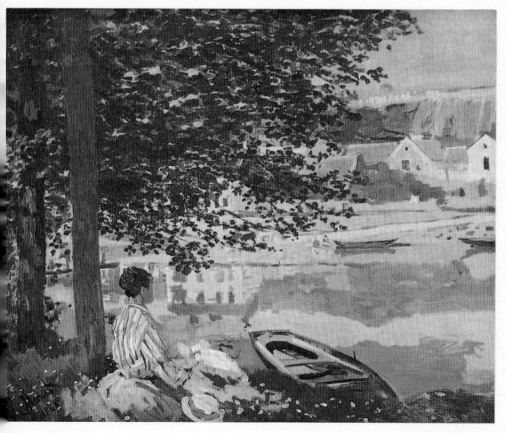

CHAPTER FOUR

Events leading to the Impressionist exhibition of 1874

By the end of 1869 all the major Impressionists knew each other well, and two of them – Monet and Renoir – had begun to paint in the technique which, when fully developed, characterized Impressionism at its height. At this time, too, the Café Guerbois (*Ill. 62*) on the Rue des Batignolles (later the Avenue de Clichy), near Manet's studio, became the headquarters of an artistic circle which was often argumentative, and even quarrelsome. Although many members of the group, for example, Renoir, Monet and Degas, confided to letters or journals their preference for the solitude of the country and their dislike of aesthetic discussion, most of them, including Monet, admitted that they had learned much from these gatherings. 'Nothing could have been more interesting', Monet recalled, 'than these *causeries* with their perpetual clash of opinions. They kept our wits sharpened. . . . From them we emerged with a firmer will, with our thoughts clearer and more distinct.' To say that one hated the wicked, expanding cities and longed for rural solitude was almost a moral obligation according to the code of Romanticism, but it is noticeable that in fact only Pissarro and Cézanne remained in the country, appearing only rarely at the Café Guerbois.

We know which painters assembled there and what they looked like, but we know less of what they talked about. We have not even the advantage of an unreliable, not to say mendacious, account such as George Moore later supplied of La Nouvelle Athènes, the successor to the Café Guerbois after the Franco-Prussian War. In the days of the Café Guerbois, Manet was apparently the dominating personality, with his ironical, sometimes cruel remarks. Degas was apt to discourse on the unsuitability of making art available to the lower classes, an attitude which might well have nettled Monet and Pissarro, whose sympathies were left-wing. Edmond Duranty described Degas as 'an artist of rare intelligence, preoccupied with ideas

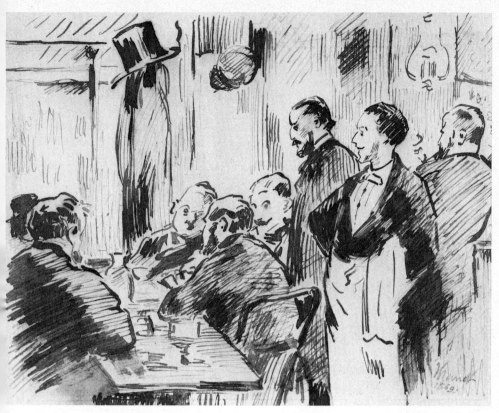

62 Manet *Café Guerbois* 1869

which seemed strange to the majority of his fellows . . . his brain was always active and boiling over; they called him the inventor of social chiaroscuro'. Duranty, although his own origins were humble, took care to proclaim that while he himself was a realist he was not a mud-stained or *déclassé* one. In saying this he was probably attacking the Courbet circle at the Brasserie Andler. As for Bazille, he apparently had sufficient academic training to be able to express his ideas clearly and to hold his own in conversation. But one can imagine that Sisley was too timid and Renoir too averse to aesthetic disputes for either to have played much part.

Rewald suggests that the group must have discussed artistic technique (the efficacy of painting in the open air, for example, and the

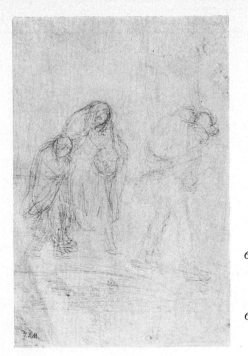

63 Millet
L'Arrivée au Barbizon 1847

64 Pissarro
Peasant Woman with a Donkey
1890 ▶

use of shadows). Manet believed that it was preferable for a painter to move abruptly from light to dark rather than to accumulate details which the eye does not see, whereas the open-air painters had become convinced that the colour of shadows was influenced by their surroundings – that they were not black, but rich in colour. Instead of dividing their work into dramatic areas of light and dark, as even Courbet did, the Impressionists used shadows to unite a picture in one dominant mood. The relationship between a spontaneous sketch and a finished picture may also have been discussed; from Delacroix onwards this was a matter of general controversy.

Nearly everyone in the group was enthusiastic about Japanese art, though each derived something different from it in accordance with his own tastes and needs. Degas appreciated the strange and unconventional viewpoints used by Japanese artists, their repudiation of post-Renaissance western perspective and their practice (which he had already imitated) of allowing figures to be cut by the picture-frame. Manet was perhaps confirmed by the Japanese in his free use

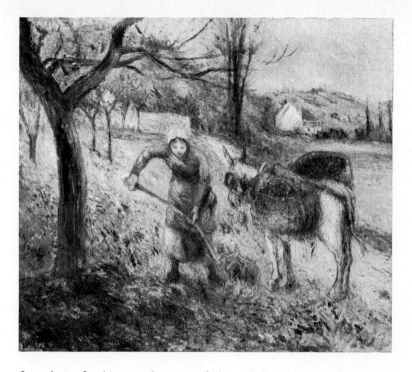

of patches of colour, and Monet followed the Japanese omission of detail in the interests of the picture as a whole.

The Impressionists' debt to Courbet and his circle is well illustrated by the cover of Duranty's short-lived periodical of 1856, *Réalisme*, in which Champfleury, Courbet's friend and the champion of realism, is shown fondling the new 'naturalism' as if it were his child. Although the painters and writers of the day often used the words 'realist' and 'naturalist' indiscriminately, as if they meant the same thing, we may perhaps use them to distinguish between the humanitarian, emotional attitude of Courbet, Millet or Proudhon, and the more dispassionate objectivity of the Impressionists. Even Pissarro, who was a socialist and anarchist, depicted peasants at their work without sentimentality and without overt compassion. (Compare Millet's *L'Arrivée au Barbizon*, 1847, *Ill. 63*, with Pissarro's *Peasant Woman with a Donkey*, 1890, *Ill. 64*.) The naturalists aimed at being more scientific than the realists and, as Baudelaire said, to 'convert delight into knowledge'.

The impromptu, immediate notation favoured by the Impressionists was not really suited to the solid documentation demanded by Zola, or for realizing Duranty's ideal that even the representation of a man's back should reveal his age, temperament and social status and whether he was coming from work or from a rendezvous. But the painters agreed entirely with the writers that the contemporary scene was their only possible subject-matter, and they did not hesitate to render the crowded, gas-lit boulevards of Paris, or informal family picnics. While this seems quite natural to us, it must be remembered that the most popular Salon pictures were still Gérôme's historical compositions (such as his *Sword Dance, Ill. 65*), which so often combined inaccurate historical details with unmistakably nineteenth-century gestures and faces. It was not long since Fantin-Latour had

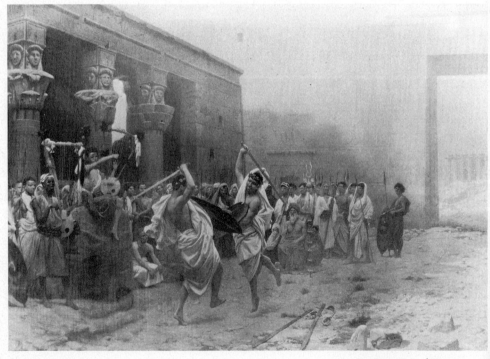

65 Gérôme *Sword Dance*

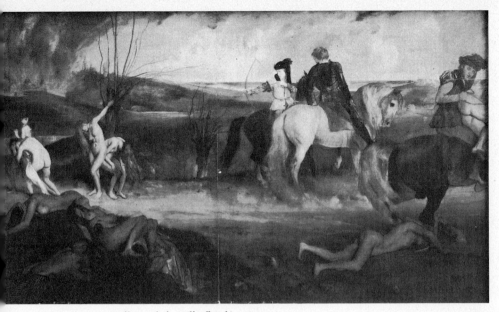

66 Degas *Les Malheurs de la Ville d'Orléans* 1865

painted the rather silly *Julia, Daughter of Augustus, Returning from a Night's Debauch* and since Degas had exhibited *Les Malheurs de la Ville d'Orléans* (1865, *Ill. 66*). A letter from Bazille to his parents in 1866 illustrates the double assumption of the Impressionists that the artist's choice of subject-matter is not really important and that, in any case, it should invariably be taken from nature and from the scene before the artist's eyes: 'I have tried to paint, as well as I can, the simplest possible subjects. In my opinion the subject matters little provided that what I do is interesting as painting. I have chosen to paint our own age because this is what I understand best, because it is more alive, and because I am painting for living people. So of course my pictures will be rejected.'

The mood of solidarity among the Impressionists at the beginning of the 1870s is expressed in several group portraits. Fantin-Latour, who had already shown a gathering of the friends in his *Homage to Delacroix* (*Ill. 67*), painted in 1870 *A Studio in the Batignolles Quarter* (*Ill. 68*), showing Manet at work in a company which includes Renoir, Zola, Bazille and Monet. (Pissarro and Sisley may have been

93

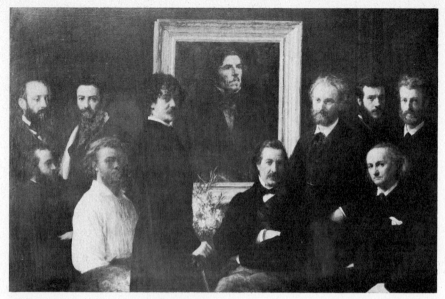

67 Fantin-Latour *Homage to Delacroix* 1864

68 Fantin-Latour *A Studio in the Batignolles Quarter* 1870

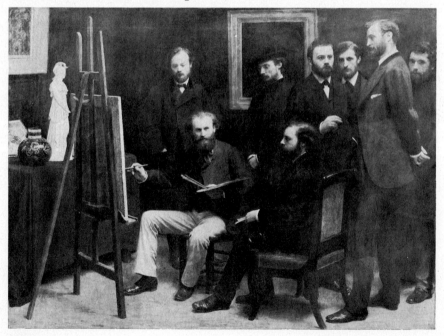

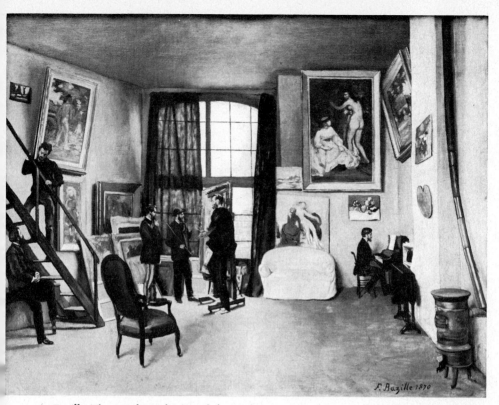

69 Bazille *The Artist's Studio, Rue de la Condamine* 1870

absent because they were less influenced than the others by Manet, or
simply because they were away from Paris at the time.) The picture
was immediately caricatured as 'Jesus Painting among the Disciples,
or the Divine School of Manet'. A more informal work, giving a
better idea of life as these young painters actually lived it, is Bazille's
The Artist's Studio, Rue de la Condamine (also 1870, *Ill. 69*). It was in
this studio that Bazille, more affluent than his friends, so often
sheltered other Impressionists. In the picture Zola is shown leaning
over the stairs talking to Renoir; Manet is inspecting the canvas on
the easel while Monet watches him, and the tall figure of Bazille,
painted in afterwards by Manet, stands opposite, holding his palette
and brushes.

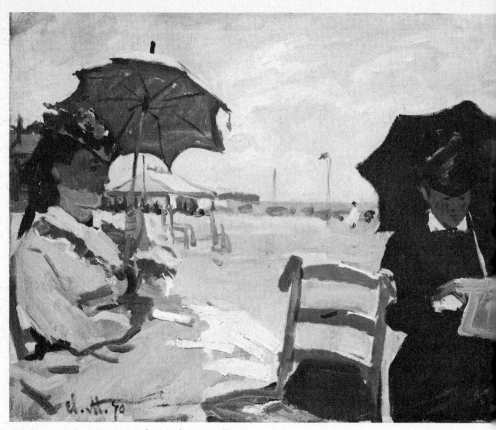

70 Monet *On the Beach, Trouville* 1870

After painting with Renoir in Bougival in 1869, Monet seems to have spent some time in the Ardennes and Paris. In June 1870 he married his model and mistress, Camille, and took her to the Hôtel Tivoli at Trouville, where he worked again with Boudin. In some of the paintings he did at this time the little figures resemble those of Boudin (*The Beach at Trouville*, *Hôtel des Roches-Noires*, and Boudin's painting on p. 34), but he also painted bolder, more powerful forms, as in *On the Beach, Trouville* (*Ill. 70*), in which the more vigorous attack has been compared with Courbet's style. One feels, however, that Courbet might have been shocked by the lack of rounded form and by the flat treatment of skirt and parasols.

96

71 Monet *The Beach at Trouville, Hôtel des Roches-Noires* 1870 ▶

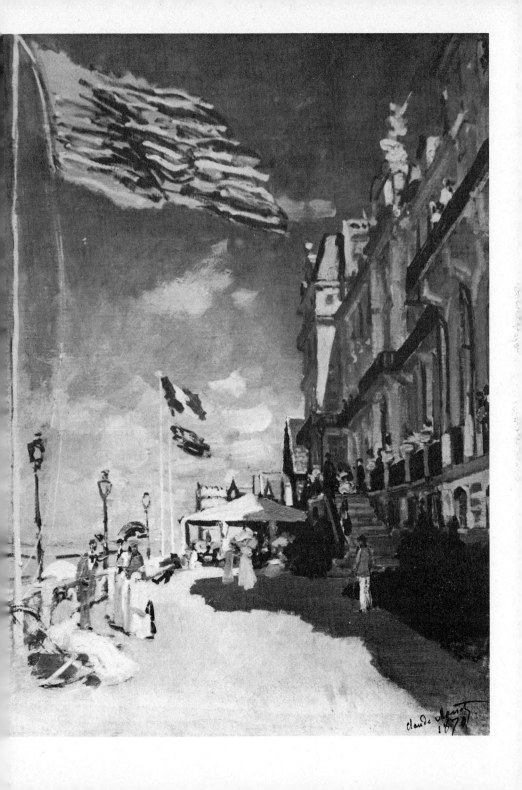

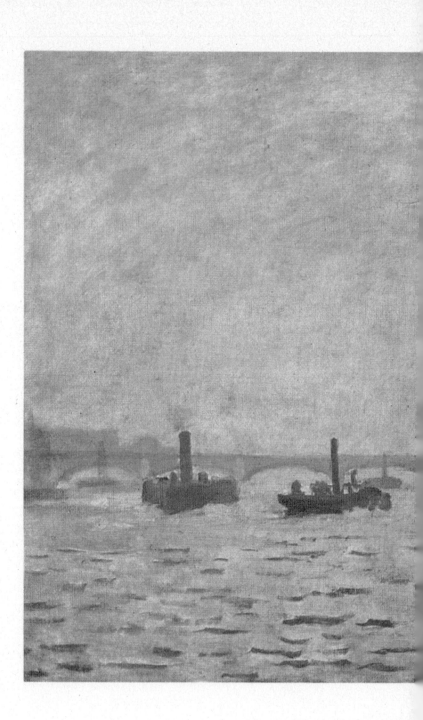

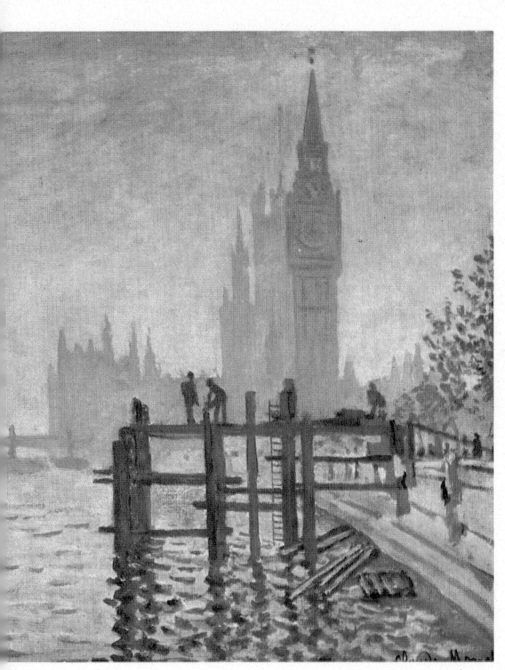

72 Monet *Westminster Bridge* 1871

In July 1870 the war with Prussia broke out, and by September Monet had witnessed the great rush to board the Channel boats going to safety in England. As a socialist and an opponent of Louis-Napoleon he felt no obligation to die for the Emperor; hence, leaving his wife with Boudin, he too fled to London. Here, once again, he was extremely poor until he met Daubigny, who had been fairly successful with his paintings of the Thames. With characteristic generosity, Daubigny introduced Monet to his own dealer, Durand-Ruel, offering to replace by his own canvases those of Monet which the dealer could not sell.

Through Durand-Ruel, Monet discovered that Pissarro had also taken refuge on the outskirts of London; here Pissarro lived with his half-sister before finally marrying Julie Vellay, who was soon to bear him a third child. Monet and Pissarro now met frequently, and painted some of those pictures which Kenneth Clark has described as 'the most complete naturalism which has ever been made into art'. Perhaps the stimulus of a strange environment and of the northern atmosphere quickened their talent; Impressionism was always a northern style, and even Renoir was far less of an Impressionist when he worked by the Mediterranean. Monet's painting had not always been as delicate as it became in London, and his great unorganized panoramas of Hyde Park (1871, *Ill. 73*) are exquisitely true to the light and particular atmosphere of the Bayswater end of the Park as it still is today. His view of Westminster Bridge (*Ill. 72*), painted in the same year, is far more ordered, especially in the careful horizontals and verticals of the wharf. Seitz has suggested that Monet may have found a precedent for such a tonal and geometric composition in Japanese prints or in the work of Whistler.

Among art historians this visit to London has become the subject of controversy, since there is a considerable difference of opinion about the extent to which Monet and Pissarro were influenced by the works of Constable and Turner which they saw at this time. The two extreme positions in this controversy – that the English painters exercised a decisive influence or that they exercised none – can only be sustained by an unrepresentative selection of pictures that the two Impressionists painted before and after the visit to England. The only first-hand accounts of this period were written nearly thirty years afterwards in letters from Pissarro to Wynford Dewhurst in 1902 and to his son Lucien in 1903 :

> Monet and I were very enthusiastic about the London land-scape. Monet worked in the parks, while I, living at Lower Norwood, at that time a charming suburb, studied the effect of fog, snow and springtime. We worked from nature. . . . We also visited the museums. The watercolours and paintings of Constable and Turner and the canvases of Old Crome have certainly had an influence upon us. We admired Gainsborough, Lawrence, Reynolds, etc., but were struck chiefly by the landscape painters who shared more in our aim with regard to *plein-air*, light and fugitive effects.

Pissarro later became more grudging :

> Turner and Constable, while they taught us something, showed us in their work that they had no understanding of the analysis of shadow, which in Turner's painting is simply used as an effect, a mere absence of light. As far as tone division is concerned, Turner proved its value although he did not apply it correctly and naturally.

73 Monet *Hyde Park* 1871

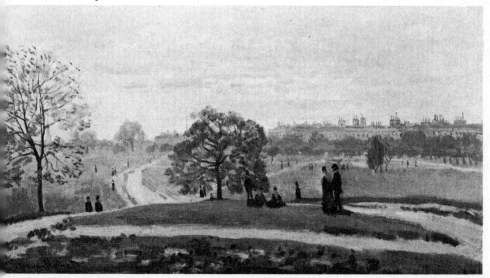

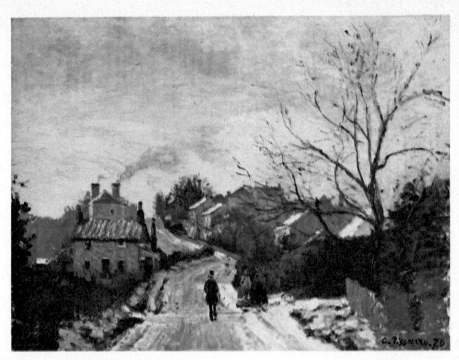

74 Pissarro *Lower Norwood, London* 1870

75 Pissarro *Crystal Palace* 1871

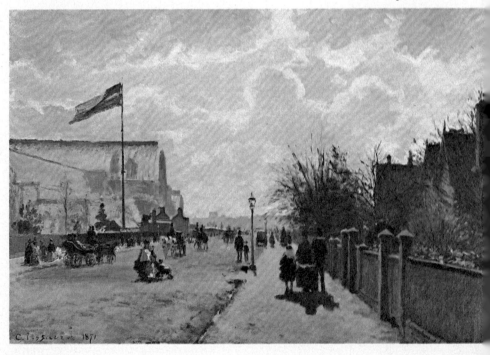

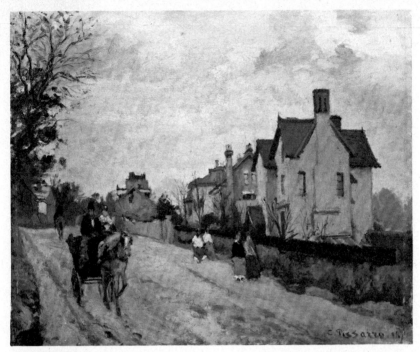

76 Pissarro *Upper Norwood, London* 1871

77 Pissarro *Dulwich College* 1871

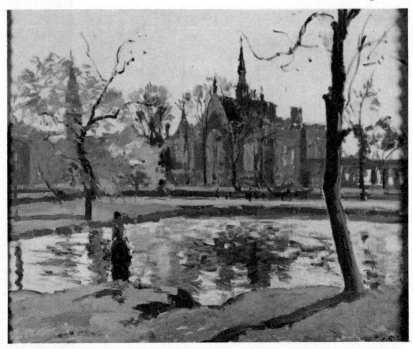

It must be remembered that before 1885, when Miss Isabel Constable gave a great number of the artist's oil sketches to the Victoria and Albert Museum, it was almost impossible to see these – the freest and most 'impressionistic' part of Constable's work. Pissarro's letter gives a hint, too, that he realized how much Turner was concerned only with 'the effect', with picture-making as opposed to naturalism. It seems likely that, in the main, Monet and Pissarro were cheered and encouraged along the path they had already chosen by the example of these English painters who had preceded them.

It also appears that Pissarro's style developed the more rapidly in England, although both he and Monet achieved a looser technique and greater lightness of colour. This was surely because Pissarro was seeing so much of Monet, who had already evolved with Renoir at La Grenouillère the small rapid touches which Pissarro now began to use. Pissarro's *Entrance to the Village of Voisins* (*Ill. 78*), painted in 1872 after his return to France, conveys the atmosphere of soft spring sunshine more effectively than any of his earlier works. It uses one of his and Corot's favourite motifs, a road, and shows that Monet, too, could learn something from his companion, who had a greater sense of construction and perspective, though far less power of conveying the continual movement of light and shade. As Benedict Nicolson writes: 'For Pissarro earth does not vary with every slant of the sun or cloud which passes; it is solid and permanent, harsh and recalcitrant as for Courbet, his real master. Light, which is Monet's godsend, is here made to play a more subordinate role.'

Durand-Ruel bought their pictures (*The Crystal Palace, Ill. 75*, was the first of Pissarro's which he acquired), but the Royal Academy rejected the works of both artists. Pissarro began to make unflattering remarks about London: 'Here there is no art; everything is a question of business.' Although a few perceptive critics, such as Hamerton, were writing about 'art for art's sake', the general taste for literal and literary art no doubt made it difficult for the English to understand the succinct and detached art of Impressionism.

At this time Monet surprised his friends by his range and variety, a variety particularly evident in the pictures painted in Holland,

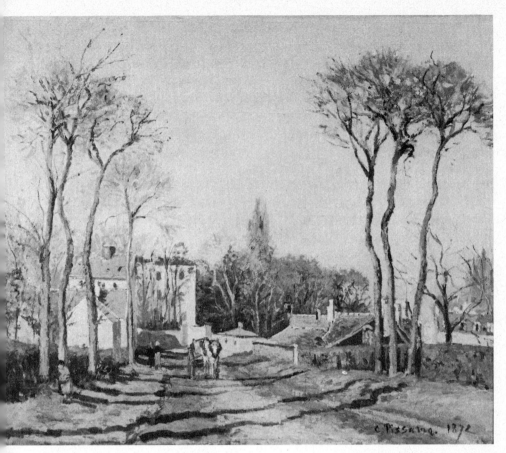

78 Pissarro *Entrance to the Village of Voisins* 1872

where he went from England in 1871 and again, from France, in 1872. These pictures were quite unlike those executed in London. Some of them have less atmospheric unity than *Westminster Bridge*, but they are freely and broadly handled with scalloped brush-strokes, which gives movement to the waves. Later he painted the canals of Amsterdam in dots, a technique that seems to foreshadow the divisionism of neo-Impressionism. A rather uncharacteristic work, *Unloading Coal* (1872, *Ill. 79*), must have been painted after his return to Argenteuil, where he rented a house until 1876. The gloomy,

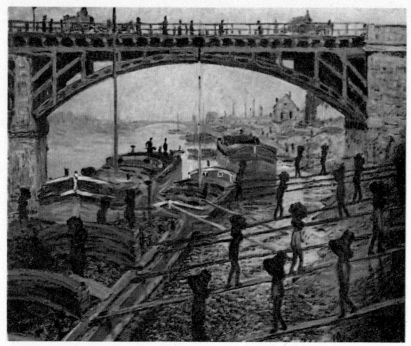

79 Monet *Unloading Coal, Argenteuil* 1872

80 Pissarro *The Road, Louveciennes* 1870

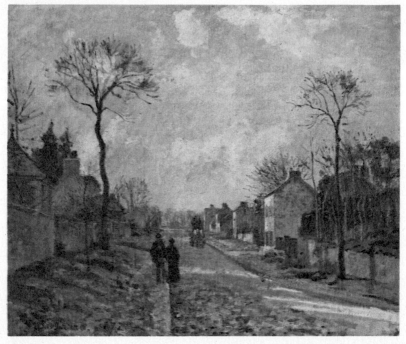

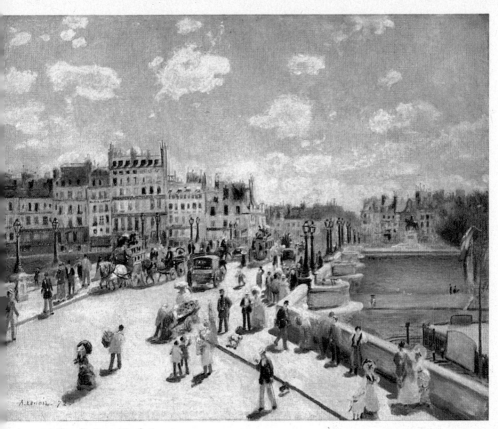

81 Renoir *Pont Neuf* 1872

dehumanized procession of men carrying coal might almost have been painted by a humanitarian or an expressionist working in a spirit of social criticism, but Monet was probably more concerned with the repeated diagonals of the gangplanks, the atmospheric subtlety of water and light, and the little figures, which may have been suggested to him by Japanese prints he bought in Holland.

In France during the war Renoir had little opportunity to paint. At the beginning of 1870, before war broke out, two of his works had been accepted by the Salon: the Courbet-like *La Baigneuse au Griffon* and his mistress painted as a *Femme d'Alger*, his tribute to Delacroix, whose influence was one of the mainsprings of his art for the next six years. Forty years later he told Vollard that Delacroix's *Femmes d'Alger* was one of the greatest pictures in the world; he made a free copy of it in 1872 and one of *The Jewish Wedding* in 1875. His visits to Algeria in the 1880s were prompted in part by this enthusiasm for Delacroix, who had been in that country in 1832.

After France declared war in July 1870, Renoir's movements were very much circumscribed. He was conscripted and sent first to Bordeaux, then to the Pyrenees with a regiment of cuirassiers. There he became so ill with dysentery that his companions gave up hope of his survival, being 'accustomed', as he wrote to Charles Le Cœur in March 1871, 'to seeing us Parisians die'. He was rescued by an uncle who took him away to recover in Bordeaux. During the Commune he was in Paris, and the years immediately afterwards, spent in Paris and near Bougival, were the period of his purest Impressionist work. At this time he painted those sparkling, sun-drenched pictures of the *Pont Neuf* (1872, *Ill. 81*) and the *Quai de Conti*, which give an extraordinarily accurate impression of Paris in the summer light. Renoir sometimes preserved the spontaneous and transitory character of such scenes by sketching, from a window, passers-by whom his brother had stopped with bogus enquiries. He had been interested earlier in painting the streets, quays and bridges of Paris, but a comparison of the *Pont Neuf* with previous pictures, such as the *Pont des Arts* (*Ill. 60*), shows how far he had advanced in the mastery of light and atmosphere. By comparison, the *Pont des Arts* or the *Champs-Élysées*, both of 1867, look stiff and resemble the work of Diaz or Courbet.

Some of the best accounts of life in Paris during the siege are those written by Berthe Morisot to her newly married sister. Her letters, sent by balloon, describe the continual noise of artillery and the gloomy prophecies of the Manet brothers, who sought to make her leave Paris by saying, 'You would be better off if you lost your hand or became disfigured.' She also reported that Manet spent most of the time changing into grand uniforms. He and Degas were both in the artillery, and this period of military service further impaired

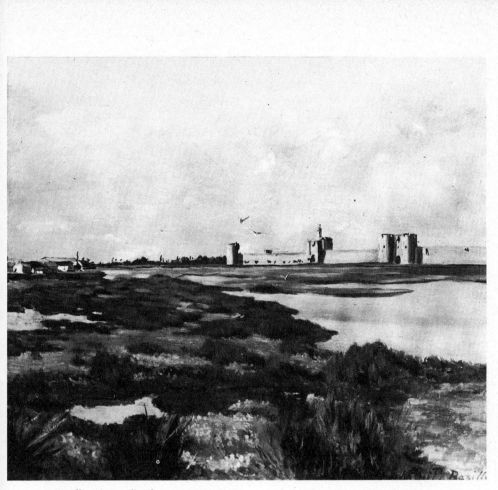

82 Bazille *The Walls of Aigues-Mortes* 1867

Degas' already weak eyesight. Although Berthe seems anxious to reassure her sister, she mentions the fact that on all their walks she and her friends come upon corpses. Manet wrote to his wife that people were eating cats, dogs and rats, since donkey- and horse-meat had become too rare and expensive.

The most tragic result of the war for the Impressionist group was the death of Bazille, who had enlisted in the Zouaves and was killed in action at the end of 1870.

Cézanne said of Pissarro that 'if he had continued to paint as he did in 1870 he would be the strongest of us all'. Although this may be unfair to some of Pissarro's later masterpieces of the 1890s, it is true that the years immediately after the war and his return from England constituted a perfect balance and delicacy in his art. His individuality was already apparent in 1870 in his wonderful *Diligence at Louveciennes* (*Ill. 83*), in which he used gleaming patterns of light and shadow applied in small dabs – a method that Renoir, Monet and perhaps he himself had discovered when painting the waters of the Seine.

Soon after his return to France in June 1871, Pissarro left Louveciennes, where he had been living before the war, and settled in the Hermitage district of Pontoise. He was joined there by several younger friends, the most gifted of whom was Cézanne. Pissarro always maintained a confidence in Cézanne which was far from general. He once wrote that Cézanne would 'astonish a lot of artists

83 Pissarro *Diligence at Louveciennes* 1870

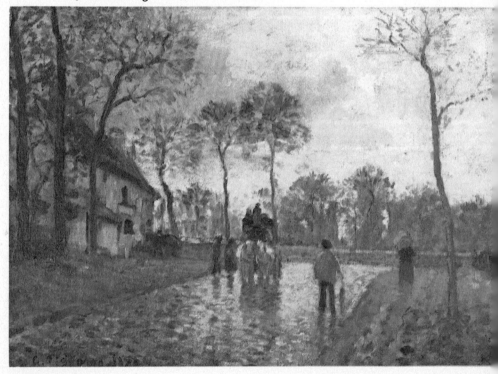

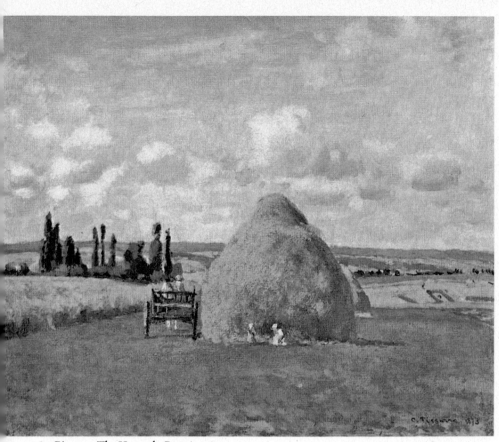

84 Pissarro *The Haystack, Pontoise* 1873

who were in too great a hurry to condemn him'. Soon after moving to Pontoise, Pissarro painted the luminous *Entrance to the Village of Voisins* (*Ill. 78*), and a scene of the River Oise which included smokestacks. These were still considered too humble a theme for artistic representation, although Degas had placed them in the background of race-scenes and Seurat was to paint them with relish a little later.

In his pamphlet on the Impressionists published in 1878, Théodore Duret described Pissarro as 'the most naturalist of them all. He sees nature and simplifies it through its most permanent aspects. . . . His canvases communicate to the highest degree the situation of space and solidity; they set free an impression of melancholy.' This is certainly true of one of the masterpieces of the 1870s, *The Haystack, Pontoise* (*Ill. 84*), in which the colours are extremely soft and varied, and a sensation of solidity is evoked by the conical haystack. Duret's judgment may have been based on the fact that the quality of Pissarro's pictures depends a great deal on the actual scene he is painting and the pleased recognition it evokes in the spectator. In other words, the fact that a painting by Pissarro may be crudely bright or heavy and mud-coloured is based on the honesty of his reporting rather than vagaries of his technique.

Immediately after the war prospects seemed relatively bright for these young artists. When Hoschedé, director of a Paris department store, sold a group of their works, the prices for the paintings of Monet, Degas, Sisley and Pissarro were fairly high. In 1873 Durand-Ruel felt confident enough to prepare a complete catalogue of the contents of his gallery, illustrated with etchings and with a preface by Armand Silvestre. But this catalogue was never published, for there was a financial crash in 1873, followed by a six-year depression, and the number of private buyers dwindled. Durand-Ruel was even forced to sell at a loss various major works of the Barbizon school in order to pay his creditors.

The Salon of 1873 was so hostile to novelty that once again a Salon des Refusés was set up. But this solution was unsatisfactory for the Impressionists, since it meant that their works would be shown with the stigma of refusal on them and in company with hundreds of mediocre pictures which had been justifiably rejected. The success of Manet's rather meretricious *Bon-Bock* at the Salon, where so many of his more serious works had been refused, confirmed their view that they could secure the admission of their pictures only by a sacrifice of integrity. Consequently from 1873 onwards many of the group abstained from sending work to the Salon.

Long before, in 1867, Monet and Bazille had conceived a plan for holding a group exhibition to be quite separate from the official Salon. When Monet revived the idea in 1873, Duret and others discouraged him. They believed that success could be achieved only at the Salon, which was the one gallery capable of attracting a public larger than the small nucleus of artists and patrons who already knew the Impressionists' work. Surprisingly enough, Degas, who had never much favoured the practice of open-air painting and refused to be identified with the Impressionists, was enthusiastic about the proposal for a new group exhibition. He wrote warmly about it to James Tissot and Alphonse Legros in London, urging them to join: 'The realist movement no longer needs to fight with others. It is, it exists, it has to show itself *separately*; there must be a *realist Salon*.'

At first it was proposed to invite some of the older masters, such as Corot, Courbet and Daubigny. But this idea was abandoned, perhaps because these established painters agreed with Corot, who was entirely against the idea. Pissarro suggested and prepared a complicated plan for a co-operative association, weighed down with cumbersome rules; but Renoir successfully opposed this in favour of an agreement that each painter should contribute to the group fund one-tenth of his income from any sales. Greater difficulties arose over questions of inclusion. Degas sensibly insisted that they should invite some 'respectable artists', who would appear less offensive and revolutionary to the general public – men such as Boudin, Stanislas Lépine and Giuseppe de Nittis. Pissarro found it difficult at first to persuade Degas or even Monet to allow Cézanne's work to be included, but he prevailed in the end. Berthe Morisot, whose work was almost always accepted at the Salon, resisted the appeals of Manet and exhibited with the group, but Fantin-Latour, Legros and Tissot were among those who refused.

Altogether thirty-nine artists participated with over 165 works, of which Degas contributed ten, the largest number by any single artist. Allocation of hanging space was decided by size and by lot; the hanging was done by Renoir on reddish-brown wallpaper and the catalogue was prepared by his brother Edmond. The latter's impatience with Monet's humdrum titles may have been the reason why Monet decided to vary them by calling one *Impression: Sunrise* (*Ill. 85*). Derisively quoted by a critic, this title ultimately gave its name to the group as a whole.

113

85 Monet
Impression: Sunrise 1872

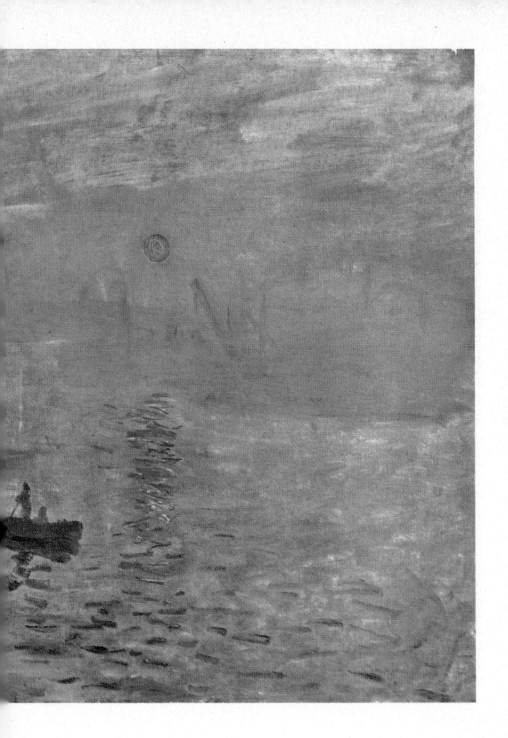

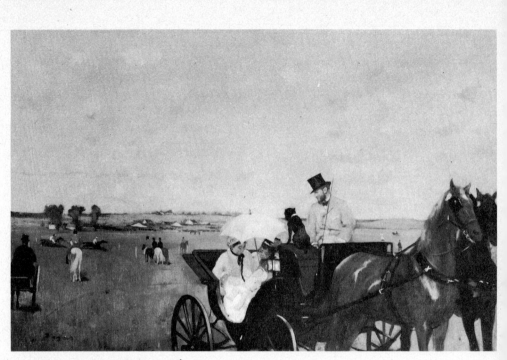

86 Degas *Carriage at the Races* 1870–3

The exhibition was open (evenings included) from 15 April to 15 May 1874 in the studios recently vacated by the photographer Nadar at the corner of the Boulevard des Capucines and Rue Daunou. Among the masterpieces shown at the first exhibition by the self-styled 'Société anonyme des artistes, peintres, sculpteurs, graveurs, etc.' were Degas' *Carriage at the Races* (*Ill. 86*), Cézanne's *Maison du Pendu*, Renoir's *Harvesters* and *La Loge* (*Ill. 119*), and Berthe Morisot's *Hide-and-Seek* (*Ill. 87*), which belonged to Manet.

The ridicule brought forth by this first exhibition is too well known to require discussion here. It is a fate common to innovators in the arts, and only with the passage of time does the public come to accept, and objectively criticize, the truly new. In view of the fluorescent tones used by Pop and Op artists of today, the brilliant colours of the Impressionists, so shocking initially, seem tame. However, it was not only the colours which were found to be offensive, but also the strange distortion of forms. The features found most laughable in 1874 were the 'cottony legs' of Renoir's dancer and the many 'black-tongue-lickings' (actually human beings) at the bottom of Monet's *Boulevard des Capucines* (*Ill. 6*). The enterprise made so little money that the 'société' had to be liquidated. Still, the exhibition had served a purpose; it had given the group cohesion and acted as a precedent for future, more successful ventures of the same kind. Between 1874 and 1886 there were eight Impressionist exhibitions.

87 Morisot *Hide-and-Seek* 1872–3

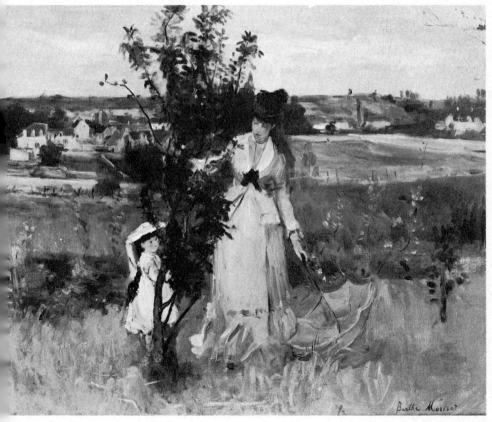

CHAPTER FIVE

The relationship of Manet and Degas
to the Impressionists

Vague or specialized definitions of Impressionism have been attempted in order to include both Édouard Manet and Edgar Degas within the movement. It is true that these two artists were concerned, like Monet and his friends, with the passing moment, with the concrete and particularized actuality of life around them rather than with the archaic and smooth generalities of Salon painting. But their relationships with the Impressionist painters were complicated and changeable. They were separated from the Impressionists by artistic aims, social class, education and, perhaps above all, by their age. Sometimes Manet and Degas seem like the more sophisticated and articulate elder brothers of Impressionism, often helpful, occasionally scornful, but not too proud to learn a trick or two from their juniors.

Born in 1832, Manet was older than Renoir and Monet by eight and nine years respectively, whereas only two years separated him from Degas, who was born in 1834. As Parisians from 'good' families, Manet and Degas had far more early opportunities than Monet and his group for contacts with writers and musicians. This helped to mould their artistic ideas and also affected the themes of their pictures, as in Degas' strange genre studies of modern life (*Ill. 89*), his scenes of the Opéra and the orchestra, and the drawings he did for the Goncourts' *Fille d'Elise*.

As young men they undoubtedly became aware of the new 'realist' movement (growing out of and replacing the humanitarianism of Daumier and Courbet), embodied in such periodicals as *Réalisme*, whose editor, Duranty, later became one of their friends. Manet's relationship with Baudelaire was close and important at the time when the poet was writing *Peintre de la Vie Moderne* (which appeared in 1863) and Manet was working on *Musique aux Tuileries* (*Ill. 51*), shown at Martinet's gallery in the same year.

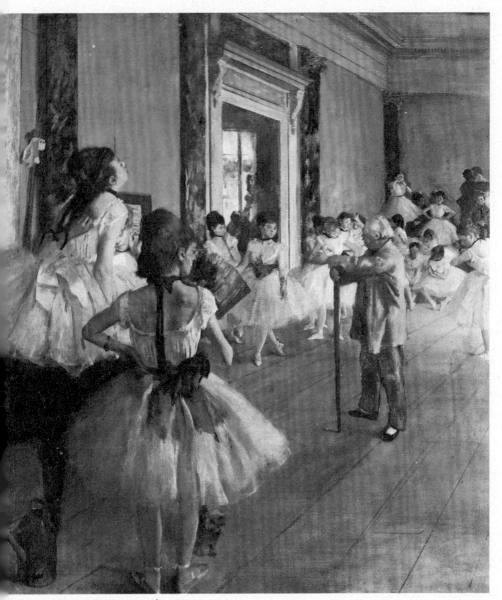

88 Degas *The Dancing Class* 1874

The early paintings of Manet and Degas, together with the latter's unpublished notebooks, show the same painful transition which the writers also had to make from idealized romantic daydreams towards what Manet's friend Zola called 'this sublime reality which comes to us from God'. 'There are certain days', Zola wrote, 'when beyond the scents and the shimmering visions . . . I glimpse the hard outlines of things as they are.' This is the same feeling which made the young Manet annoy the models at his master Couture's studio by asking them whether they assumed such exaggerated poses when they were buying radishes in the market. Degas expresses a similar attitude in an early jotting in a notebook: 'M. Beaucousin's *Ariosto* appeals to me very much, but how can we find a composition which paints our time?' and in the more celebrated and classical cry: 'Oh Giotto, don't prevent me from seeing Paris and you, Paris, don't prevent me from seeing Giotto!' Baudelaire epitomizes this strain in contemporary feeling when he declares, in *Les Fleurs du Mal*: 'The man who does not accept the conditions of ordinary life sells his soul.'

The mature paintings of Manet and Degas have far greater unity and economy than the more sprawling compositions of Courbet and the Barbizon painters. In this respect they can be seen to inhabit the same mental world as their literary friends, who were reacting against the longwindedness, and the *penchant* for fantastic 'Gothick' details, of so many of the Romantic writers. When *Les Misérables* appeared in 1862 even the great Hugo was ridiculed for his prolixity. At the other extreme, Stéphane Mallarmé (1842–98), whom Manet saw almost daily for ten years, insisted that, in the cause of brevity, the word *comme* must be struck out of the poet's vocabulary. According to Manet's friend Antonin Proust, Manet often said that he loathed all that was unnecessary in painting: 'Concision in art is a necessity and an elegance. The verbose painter bores: who will get rid of all these trimmings?' The answer was, of course, Manet himself and, still more, Degas, whose rapid line and uncluttered pictures are the counterpart of his own swift, epigrammatic wit. To a considerable extent their economy and directness were adopted by the Impressionists, who ceased to include small details in their pictures just as they ceased to labour for a high finish.

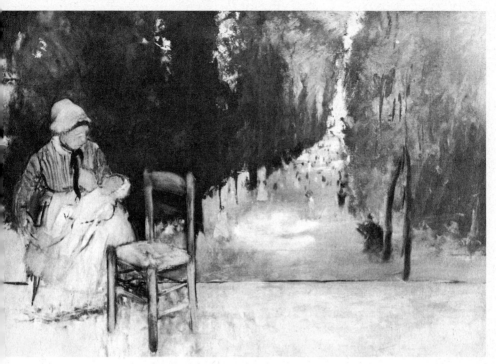

89 Degas *Nursemaid in the Luxembourg Gardens* 1871–2

The detached, impersonal quality of the art of Manet and Degas has perhaps been over-stressed ever since the radical critic Thoré-Burger complained that Manet's vice was to value a man's head no more than a slipper. Meyer Schapiro, in a classic review, has shown that this criticism rests upon a confusion and that the cool, impersonal tone of Manet and Degas does not in the least imply that choice of subject was a matter of indifference to them. Indeed, it seems odd that the contrary opinion can be maintained in view of the highly original and personal themes selected by these painters, so much more varied than those of the Impressionists. Their originality and range can be seen in Manet's novel type of modern historical picture, such as *The Kersearge and Alabama*, depicting a naval battle in the

American Civil War, and in Degas' genre scenes from everyday life, for example, *The Pedicure* (*Ill. 90*) and *The Cotton Exchange* (*Ill. 91*).

The detached air of their painting was partly a matter of temperament. In spirit, if not by birth, they were both fastidious aristocrats who wished to efface themselves behind their work. Their natural reticence was further strengthened by the contemporary reaction against the unleashed feelings and autobiographical indiscretions of the Romantics. Monet, Renoir and Pissarro also distrusted the

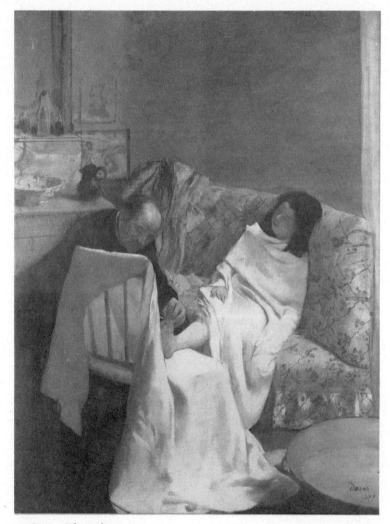

90 Degas *The Pedicure* 1873

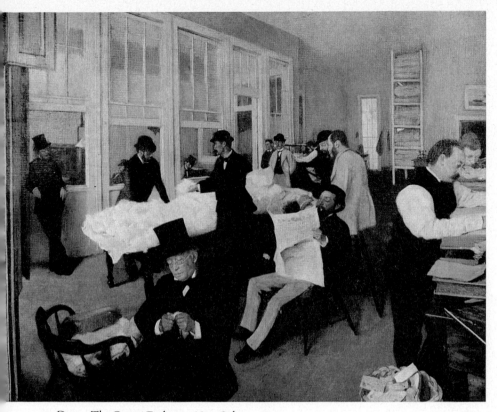

91 Degas *The Cotton Exchange, New Orleans* 1873

rhetoric and pathetic fallacies of earlier 'nature' painting; but in so far as their art was detached this was less obvious in their landscapes than in their figure painting, and therefore less enraging to critics. Besides, they did not and could not aspire to the role of the dandy, the *flâneur*, the elegant Parisian stroller, the sophisticated commentator on modern life, as Manet and Degas did. N. G. Sandblad has suggested that Manet's *Musique aux Tuileries* (*Ill. 51*) owed much to the artist's conception of himself and his friends as upper-middle-class *flâneurs*. At the time that picture was painted the Tuileries Gardens were just replacing the Palais-Royal as the meeting-place of the élite, and Manet, who loved parties and the fashionable world, was choosing an extremely up-to-date theme.

There were other respects in which Manet and Degas differed from the Impressionists. As Parisians, they did not have the same early contact with the open-air landscape painters of Normandy and Barbizon; this influence came to them only later, from their juniors. More important, perhaps, they were both old enough to dislike the brash and noisy propaganda for an art of social realism which emanated from Courbet and his satellites in the Brasserie Andler. In fact, Manet was influenced by Courbet's art and example (for instance, in *Le Déjeuner sur l'Herbe*, with its strong greens and bright nude against a dark background), but as soon as Manet began to exhibit, he and his critic-friends felt the need to distinguish his art as sharply as possible from the works of Courbet and, even more, from Courbet's socialist interpreters. In this respect Manet was in harmony with the doctrine of *l'art pour l'art* preached by Gautier, the Parnassian poets and many other writers. When Prudhon, in *Du Principe de l'Art* (1865), made a plea for a humanitarian, morally elevating and semi-propagandistic art, Flaubert wrote to the Goncourts: 'I have just read Proudhon's work on art. Every word of it is filth.' Zola, who was to be neither right-wing nor politically indifferent, addressed the humanitarian followers of Proudhon: 'Artists are not at anyone's service – and we refuse to enter yours.'

On the other hand, Courbet and his friends were somewhat jealous of Manet for replacing Courbet as a *succès de scandale*. 'This young man shouldn't play the role of a Velasquez in front of us,' Courbet said. Manet and Degas were further alienated from Courbet's circle by their pessimism and political disillusionment. Their disenchanted melancholy, and their distrust of the big resounding phrases which had been characteristic of earlier writers and politicians, were based partly on their disappointment at the outcome of the 1848 revolution and their disgust with the moneyed mediocrities of the Second Empire. Baudelaire wrote of Gautier and Leconte de Lisle, 'Without any difficulty both know how to avoid ever being taken in'; and Manet and Degas could have been described in the same words.

But within this framework of patrician disgust, the two painters differed profoundly about politics, as they did in many other fields. For such an intelligent man, Degas seems to have been politically

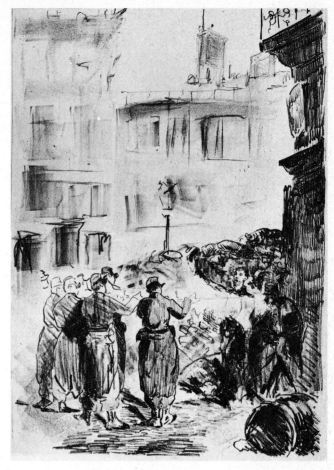

92 Manet
The Barricade 1871
(S. P. Avery
Collection,
The New York
Public Library)

hidebound. He was a banker's son who scorned the rabble and loved tradition so much that he said of Louis XIV's court: 'They were dirty perhaps, but distinguished; we are clean but we are common.' He was a fanatic anti-Dreyfusard and separated himself from his dearest Jewish friends, including the Halévys, for many years; he would even question a model about her race and dismiss her if she were Jewish.

Manet, on the other hand, was a left-wing Republican and a consistent enemy of the Empire from the age of sixteen, when he wrote to his father from Rio de Janeiro: 'Try to keep a good Republic for us against our return; I'm afraid Louis-Napoleon is not a very good Republican.' This political allegiance affected the themes of his pictures, as in the fragment *The Execution of Maximilian* (1867, *Ill. 94*) in the Kunsthalle, Mannheim. He represented the firing squad in French, not Mexican, uniforms as a way of criticizing French policy. During the Commune of 1871, together with Corot, Courbet and Daumier, Manet was elected to the Fédération des Artistes de Paris, and his barricade scenes (*Ill. 92*) recall the work of Goya in their horror at the cruelties of the oncoming army. He also painted such Republican heroes as Gambetta and depicted the escape of Rochefort, a Communard journalist, from a penal colony by boat.

Many of the characteristics Manet and Degas had in common may be attributed to the fact that both were eldest sons, with all the pioneering qualities and sensitivity (not to say neuroses) which this

93 Degas *Semiramis Founding a Town* 1861

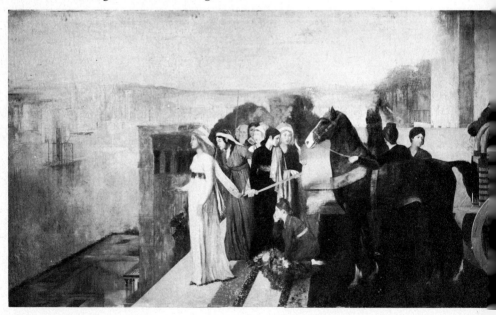

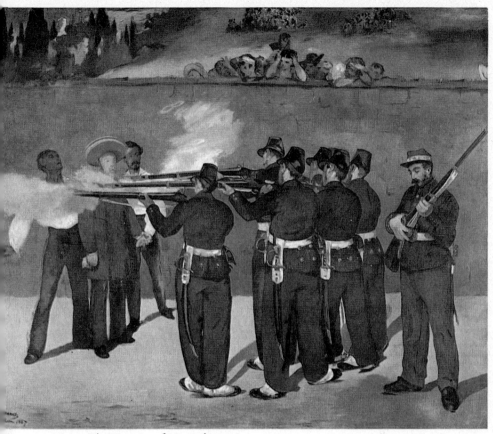

94 Manet *The Execution of Maximilian* 1867

position in a family sometimes breeds. Degas' beautiful Creole mother died when he was a boy of fourteen, and he soon developed a mask of toughness to hide his susceptibility. But Manet showed so clearly how much he minded criticism of his work that in 1865 Baudelaire wrote to him, 'It's really stupid that you should get so worked up. You're laughed at, your merits are not appreciated. So what? Do you think you're the first man to be in that position?'

Manet was far more addicted than Degas to the Salon, which he called 'the real field of battle', and he advised his friends to put on

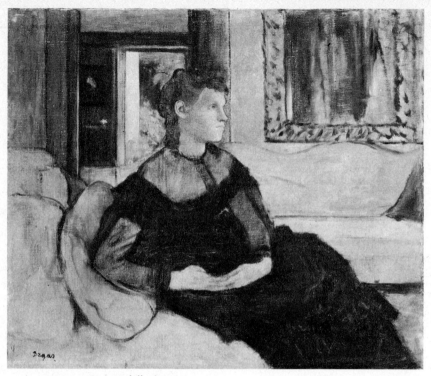

95 Degas *Mme Gobillard-Morisot* 1869

tail-coats and go out more in the world. 'Why slop about in slippers?' he asked them. Degas was by no means a bohemian, and for years he loved parties, but he was far less conformist than Manet, and when the latter advised him to accept a medal he exploded: 'This is not the first time I have realized what a bourgeois you are, Manet.' In return, Manet was often heard to remark that he was already painting his contemporaries while Degas was still busy painting ladies like Semiramis (*Ill. 93*). This distinction does not in fact hold good, and the two men continually exercised a reciprocal influence on each other. There were occasional storms, notably when Degas painted Manet's wife playing the piano and Manet, finding the portrait unflattering, cut it in half. But generally they had the utmost respect for each other's genius. 'Manet, that tremendous talent,' Degas would say.

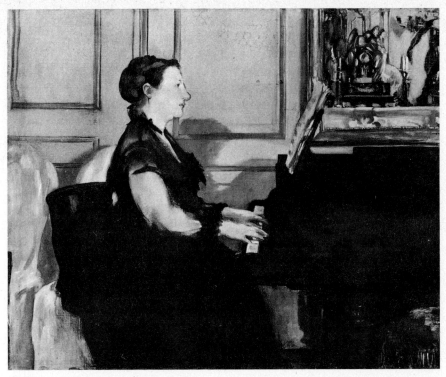

96 Manet *Mme Manet at the Piano* 1867

This respect was whetted by the many differences in their attitude towards painting. Degas, who had been trained by the disciples of Ingres, saw himself primarily as a draughtsman. He complained that he had tried to urge his friends in the same direction but that they were all preoccupied with colour. Those who most felt his influence (Lautrec, Gauguin and Suzanne Valadon) were preoccupied with line. Manet, who was far more painterly than Degas, used a rich, loose brush-stroke and gloried in a style that was rapid and spontaneous: 'There is only one important thing. . . . Put down what you see the first time. If that's it, that's it.' Whereas Degas said: 'There is nothing less spontaneous than my art.'

Both were interested in new techniques. Manet employed what was called *la peinture claire*, laying on light passages in flat areas of paint and adding the dark passages before the others had time to dry.

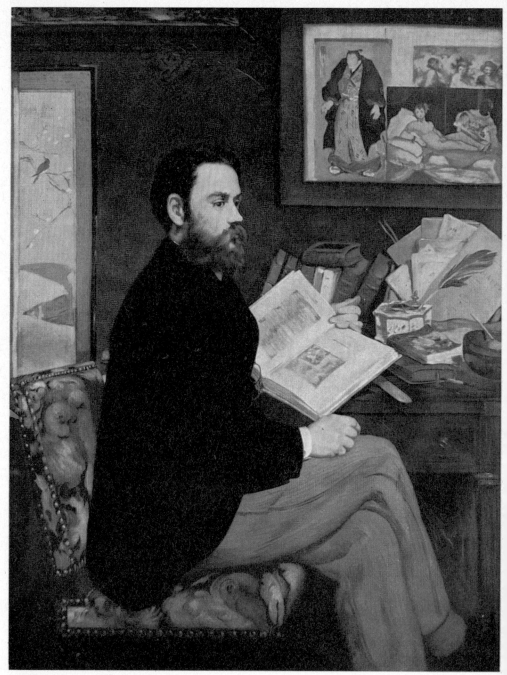

97 Manet *Portrait of Émile Zola* 1868

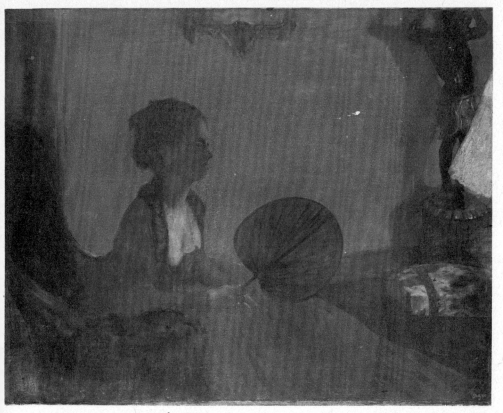

98 Degas *Mme Camus with a Japanese Screen* 1870

Like Chardin or Renoir, he apparently did not work all over the canvas at the same time, as can be seen in the watercolour sketch for *Le Déjeuner sur l'Herbe* (*Ill. 54*). He also liked to use pure, flat colours without shadows, and he painted with the light behind his head, which flattened the object and obviated the need for modelling. This caused Courbet, who liked dense and substantial forms, to complain that Manet's *Olympia*, shown at the Salon of 1865, looked like the Queen of Spades on a playing-card. Degas sometimes said that painters were too fond of using an over-loaded brush; his own paint is often thin or refined with essence.

Manet and Degas resembled each other chiefly in being the supreme illustrators of Parisian life in their time and, as S. Lane

Faison has pointed out, because they both 'insisted on fitting what they saw of the brilliant passing show into a language of pattern, of attenuated shapes of infinitely subtle colour relationships disengaged from a particular moment in time. At heart they were both – to use a modern term – abstract artists.' Manet was interested in rendering elegance and charm, whereas Degas explored the beauty of the *jolie laide* and of attitudes generally considered unbecoming, such as yawning or scratching the back. When the two men first met it was Manet who had most to teach the other. Degas had hitherto found his closest friends among painters of academic or historical subjects, such as Léon Bonnat and Gustave Moreau, even while he was longing to depict contemporary life. But one suspects that any such discrepancy between them in experience was soon balanced by the far more acute sense which Degas possessed of the harmony and composition of a canvas as a whole. As evidence of Degas' influence on Manet, Faison has cited Degas' *Collector of Prints* (1866) and Manet's *Portrait of Émile Zola* (1868, *Ill. 97*). I would add Degas' portrait of Mme Gobillard (*Ill. 95*) and Manet's *Mme Manet at the Piano* (*Ill. 96*).

In the 1870s Renoir, Monet and Sisley were usually known as 'la bande à Manet'. Manet was regarded as their leader, having replaced Courbet as the figurehead of the adventurous younger generation. Manet was an ambivalent, complex artist, and his relations with the Impressionists were no simpler than anything else about him. It is hard to think of any other great nineteenth-century painter whose originality and whose legacy to succeeding generations have been so foolishly belittled, not only in his lifetime, which is understandable, but right down to the present day. Books have been written with such titles as *Manet, or the Lack of Spirituality*, and critics have concentrated on bewailing his worldliness and his artistic borrowings. His reputation in France may have suffered from the hostility of Degas' supporters (such as Jacques-Émile Blanche) and in England from the success of flashy, academic portraitists like Orpen, who imitated Manet's ease of manner without having his genius.

But if Degas' friends undervalued Manet, it is clear that Degas himself and the Impressionists did not. In their period of development, Monet and Renoir in particular owed a great deal to Manet's free, vigorous brush-strokes, his habit of painting directly onto a white canvas, his blond colours, and the concision and overall unity of his compositions. His elimination of half-tones, by exploding the academic doctrine that a painting must be based on intermediate tones progressing from dark to light, established the Impressionists' right to paint in whatever colours or tonalities they wished, and they quickly availed themselves of this right. Even more exhilarating, perhaps, was Manet's accurate sense of the everyday life of contemporary Paris, whether it was embodied in a picture of a fashionable stroll or of a queue at the butcher's shop during the siege (*Ill. 99*). Part of Manet's fascination for the Impressionists lay in the fact that he was the 'peintre de la vie moderne' that Baudelaire had demanded.

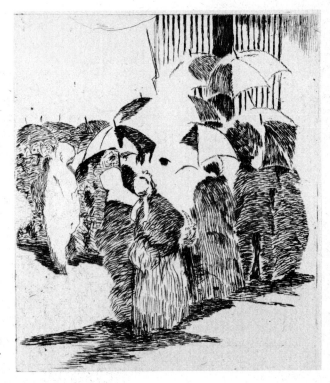

99 Manet
Queue in front of the
Butcher's Shop 1871

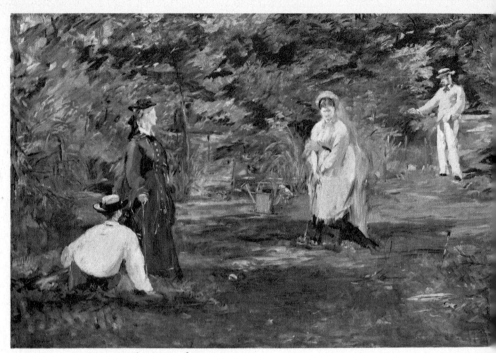

100 Manet *The Game of Croquet* 1873

101 Manet *River at Argenteuil* 1874

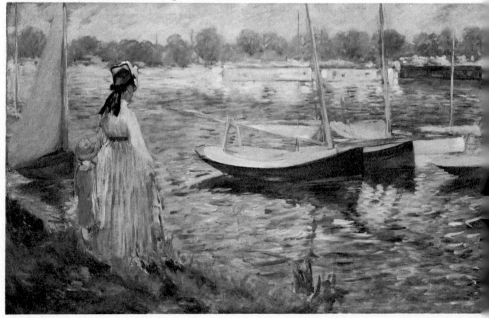

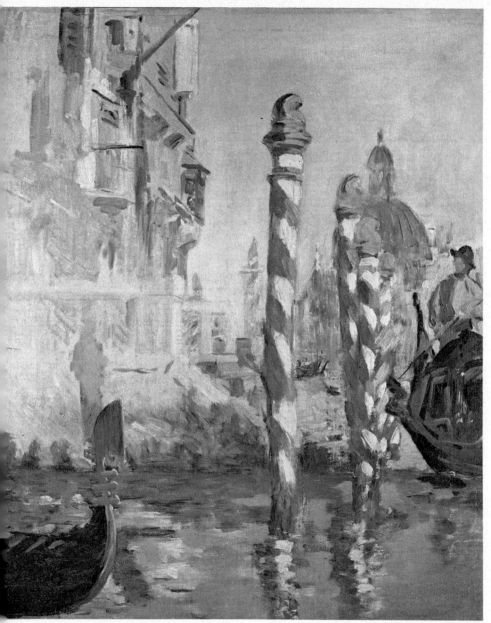

102 Manet *The Grand Canal, Venice* 1875

In their turn the Impressionists exerted a reciprocal and invigorating influence on Manet's own painting. In the 1920s contradictory theories were aired on this subject, Severini denying that Manet's art had ever been influenced by Impressionism, and Roger Fry declaring that Manet's Impressionist work was a deplorable aberration. The fact is that even in his most 'Impressionist' period Manet was never primarily a painter of landscape or reflected light, he never abandoned local colours or black, and most of his works were executed in the studio, from drawings made in front of the subject itself.

Manet had begun his studies under Thomas Couture, a disciple of the Romantic painter Baron Gros, a man neither illiberal as a teacher nor incompetent as a painter. Manet learned much from him and comparisons are often made between the compositions of Couture's *Romains de la Décadence* and Manet's *Musique aux Tuileries*. Some of Couture's work shows an attempt to abandon transitional tones and a taste for strongly opposed tonal extremes massed together, such as Manet achieved in *Musique aux Tuileries*. Unfortunately Couture was a fanatical anti-realist and had even painted a satirical picture which showed a 'realist' student drawing the snout of a pig. Enraged by Manet's jeers at the Prix de Rome ('But we are not in Rome and we don't want to go there'), Couture told him slightingly that he would never be anything but the Daumier of his day. After that, like many of his contemporaries, Manet made his own personal synthesis from the fashionable Spanish painting (which could be seen in the collections of Baron Soult, Louis-Philippe and the series of engravings from Goya published in 1819), from Japanese prints and from photographs.

It was maintained in the preface to the catalogue of his exhibition at the 1867 World's Fair in Paris, 'Manet has no pretensions either to overthrow an established mode of painting or to create a new one.' Berthe Morisot, writing to her sister, gives a vivid account of Manet's obvious apprehensions about the reception of his pictures when they were to be shown at the Salon. During the years 1867 and 1868 he apparently painted fewer pictures than ever before (only six in 1867, seven in 1868) and he destroyed many canvases unfinished. The failure of his one-man exhibition in 1867 and his constant rejections by the Salon had shaken his nerve. Never regarding himself as a rebel, he longed for appreciation and was far less resigned to the role of artistic outlaw than his wise or more cynical friends Baudelaire and Degas. His loss of confidence was particularly unfortunate at this time, for he had recently achieved considerable artistic maturity in such works as *Lunch in the Studio*. But he was to be saved from this sterility by the encouragement and influence of the Impressionists who had learned so much from him – particularly the young Berthe Morisot.

Though the years 1869–74 are usually considered to be Manet's most Impressionist period he never submitted entirely to this idiom. Yet his art was to be affected by Impressionism until the end of his life. This was because of the affinity which already existed between Impressionist painting and his own. It was merely a happy accident that the charming and congenial Berthe Morisot was his guide; he learned also from the stronger talent of Monet. Leon Rosenthal, in his book on Manet's engravings and watercolours, maintains that in these techniques he was able to be more 'advanced' at an earlier period than in the oil paintings; he showed considerable interest in light, and the harsh 'playing-card' contour of his figure painting had virtually disappeared long before the luminous and unconventional *Queue in front of the Butcher's Shop* (1871).

A great deal of nonsense has been written about Manet's plagiarism and his compositional difficulties. Critics do not object to Degas or the young Picasso using the works of older artists, yet they deplore this practice in Manet. Alan Bowness wonders why we should be so critical of his compositional difficulties. One cannot seriously believe that anyone with as thorough a training as Manet could not have correctly adjusted his proportions and perspective if he had wished to. Bowness is convincing in his statement that Manet, as a young man, though he did not think of himself as an innovator, was trying to do something new: 'He was seeking to develop an informal type of composition which would nevertheless be as tightly organized on the surface as the pictures of Velasquez.' Manet copied the picture *Petits Cavaliers*, which was then believed to be by Velasquez; it had an important influence on such paintings as the *Musique aux Tuileries*.

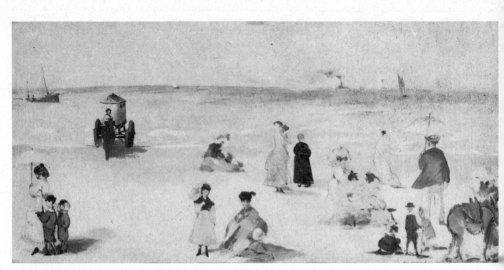

103 Manet *On the Beach at Boulogne* 1869

104 Degas *At the Seaside c.* 1876

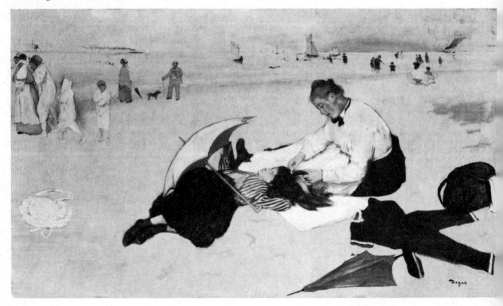

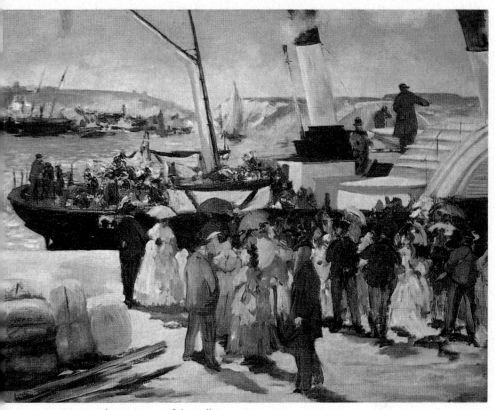

105 Manet *The Departure of the Folkestone Boat* 1869

This was to be of capital importance for twentieth-century art. Clement Greenberg, in an article on *avant-garde* art, declares that Manet's are the first 'modern' paintings by virtue of the frankness with which they declare the nature of the surface on which they were painted. But such a judgment seems to imply that Manet, rather than Renoir or Cézanne, was the first Post-Impressionist.

In the summer of 1869, while Monet and Renoir were perfecting their new style by the river, both Manet and Degas were at Boulogne, and here a new Morisot-like freshness and sense of atmosphere invade Manet's art, particularly in *The Departure of the Folkestone Boat (Ill. 105)*

139

and *On the Beach at Boulogne* (*Ill. 103*). The latter is a transitional work and Alain de Leiris has shown from the preliminary sketches now in the Louvre that it was composed in the studio and not on the scene. In contrast with Boudin or Degas (in the later *At the Seaside, Ill. 104*), Manet seems to have purposely emphasized individual figures or groups and given his figures a random, haphazard quality at the expense of the unity and harmony of the whole. The man holding the umbrella, for instance, seems too big in proportion to the other figures. Manet was transcribing from brief sketches made on the spot, seeking to maintain the truth of his original perception.

When war broke out in the following year Manet and Degas enrolled as gunners. Manet served under the painter Meissonier and stayed in Paris until the surrender of the French armies in January 1871. His experiences inspired two lithographs, *The Barricade* (1871, *Ill. 92*) and *Civil War*, taken from drawings made on the spot with rapidity and directness – Manet actually saw these corpses at the corner of the Boulevard Malesherbes.

In February 1871 he left to join his family at Olaron-Ste-Marie. Now he broke more decisively with his indoor habits and painted seascapes, landscapes and port scenes with far greater attention to light and atmosphere. John Richardson considers that Berthe Morisot's tendency to softness, sketchiness and looseness had an unhappy influence on Manet's somewhat wavering and eclectic style at this time. If this is true, however, he soon recovered from his vacillation. After a burst of unpleasant reversion to convention in the somewhat Hals-like *Bon-Bock* (which pleased the critics, as he had hoped) Manet, for a few years, approached as closely to Impressionism as he ever would.

The culmination of his Impressionist phase took place during the summer of 1874 when he painted at Argenteuil on the Seine (*Ill. 101*) with Monet and Renoir. Monet had been living in Argenteuil since 1872; it was here, with the help of a neighbour, Gustave Caillebotte, a marine engineer and amateur painter, that he fitted out a floating studio – an idea he adopted from Daubigny. When he returned to Argenteuil from the first and singularly unsuccessful Impressionist exhibition in Paris, he was threatened with eviction, but Manet was

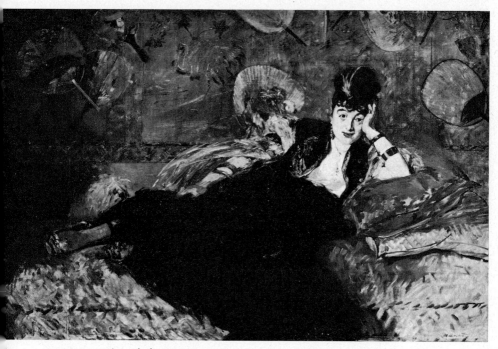

106 Manet *Lady with the Fans* 1873–4

instrumental in finding him another house. When Manet joined
Monet and Renoir that summer he had already learned how to unite
his figures with their settings and to share the exhilarating Impressionist experience of losing oneself in the physical impressions of the
moment (something that Degas never quite shared). It was this
experience of working side by side with Renoir and Monet, painting
in Monet's garden and along the river, that convinced Manet of the
value and advantages of open-air painting.

Later in 1874 he went to Venice with James Tissot, the French
genre painter who lived in London. Here, in stippled, Impressionist
brush-work, he painted *The Grand Canal* (*Ill. 102*). In France, three
years later, he painted what is perhaps (together with the earlier
Lady with the Fans, Ill. 106) his most delicious, airy, Impressionist
work: *The Road Menders in the Rue de Berne* (*Ill. 107*).

141

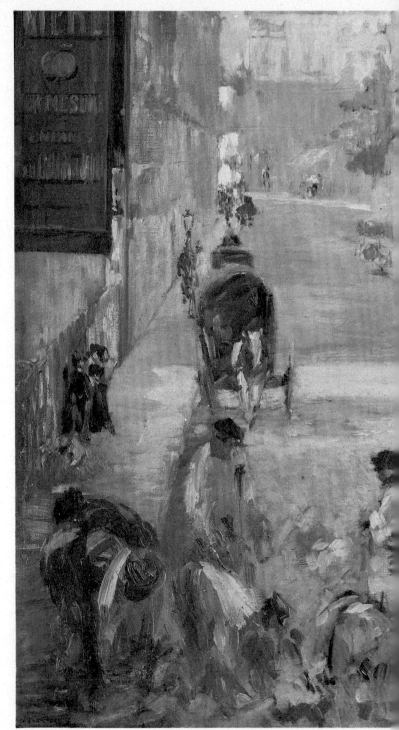

107 Manet
*The Road Menders
in the
Rue de Berne*
1877–8

142

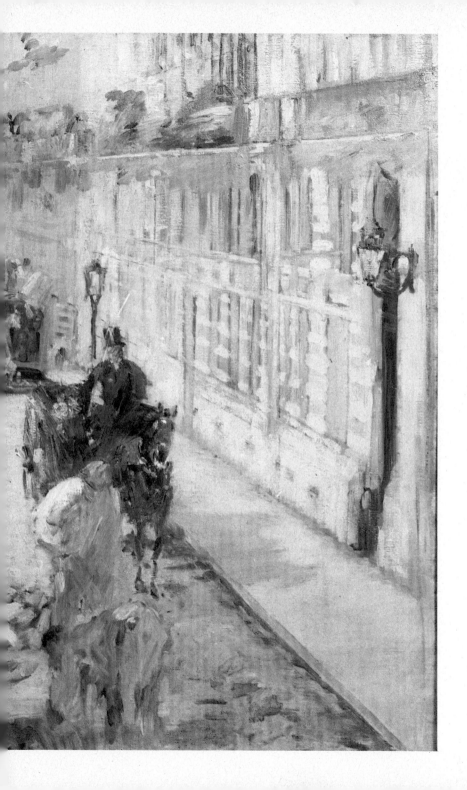

At the end of the 1870s the Impressionists themselves were beginning to split up, to have doubts, and to find their exhilarating art inadequate. Manet did not, of course, then discard all his Impressionist qualities and paint pictures like the flat 'playing-card' works of the 1860s, but he did revert to his most constant role as 'painter of modern life' – in particular the Paris of the Third Republic. Actresses, barmaids, skaters and courtesans are all as brilliantly and dispassionately observed in these later paintings as the women in Maupassant's stories. Just when Manet was acquiring favour with the Salon and developing a wider range both imaginatively and technically, he became ill and was forced to work on a minor scale in the suburbs, always pining for his beloved Paris. Finally, in 1883, his left leg had to be amputated because of gangrene caused by paralysis. But the operation did not save him, and he died on 30 April.

The recorded remarks of Manet's friends, and not least those of the Impressionists themselves, tend to confirm my own view that the friend of Baudelaire, Mallarmé, Degas and Monet cannot have been a derivative and worldly dullard. The Impressionists certainly did not think so. And why should they not be right, rather than Zervos, Roger Fry, Waldemar George or John Rewald, who seems so misguided when he traces the descent of modern painting from Degas, Seurat, the Classicists and Picasso, and claims that Manet had no posterity? Much earlier, Matisse had said wisely that Manet was the first great modern artist because his free and spontaneous brush-work liberated the artist's instinct.

Degas always said roundly that he was not an Impressionist. He personally repudiated the description, and even when, after the third Impressionist exhibition of 1877, those painters who had displayed the characteristics which gave rise to the term became resigned to adopting it, he was opposed.

Of those who persist in defying the painter himself and classifying him as an Impressionist, one of the most convincing and most cautious is Jean Boggs in her book on Degas' portraits. She admits that he was primarily a draughtsman and more interested in human

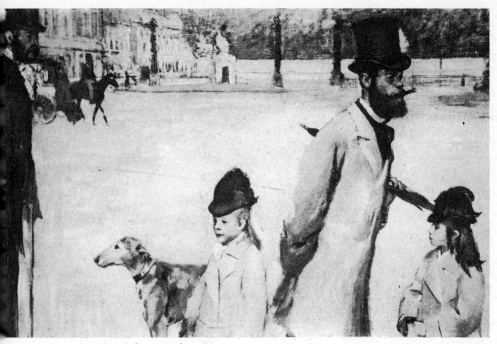

108 Degas *Place de la Concorde c.* 1875

beings than in country scenes, that he rarely used small, juxtaposed
strokes of colour, that he was more concerned with bodily movements than with light and colour, and that he made a co-ordinated
design even when he was trying to re-create the trivial and ephe-
meral. But one must also allow, as she insists, that his paintings
gradually became more suffused with light, and his colours brighter,
and that, like Manet, Renoir and Pissarro, he developed a formal
vocabulary to produce the visual sensation, although selected and
intensified, of something he had actually seen. This is especially
apparent in such works as *Place de la Concorde* (*Ill. 108*) and in his
subtle way of capturing the crucial point of a movement. 'A painting', he said, 'is an artificial work existing outside nature and it
requires as much cunning as the perpetration of a crime.'

145

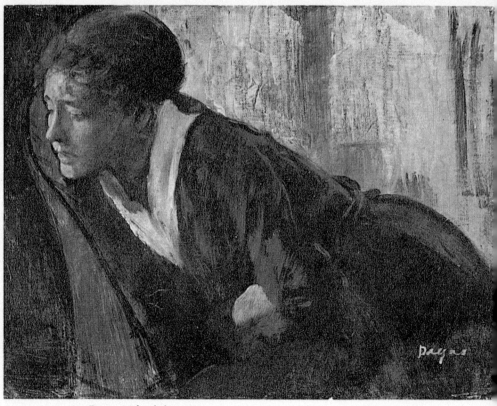

109 Degas *Melancholy c.* 1874

Degas' chief contribution to the Impressionists may have been the originality of his compositional and iconographic invention. But he conferred a further benefit on them by introducing into their circle the painter Mary Cassatt, with her American connections. The daughter of a Philadelphia banker, Mary Cassatt was of the same generation as the other Impressionists, but slightly younger. She had spent her childhood in France and returned to Europe in 1868. Like Degas she studied the old masters and, like Manet, was especially impressed by Velasquez. After her portraits had been rejected by the Salons of 1875 and 1877, Degas suggested that she join the Impressionist group. Later, he said of her that she and he had identical intellectual dispositions and an identical predilection for drawing.

146

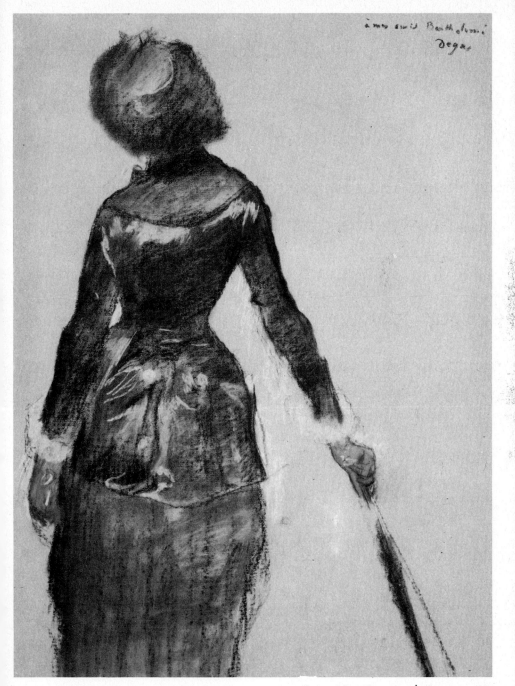

110 Degas *Mary Cassatt at the Louvre c.* 1880

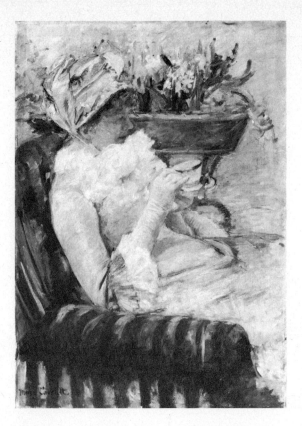

111 Cassatt
The Cup of Tea

They were certainly very close friends and it was generally assumed that they were lovers. She often showed considerable tact in dealing with this complex and cantankerous man, but after he had made some biting remark about her work she refused to meet him for several years. She had posed for him as a model even more often than Berthe Morisot posed for Manet, sometimes as an anonymous woman, such as a milliner, and at least six times in her own identity. It was scarcely flattering to her that in the many figures of Mary Cassatt in the Louvre (see *Ill. 110*), Degas was trying, as he told a friend, to show 'a woman's crushed respect and absence of all feeling in the presence of art'. But their intimacy is suggested by the fact that one of his notebooks contains not only a list of his own proposed contributions to the fourth Impressionist exhibition, but also another list of eleven works by Cassatt to be submitted at the same time.

148

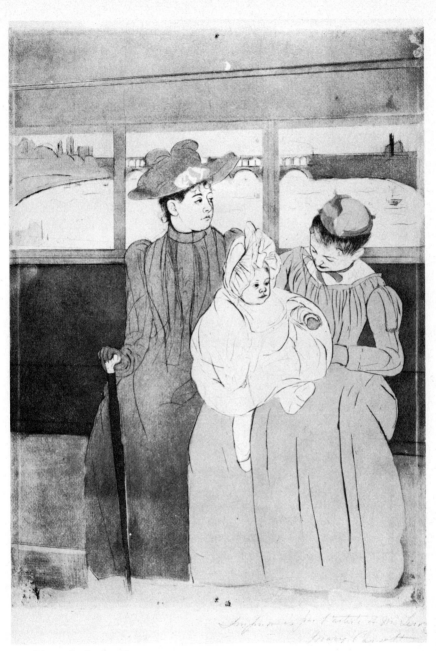

112 Cassatt *In the Omnibus* 1891

The contrast between the art of Berthe Morisot and Mary Cassatt is obvious and has often been noted. Both women treated themes which were derived from their knowledge of a woman's life; but Morisot is far more Impressionistic and informal than Cassatt, and less linear in style. Her sitters (like herself) seem softer and more tender than the rather stiff, seemingly Puritanical characters portrayed by Cassatt.

Mary Cassatt became a friend of Mallarmé and Pissarro, and with the latter she made coloured lithographs and etchings which are among her most successful works (*Ills. 112, 113*). She was rich enough to buy Impressionist paintings herself, and she always tried to interest her American friends in the group's work. Like Degas, she seems, in her later paintings, more akin to the Post-Impressionists than to the artists who are the main subject of this book.

113 Cassatt *Feeding the Ducks* 1895

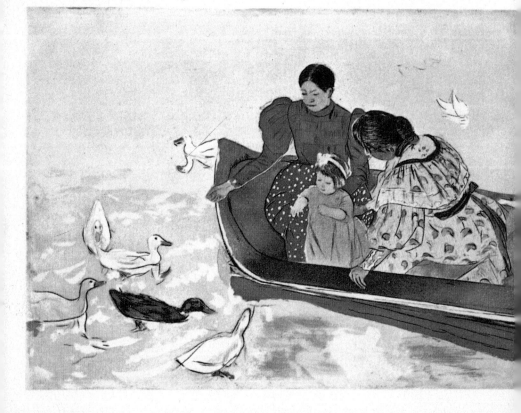

CHAPTER SIX

The period of High Impressionism: 1874 – *c.* 1880

The years between the first Impressionist exhibition and about 1881 are generally regarded as the period of mature, or 'high', Impressionism. It is a puzzling fact that the heyday of this new style should have lasted for so short a time. One is inclined to argue that surely, after so great a struggle, the Impressionists might have realized that they had developed a valuable and original idiom, and they might have continued for many years to draw upon the implications of their discoveries. Yet by and large they did not. Kenneth Clark finds one explanation for this in the inherent limitations of a style which attempts to transcribe nature: 'To go on producing clear, objective transcripts of natural appearance without loss of freshness, requires very rare gifts of simple-heartedness and calm. . . . Even such a beautifully endowed painter as Sisley suffered a gradual decline in sensibility and conviction.' Sisley's own falling-off can be attributed to independent causes: he had never been one of the dominant Impressionists, and in later life he suffered from bad health which further impaired his relatively modest talent. As for the others, however, it was partly because they came to realize that they were *not* merely transcribing nature (which the camera could do better), but epitomizing and abstracting from what they saw, that they found themselves in a stylistic impasse and eventually opened the way to many new developments.

The years of high Impressionism, before this impasse, are especially well represented in the art of Renoir and, to a lesser extent, Sisley. It is true that Monet painted his magnificent Gare St-Lazare series at this time, but he was hampered throughout by financial anxieties, and by the illness and eventual death of his wife.

Renoir, unlike Pissarro, was never so overwhelmed by the forcible genius of Monet as to lose his personal identity. During the 1870s he forged a style of rendering the life of his own day which was a counterpart of eighteenth-century *fêtes champêtres* paintings. But whereas a *fête champêtre*, as Watteau represents it, is a fantasy, idealized and romantic, the characters of Renoir who dance at the Moulin de la Galette in Montmartre (*Ill. 116*) or attend boating parties at Chatou are solid, ordinary *petits-bourgeois* enjoying their real and characteristic pastimes. It has been said that Renoir's response to life is that of an adolescent who glories in luscious food and plump, pink girls, and it is certainly true that his sensual preferences are unsubtle and crude in comparison with the more sophisticated tastes of Manet and Degas. But the way in which Renoir painted these simple and direct subjects was far from naïve. He was in many ways the most instinctively professional painter of the whole group, with a light,

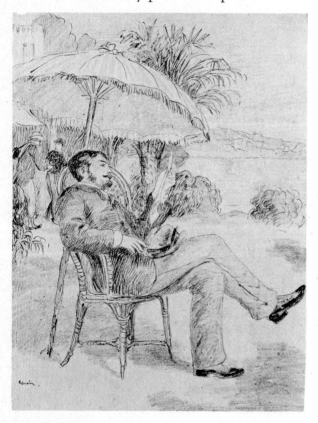

114 Renoir
*Edmond Renoir
by the Mediterranean* 1881

sweeping, feathery brush-stroke and greater delicacy and rhythmic unity than Pissarro or even Monet. This showed to particular advantage in his renderings of shimmering light or delicate young skin.

Renoir, who admired Veronese as well as Watteau, was well equipped to translate the visions of a golden age into modern terms. He was the only Impressionist who invested contemporary life with a touch of social glamour, and it is worth noting that during the 1870s Degas and Manet were producing very different versions of the modern scene (as in Degas' *The Pedicure* and Manet's *Nana*). But Renoir was also capable of their more realistic approach, as can be seen in his drawing of his brother at Mentone (*Ill. 114*).

After the failure of the first Impressionist exhibition, Renoir was largely responsible for a sale of the group's work which took place at the Hôtel Drouot auction-house; but this proved to be no more successful than the exhibition. Fortunately, in 1875 a young and generous customs officer, Victor Choquet, was introduced to the group. He became a particular friend and patron of Renoir, finding an affinity between his work and the painting of Delacroix, which of course Renoir had admired and copied. Choquet was painted more than once by Renoir, as well as Cézanne (*Ill. 149*).

In 1876 the Impressionists held their second exhibition, to which Renoir contributed fifteen works, six of which had already been bought by Choquet. It was on this occasion that Albert Wolff of *Le Figaro*, who had always been a hostile critic, called the show a 'disaster' and wrote of a Renoir nude: 'Try to explain to M. Renoir that the torso of a woman is not a mass of decomposing flesh, with green and purple patches like a corpse in a state of utter putrefaction.' The Impressionists were more affronted by what they considered to be the obtuseness of their friend Duranty in his pamphlet *La Nouvelle Peinture* (1876), which was ostensibly produced in their defence. Duranty warmly praised Degas, without naming him, but expressed certain reservations about other members of the group. Monet, Renoir and Pissarro were extremely irritated, not only with Duranty but also with Degas, whom they wrongly suspected of having a hand in the pamphlet's composition.

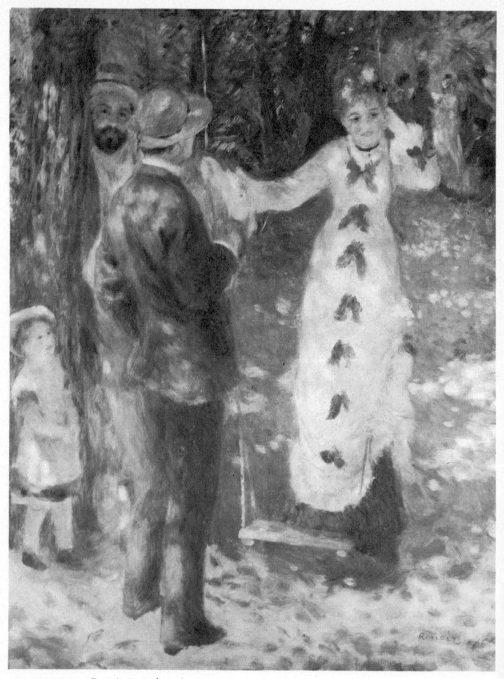

115 Renoir *La Balançoire* 1876

116 Renoir *Le Moulin de la Galette* 1876 ▶

117 Renoir *Mme Charpentier and her Children* 1878 ▶

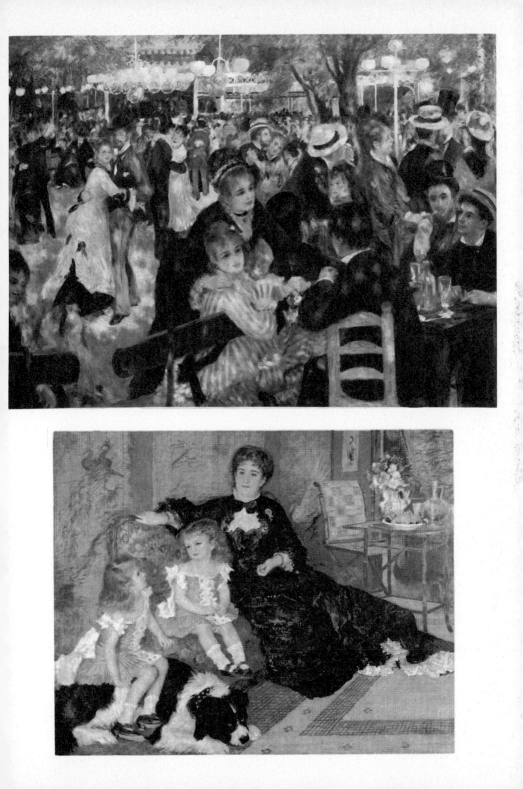

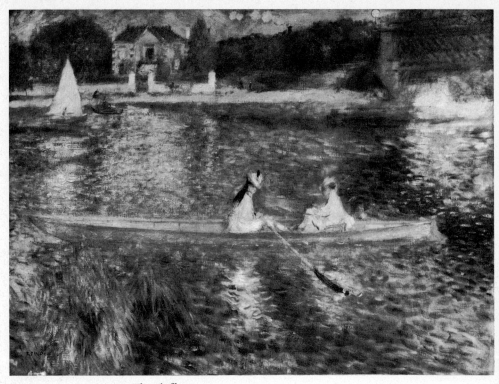

118 Renoir *The Skiff* c. 1879

The year 1876 was an *annus mirabilis* for Renoir; during its course he painted at least two of his most celebrated works and met a patron who was to be even more helpful to him than Choquet.

Renoir often spent Sunday afternoon or evening in the public dancing hall at the Moulin de la Galette. He preferred to paint the young girls who came to dance there rather than professional models, and eventually he found a studio nearby from which he could work in the open air. In the famous pictures referred to above, *La Balançoire* (*Ill. 115*) and *Le Moulin de la Galette* (in two versions, see *Ill. 116*), he used the effects produced by dappled light striking through trees on a summer's afternoon or night. Both works show Renoir's great talent for unifying and giving a flowing rhythm to a large number of figures.

156

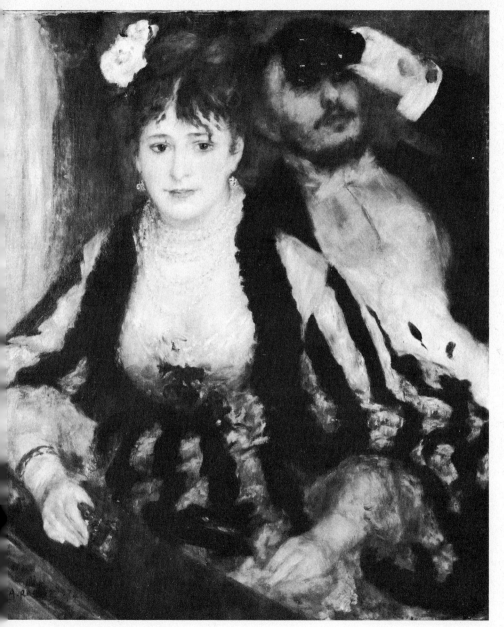

119 Renoir *La Loge* 1874

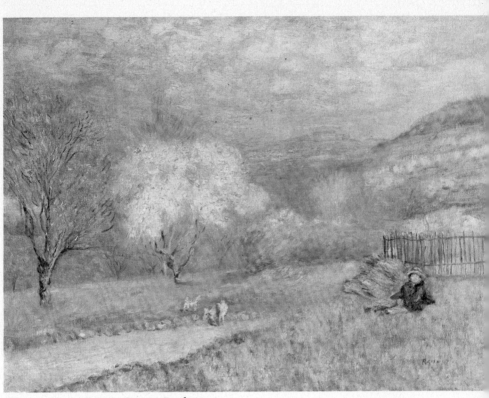

120 Renoir *Country Road* 1873

His new patron was a young publisher called Georges Charpentier, whose wife kept a salon frequented by such diverse and eminent figures as Yvette Guilbert, Edmond de Goncourt and Gambetta. Renoir, a classless, unselfconscious man, felt perfectly at ease there and had soon painted five portraits of the Charpentier family, including the well-known *Mme Charpentier and her Children* (1878, *Ill. 117*). This painting has a skilful and almost classically organized composition, which depends partly on the lines of the carpet which converge on the main figure. In the Charpentiers' house Renoir also met the fashionable young diplomat Paul Bérard, who asked him on several occasions to stay on his estate at Wargemont in Normandy. Renoir often painted his host's family, notably in *The Children's Afternoon at Wargemont* (1884). Renoir's portraits of men were sometimes criticized as being too soft and effeminate, and it is not surprising that his particular gentleness and grace were soon thought to be ideally suited to the portrayal of children. In the year 1880–1, just before stylistic problems began to worry him and to herald his so-called 'sour period', he received many commissions for portraits of rich bourgeois children, not always those of his friends. In 1878 one of his paintings, *The Cup of Coffee*, was accepted by the Salon; after that he submitted other pictures there and did not participate in the fourth, fifth and sixth Impressionist exhibitions in 1879, 1880 and 1881.

121 Renoir *Monet working in his Garden* 1873

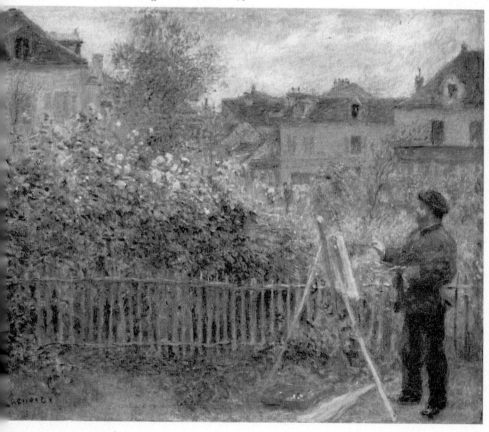

In spite of his growing success, Renoir was by no means secure
financially. This is perfectly evident from the number of requests for
money which he was forced to address to his new patrons. Even so,
he was in a better position than Monet, whose less seductive and
graceful art had not yet found rich and fashionable admirers. In the
winter of 1875 Monet was painting snow scenes in Argenteuil;
the next year he showed some of his La Grenouillère pictures at the
second Impressionist exhibition. Then he began to paint his series of
masterpieces depicting the Gare St-Lazare (*Ills. 123, 124*). Railway
stations even now retain some drama and glamour for us, and it is
easy to see how these qualities must once have been enhanced by their

122 Renoir *Mme Monet and her Son in their Garden at Argenteuil* 1874

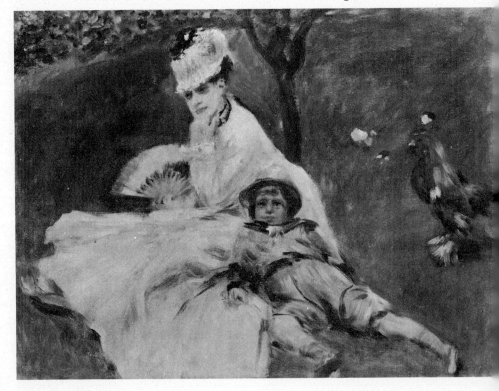

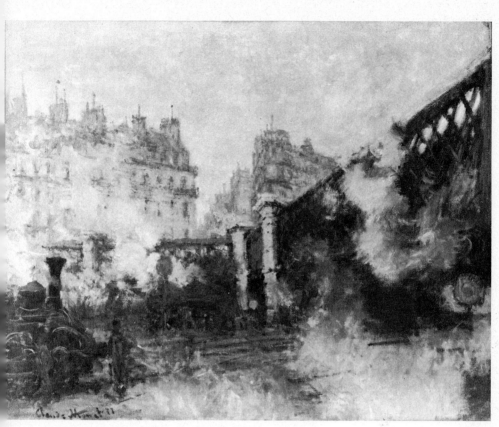

123 Monet *Le Pont de l'Europe, Gare St-Lazare* 1877

comparative novelty. In 1868 Gautier was writing that stations would soon be 'the new cathedrals of humanity, the centres where all ways converge', and earlier the Romantic poet de Vigny, in *La Maison du Berger*, transformed a railway engine into a roaring bull. This, however, is remote from Monet's intention, which was to distil poetry from a very exact naturalism.

Forty years later Renoir laughed as he told his son about the events leading to the Gare St-Lazare series. According to his story, Monet was annoyed when critics of his pictures said that fog was not a suitable subject for a painting. So he decided to execute a painting

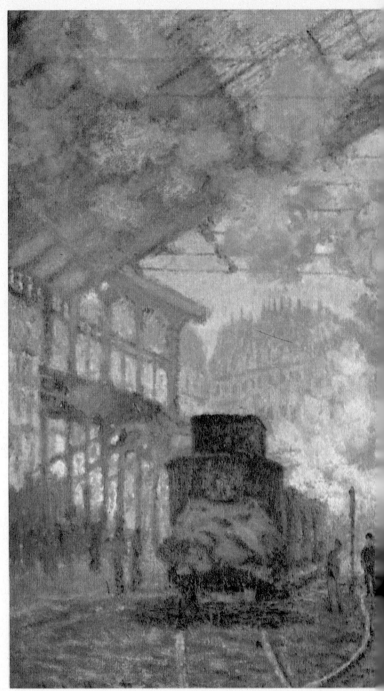

124 Monet
Gare St-Lazare
1877

162

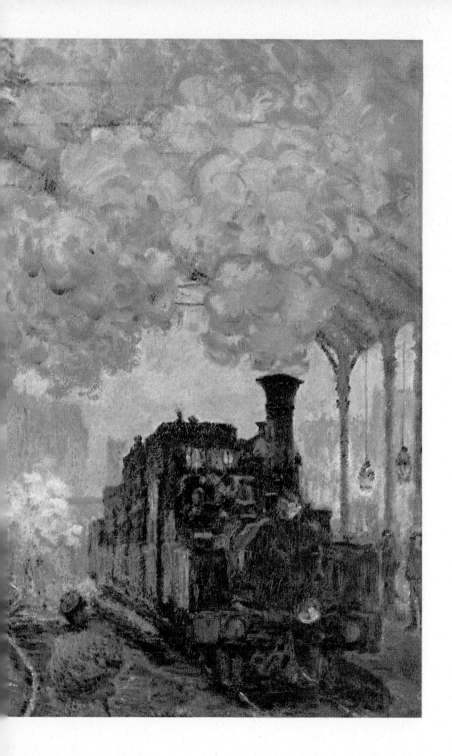

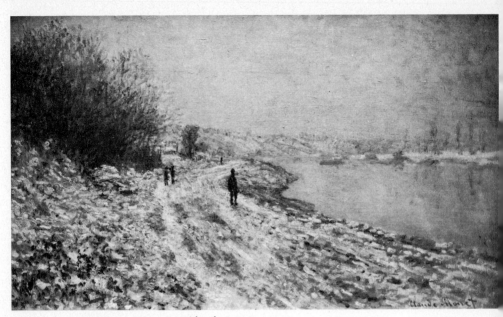

125 Monet *Winter in Vétheuil* 1878-81

with a subject even foggier than any he had used before. 'Why not a scene of Negroes fighting in a tunnel?' he suggested. When he finally decided on a view of the Gare St-Lazare, 'with smoke from the engines so that you can hardly see a thing', Monet, who had scarcely a *sou* at his disposal, put on his best clothes and went to call on the Superintendent of the Chemins de Fer de l'Ouest, introducing himself as 'the painter Claude Monet'. The official, who knew nothing about painting, suspected that his visitor was a famous Salon artist, and gave Monet permission to do exactly what he wanted. 'The trains were all halted; the platforms were cleared; the engines were crammed with coal so as to give out all the smoke Monet desired.' Afterwards, he was bowed out by uniformed officials.

The irony of this story, no doubt heightened by Renoir in retrospect, lies in the hideous poverty of Monet and his family between 1876 and 1880. He constantly had to ask for financial help from Manet, Zola and others to pay off his landlord in Argenteuil. Finally

164

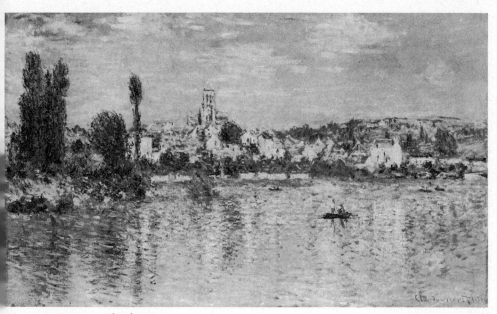

126 Monet *Vétheuil* 1884

he could no longer afford to live in that neighbourhood and had to rent a house farther away from Paris, at Vétheuil. How little direct self-projection there was in his work is proven by the fact that during these years of misery and despair he painted such pictures as his bright, tumultuous *Rue Montorgueil Decked out with Flags* (*Ill. 127*), in which all realistic detail is submerged in a riot of colour and of perceptible brush-strokes. This is quite unlike the more naturalistic treatment of a similar subject by Manet, *Rue Mosnier with Flags*.

By 1878 Monet's patron Hoschedé had been ruined and Mme Hoschedé, who later became the artist's second wife, came with her six children to live with the Monet family in Vétheuil. The following year marked the nadir of Monet's fortunes. In the spring he had been too poor and depressed even to submit his pictures for the fourth Impressionist exhibition (though Caillebotte collected twenty-nine and sent them in for him) and in September his wife Camille died. Along with this break in his life came the end of his close friendship

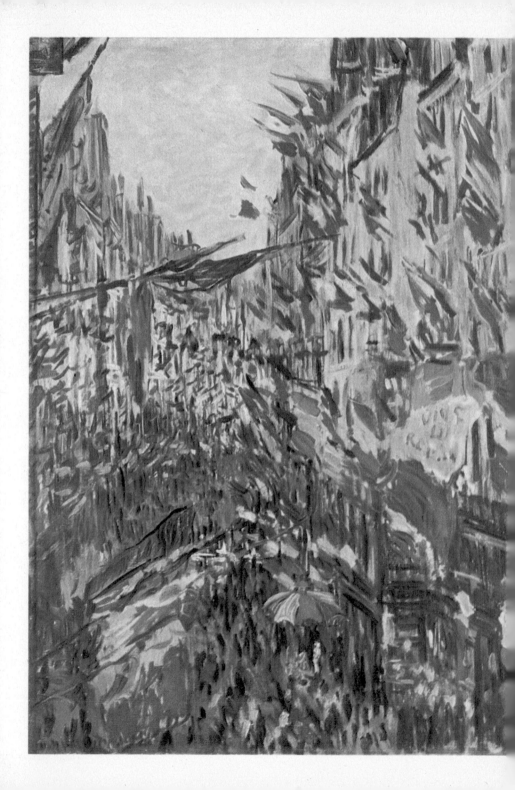

with the other members of the Impressionist group. In 1880, when he held a one-man show at the offices of a newspaper called *La Vie Moderne*, he said: 'I am still and always intend to be an Impressionist – but I very rarely see the men and women who are my colleagues. The little church has become a banal school which opens its doors to the first dauber.' He was probably referring to the disputes which occurred increasingly among the group when artists had to be chosen to exhibit with them. Pissarro had already caused dissension in 1879 when he invited Gauguin, and his insistence in 1886 that Seurat should join the group may well have given the final blow to its unity, particularly as Seurat's *Un Dimanche à la Grande Jatte* was apparently painted as an anti-Impressionist manifesto.

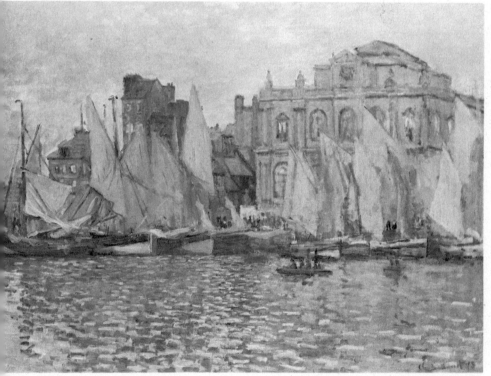

128 Monet *The Harbour, Le Havre* 1873

167

◀ 127 Monet *Rue Montorgueil Decked out with Flags* 1878

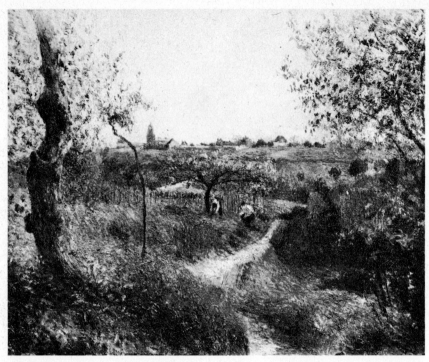

129 Pissarro *Path through the Fields* 1879

130 Pissarro *Harvest at Montfoucault* 1876

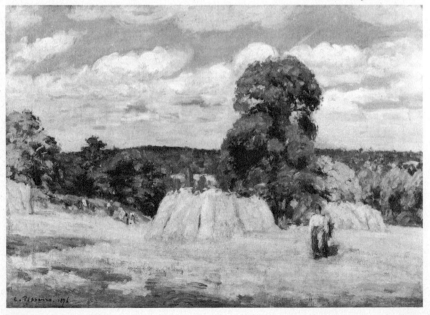

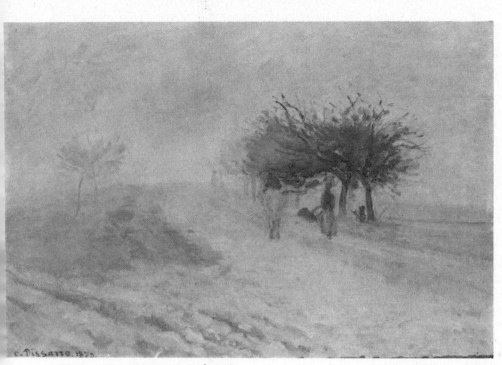

131 Pissarro *Misty Morning at Creil* 1873

Most of Pissarro's works from the mid-1860s to the mid-1870s have
a more architectural quality than those of Monet and Renoir; this
can be seen in *Le Pont de Chemin de Fer, Pontoise* (1873). He also used
lines to define volumes more than they did. But this perfect balance
between naturalism and semi-intellectual design was to be broken,
in the late 1870s, by Pissarro's new style of deliberately cultivated
'Impressionism', which never suited him so well. Now roads and
houses were supplanted by tree-branches, leaves and sometimes
water; and his old firmness disappeared, without being replaced by
the heightened colour and lyrical intensity of Monet. Jerrold Lanes
suggests that Pissarro was too obsessed by the examples of Renoir
and Monet, and that his new style (patchy and rather febrile), since
it seems to have no purpose behind it, appears contrived, almost

169

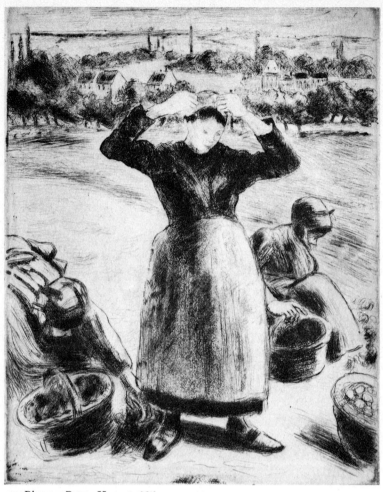

132 Pissarro *Potato Harvest* 1886

decorative. For a time, too, Pissarro's need to sell his work prompted
him to produce genre pictures (*Ills. 132, 133*); these sometimes have
the sentimentality of Millet.

Renoir's friend Georges Rivière had been asked by the Impressionists to write about their third exhibition (1877), partly to
forestall a commentary by Duranty, whose previous pamphlet had

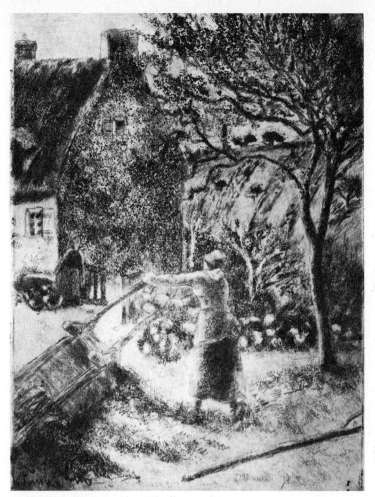

133 Pissarro *Woman with a Wheelbarrow* 1880

so irritated them. Rivière had already declared that Impressionism
consisted of treating a theme in terms not of the subject-matter, but
of tone. This may more appropriately be said of the Impressionists
in general than of literary painters such as the English Pre-Raphaelites,
but it is not true that the Impressionists were wholly indifferent
to subject-matter. The impressive qualities of Pissarro's harvest and

171

haystack scenes, for example, derive to a great extent from his feeling for the dignity of man's traditional labour. This is also true of his peasant figures carding wool or minding sheep, and it was also characteristic of him, as it was later of Seurat, not to think that such themes as factory chimney-stacks were unworthy of an artist's attention. Indeed, their vertical shapes, seen against water, are formally most pleasing.

Among the Impressionists, Pissarro had the best analytical brain, and it is fitting that he should have been the one to attempt to expand Impressionist technique. When questioned, he was prone to say that the method was easy to explain but that it took a lifetime to learn how to practise it. In his view, the chief characteristics of the method were the use of coloured light reflection and of unmixed colours.

134 Pissarro *The Seine at Marly* 1871

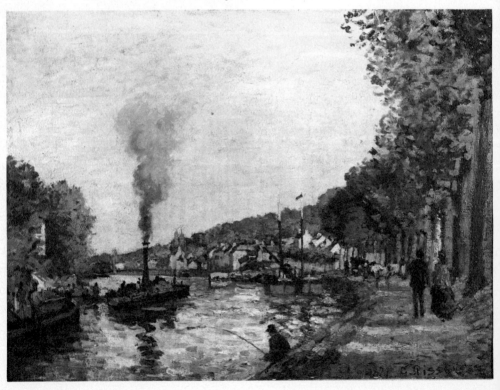

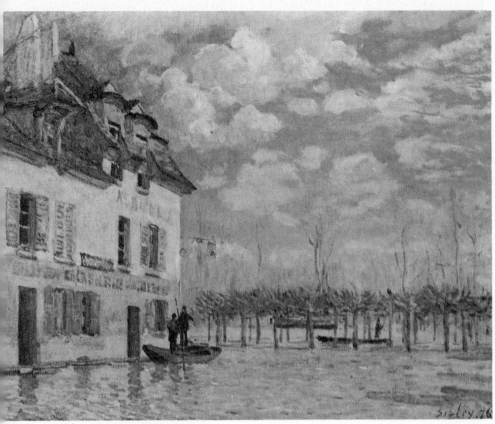

135 Sisley *Floods at Port-Marly* 1876

In any survey of Impressionism at its peak, the work of Sisley deserves attention, for he was in some ways the most consistent member of the group and never developed another manner of painting, as all the others did. He almost invariably painted landscapes – never portraits or still-lifes. His work in the 1870s was his best and most typical. Until the Franco-Prussian War he had been partly subsidized by his father, but after his father's death Sisley, lacking the toughness or the habit of poverty which had conditioned his friends, was forced by financial need to paint a great deal more than before.

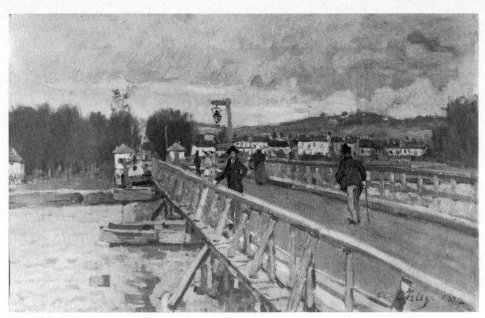

136 Sisley *Wooden Bridge at Argenteuil* 1872

137 Sisley *Bridge at Hampton Court* 1874

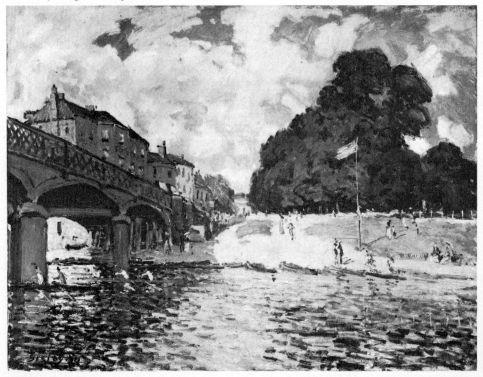

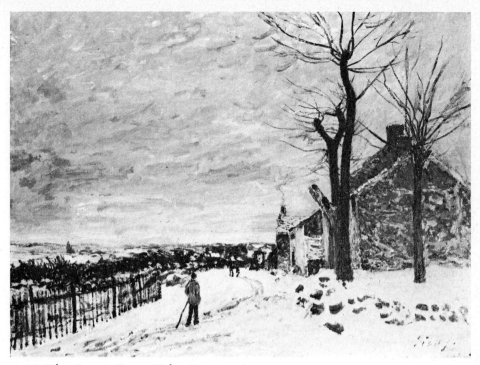

138 Sisley *Snow at Veneux-Nadon* 1879–82

His early works had been sober in tone, often made up of browns, greens and greys which bear witness to his admiration for Corot, Courbet and Manet. Like Corot, he had an exact feeling for tonal values, and he was more interested than any of the other Impressionists except Pissarro in construction and space. After 1870 he lightened his palette and his brush-strokes became freer. He had always excelled at evoking snow in all its various aspects, and now he showed the same subtlety when depicting mist (*Ill. 139*). It is generally held that his masterpieces are the three pictures he painted in 1876 of the *Floods at Port-Marly* (*Ill. 135*). In the Jeu de Paume in Paris one of these is shown in a triple frame with works by Renoir and Monet, and here, for once, Sisley does not suffer by comparison.

Sisley's best work had always been tender and melancholy in style, but after 1880 he used brighter colours; what he gained in effect he lost in grace and finesse. The leaves and skies in these later works are comparatively heavy and lifeless. Of all the Impressionists he was the only one during the 1870s who was not preoccupied with stylistic change. Degas said of Zola's novel *L'Œuvre* that its Impressionist hero should not fail from too much artistic ambition but from a kind of dilettante sketchiness, which Degas felt was the Impressionists' peculiar vice. Sisley, though a slight and delicate artist in comparison with the forceful Courbet or Manet, did not eventually fail from sketchiness or monotony. A more likely explanation is that whereas he had at first painted only occasionally and when moved by inspiration, his loss of income and the consequent need to provide for his family forced him to paint whether or not he had any compelling urge to create.

From the viewpoint of the historian of Impressionism, the 1870s and early 1880s are easier to discuss than the earlier period of experiment and development, for now at last these artists and their friends, hitherto so tantalizingly reticent, began to talk or write letters about their new technique. Monet, it is true, did not say much until he gave an interview to F. Thiébault-Sisson in 1900, but Pissarro began writing on the subject to his son in 1883. These letters, although their main subject is Lucien's artistic education, are vivid and revealing of Pissarro's attitudes. He inveighs against the new artistic trends, and attributes them partly to political reaction. 'The *bourgeoisie*, frightened, astonished by the immense clamour of the disinherited masses . . . feels that it is necessary to restore to the people their superstitious beliefs. Hence the bustling of religious symbolists, religious socialists, idealist art, occultism, Buddhism, etc.' He has no doubts about his own form of art and its meaning: 'The Impressionists have the true position, they stand for a robust art based on sensation, and that is an honest stand.'

Even Sisley, in spite of his timidity, made a few pronouncements about painting in letters to friends. He wrote to the critic Adolphe Tavernier: 'The sky cannot be merely a background. On the contrary, it contributes not only through the depth given by its planes (for the sky has planes just as the earth has), it also gives move-

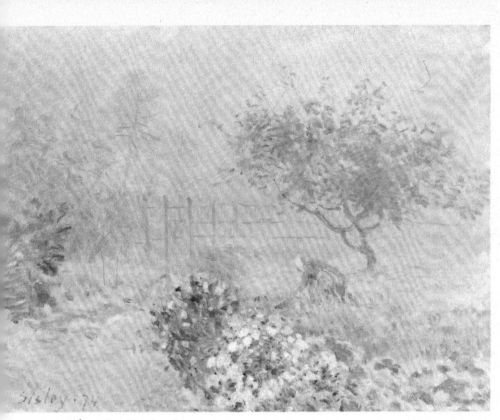

139 Sisley *Misty Morning* 1874

ment by its form, by its arrangement in harmony with the effect
or composition of a picture.'

Sisley was also the only Impressionist to write about the diversity
and un-stereotyped quality of the Impressionists' brush-work. In this
respect, he wrote to Tavernier, he favoured using a different manner
in different parts of the same picture – a theory which he put into
effect in his pictures of Hampton Court. In these the sparkling water
is represented by little fragmented touches of vibrant colour, whereas
the fields and sky are more smoothly and softly rendered. This
variation of brush-work was practised by all the Impressionists.

In 1883 Jules Laforgue, a perceptive critic who was as close to
the mature Impressionists as Baudelaire was to Manet, discussed

Impressionism in a review of a small exhibition held in Berlin. Laforgue is one of the few contemporary critics who really add to our understanding of Impressionism, and his article is an admirable blend of the semi-scientific and the lyrical:

> The Impressionist eye [he writes] is the most advanced in human evolution, the eye which has grasped and rendered the most complicated combination of nuances and tones. According to the Young-Helmholtz theory of colour-vision there are three elementary retinal and post-retinal processes which produce sensations of red, yellow, green and blue: 'A natural eye forgets tactile illusion and the conventional dead language of line and acts only according to this prismatic sensibility.' The Impressionists abandoned the three supreme illusions by which the academic painters lived – line, perspective and studio lighting. Where the one sees only the external outline of objects the other sees the real living lines, built not in geometric forms but in a thousand irregular strokes which, at a distance, establish life. Where one sees things placed in regular perspective planes according to theoretical design, the other sees perspective established by a thousand trivial touches of tone and brush and by the varieties of atmospheric states.

Laforgue stresses the great speed with which the Impressionists were forced to work in order to capture the changing effects of light. Monet sometimes painted for only fifteen minutes at a time on a canvas, but he was able to work on the same canvas again if similar light conditions prevailed on another day. Laforgue points out that even if the painter remains only fifteen minutes in front of a landscape his work can never be the real equivalent of a fugitive reality, because even when he merely looks down to load his brush with another colour, the fresh impression of his eye will immediately be modified by the colour of his shirt or other objects that he involuntarily glimpses. An Impressionist work cannot, therefore, be an accurate transcription, but rather 'the record of the response of a certain unique sensibility to a moment of time which can never be exactly reproduced.'

178

CHAPTER SEVEN

Impressionism in the art of Cézanne, Gauguin and Van Gogh

Some of the most concentrated and powerful works in the Impressionist idiom were produced by the great painters who are often, if loosely, classified as Post-Impressionists. These men, who used and transformed Impressionist discoveries for their own artistic and personal ends, eventually helped to forge the art of the twentieth century, and to abolish that direct concern with actual everyday reality on which Impressionism was based. The Impressionist movement did not, of course, peter out immediately, as the adventurous and articulate younger painters and critics of the turn of the century would have wished. Like Charles II, Impressionism was an unconscionable while a-dying; in 1919 the word could still be used by an *avant-garde* classicist such as Cocteau in order to describe the enemy: 'Impressionism has fired its last rocket; it is for us to set the fireworks for a new fête.'

Working in the changed cultural climate of the mid-1880s, the Post-Impressionists were different *as men* from their predecessors. We have seen that Renoir, Monet and Sisley were not always lighthearted and spontaneous, but at least most of their troubles had external causes. Not only was it difficult for them to realize a momentary vision on canvas in the short time available before the light changed, but they suffered from extreme poverty and lack of public recognition. Cézanne, Van Gogh and Gauguin were far more deeply at odds with themselves and society, far more concerned in both their art and their lives with answering Gauguin's questions: 'Where do we come from? What are we? Where are we going?' Van Gogh was nearly always driven by suffering (and so, frequently, was Gauguin) to discover and communicate something more permanent than the chance play of light on trees at some particular moment. Both by reason of their temperaments and because they were painting in the late 1880s, neither painter wished or could afford to have a simple and passive attitude towards nature. Gauguin was an iconoclast who desperately needed to destroy and invent, while Van Gogh used the outside world to embody the stresses and strains of his own nature and sometimes as an anchor against his forebodings of impermanence.

In mental outlook, as in other respects, the mature Cézanne was more of an Impressionist than either Gauguin or Van Gogh. He did not search the world for idyllic communities of amorous and instinctive natives, nor yearn for the old brotherhoods of religious artists. Still less did he seek to paint what Gauguin's literary friends called the *au delà* (the beyond). He was of the same generation as Monet, Renoir and Zola, his college friend; he grew up, as they did, in the aftermath of Romanticism and eventually became exhilarated, as they had been, by the extraordinary variety and splendour of the everyday world.

Cézanne knew the Impressionists from the early 1860s, when he first came to Paris in revolt against his strict bourgeois family and the law career which they had prepared for him. He must have been thoroughly conversant with the aims and practices of the Impressionists long before the time when he was to learn most from them – that is, the period during the early 1870s which he spent painting with Pissarro. He made an early impression on Pissarro. 'Didn't I judge rightly in 1861', Pissarro wrote to his son in 1895, 'when Oller and I went to see the curious Provençal in the Académie Suisse, when Cézanne's figure drawings were ridiculed by all the important artists?'

Apart from his friendships with Zola and Guillaumin, Cézanne was somewhat isolated during his early days in Paris. We know something of the workings of his imagination just before he arrived in the capital from the letters and poems he sent to Zola, who had preceded him. The poems are sometimes comic but more often macabre and melodramatic, dealing with scenes of violence and horror, as did some of his early pictures and many of Zola's writings. Cézanne was obsessed with the two great romantic themes of tragic eroticism and death. Thus one of his poems, 'Une terrible histoire',

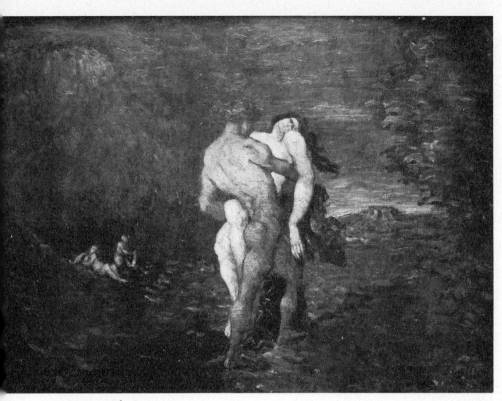

140 Cézanne *The Rape* 1867

recounts a dream in which he encountered a beautiful woman who turned into a skeleton when he kissed her. Equally significant are the poems written to a terrifying father, for we know that Cézanne's own father, although himself not married when Paul was born, had later become formidably respectable and overbearing.

Paintings typical of this period are *The Rape* (*Ill. 140*) and the grim *Autopsy*, which the local hospital in Aix had understandably refused. *The Picnic* (c. 1869) shows a mysterious, dream-like scene, far from the world of Manet's *Déjeuner sur l'Herbe* and lacking the usual care-free associations with the title. None of these early works give any hint of the Impressionist period upon which Cézanne was shortly to embark, and only in the boldly contrasted lines of the *Black Clock*

181

(1870, *Ill. 141*) and, still more, in the wonderful *Melting Snow at L'Estaque* (1870–1), with its sharp diagonals and immense horizontal sweep of overhanging grey clouds, is Cézanne's future as the greatest painter of his day foreshadowed. It is conceivable that the *Black Clock* was the outcome of a painting expedition undertaken in the autumn of 1867 with Pissarro and Antoine Guillemet, a pupil of Corot and Courbet. In a letter sent from Yport after visiting Monet, Guillemet had written to Pissarro: 'I absolutely count on you for La Roche. It will be marvellous for me to see good painting again and to work with a real comrade like you. Cézanne will probably come too.' While Pissarro did go to La Roche, it cannot be proven whether Cézanne accompanied them or not, but he certainly declared that at about this time Pissarro advised him to use only the three basic colours and their direct variants.

Cézanne was noted for his vehemently sarcastic pronouncements on the subject of 'official' art. But the violence and habit of acting the *enfant terrible*, for which he was remarkable even among Monet's turbulent friends, appear to have concealed a considerable timidity. In youth he would sometimes agree with Monet (against Renoir) that the Louvre ought to be burnt down. Nevertheless, we know that he copied pictures there and was much influenced by Rubens, Delacroix (particularly in his use of emerald), the Venetians and the grandiose Baroque painters of the seventeenth century, whom he was trying to rival without possessing the necessary technical equipment or competence. Cézanne might never have become a painter at all in any previous century, for he lacked the ordinary imitator's skill that would have been demanded by a workshop or guild. Certainly his early figures are often grotesquely disproportionate in scale, and many of the qualities we enjoy most in his mature work were absent from the feverish and frustrated pictorial fantasies of his youth. But from the first, Cézanne revealed a strong and individual gift for building a picture and an odd, subtle feeling for the interrelationships of colour. It is noticeable, too, that even the imaginary figures in his early works were nearly always dressed in modern clothes. The disgust expressed by Manet and Baudelaire with fustian and fancy dress had no doubt affected him.

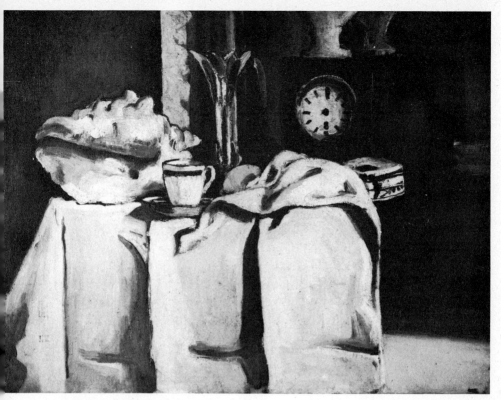

141 Cézanne *The Black Clock* 1870

Cézanne's early paintings of imaginary subjects were often exe-cuted in a thick, rich impasto laid on with a palette knife. He himself called this violent, impulsive style (often made up of curly and snake-like brush-strokes) his *couillarde* manner. He would also use fierce contrasts of black and white, as in the well-known portraits of his uncle Dominique (*c.* 1866). But around 1867 he developed in a way that prepared him for the decisive years of painting with Pissarro. He produced some still-lifes which were more objective, more like Manet's work; the paint was still thick, but it was now applied more evenly, and the forms were more fluid and more harmoniously linked together. Often he used yellows, greys and browns (colours typical of Manet), as in the *Tannhäuser Overture*. It was in this transitional style that he painted his father reading

183

L'Événement, a newspaper in which Zola had written a favourable review of his friend's work, and the impressive portraits of his friends Boyer, Valabrègue and the dwarf Achille Emperaire.

Cézanne wrote to Zola in the autumn of 1866 that it was far better to paint in the open air, and his friend Marion de Morstatt observed the difference in a letter: 'He has painted some really beautiful pictures, no longer with the knife but just as vigorous.' The *couillarde* style was already being replaced by smaller, more nervous touches, and there were no longer such violent contrasts of dark and light.

In later life Cézanne said that Pissarro had been like a father to him. (He certainly needed a sympathetic father-figure to counteract Auguste Cézanne's intermittent bullying and authoritarianism.) In 1872 he went to Pontoise to join Pissarro, who had recently moved there; this was his first prolonged contact with a landscape painter

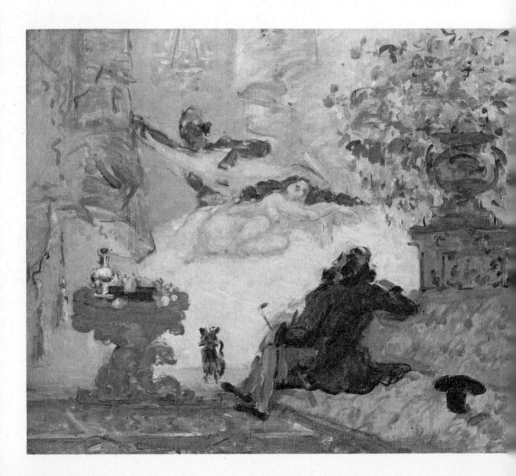

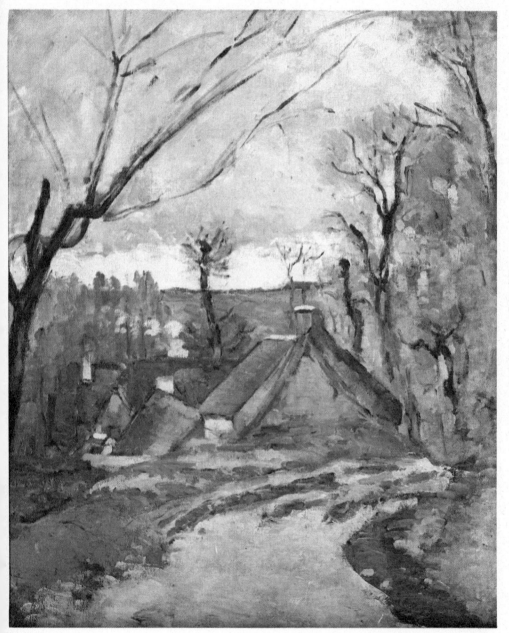

143 Cézanne *Les Chaumières à Auvers* 1873

◀ 142 Cézanne *A Modern Olympia* 1872–3

who was also a man of intense and patient observation. Cézanne now finally abandoned his big, curling brush-strokes in favour of smaller, more restrained dabs of paint which were sometimes applied with special knives. These were long, flat and supple, and enabled him to cover the canvas with dense layers of superimposed paint. In this way he could capture such phenomena as the play of light on a wall at Auvers. He also achieved a great subtlety of surface and colours which were mosaic-like. His palette became more luminous and his colours more vibrant and various. He virtually abandoned dark, earthy colours, as Van Gogh and Gauguin, also under Pissarro's tutelage, were later to do. Cézanne was becoming that 'self avid of non-self' which we recognize in his mature art, and which he so deeply needed to escape what was an innate self-disgust and timidity. One cannot imagine Cézanne dramatizing himself with the ebullient self-satisfaction of Courbet in *Bonjour Monsieur Courbet*, or painting Christ's face in the likeness of his own, as Gauguin did.

During the 1870s Cézanne painted far more still-lifes than before; they show him using changes of colour to express modelling and changes of plane, as he was to do in his maturity. These still-lifes often have a very marked central line and strongly emphasized verticals – a characteristic probably imitated by Gauguin in his still-lifes of 1885–6, such as *Still-life with a Mandolin*.

As Pissarro's disciple, Cézanne copied a large *View of Louveciennes* by his master (*Ill. 145*). At times they both painted the same subject, for example, their two versions of *The Hermitage at Pontoise* and *Street in Pontoise, Winter* (*Ill. 144*). But here there is none of the difficulty which Monet and Renoir are said to have experienced even themselves in determining which picture of a duck-pond had been painted by which artist. Cézanne's pictures of this period are less solidly constructed than much of his later work, but they are more dense and concentrated, less atmospheric and even less prolix, than those of Pissarro. Yet the tonality of such works as Cézanne's *Maison du Pendu* has much in common with Pissarro's art, and one can scarcely over-estimate the value to Cézanne of this soothing and encouraging friendship. He became more detached, more controlled and subservient to the impressions of nature; his pictures ceased to

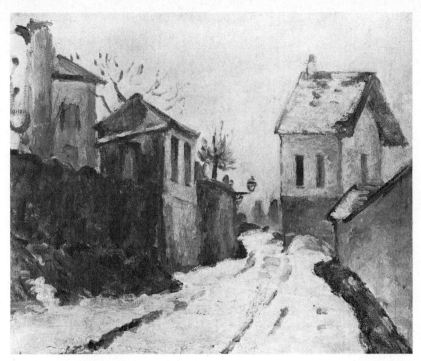

144 Cézanne *Street in Pontoise, Winter* 1873

145 Cézanne *View of Louveciennes* 1873

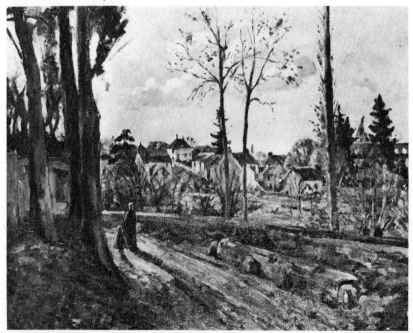

be important for the literary or personal associations of their subject-matter. He achieved structure and volume through a use of colour unknown to him before. This enrichment of his style proved to be one of the most important legacies of the Impressionists to the art of the twentieth century.

Cézanne's need to experience nature directly and to obliterate his own personality set him apart from Van Gogh or Gauguin. When photographs of the scenes he painted are compared with his pictures, one can recognize his greater verisimilitude and his deep attachment to the countryside, particularly around Aix. 'When one is born down there nothing else seems to matter,' he wrote. Yet there were many ways in which he was basically separated from the Impressionists. He was always far more concerned than Monet, for example, with solidity and composition, with balance and structure. His colours and forms are less naturalistic but have more weight, so that, as Meyer Schapiro says, 'Sea, land and sky seem to engage one another . . . and make his water heavy.' He did not relish shapeless open space, as many Impressionists did, being far more engrossed by closed and interlocking forms (see *L'Estaque*, *Ill. 146*). Indeed, he stressed the importance of neighbouring forms as the Impressionists emphasized the primacy of neighbouring colours. His works often give the sensation of permanence (as he wished them to) rather than of some passing effect of light. This, like the Mediterranean atmosphere of his work, made him more 'classical' and therefore more sympathetic to later classicists than the Impressionists were.

Cézanne's Impressionism has been discussed at some length because he is the greatest of the moderns, not because his art is susceptible to verbal explanation. As he himself desired, it is far less easily described than the art of Gauguin or Van Gogh. Cézanne needed his privacy, and even now it is hard for critics to violate it, although his slightest utterances have been seized upon and enlarged by twentieth-century doctrinaire writers. It is a sinister fact, as Benedict Nicolson has observed, that 'the views he is believed to have expressed in conversation always seem more articulate, more prophetic of the course of twentieth-century painting, than anything to be discovered in his letters.'

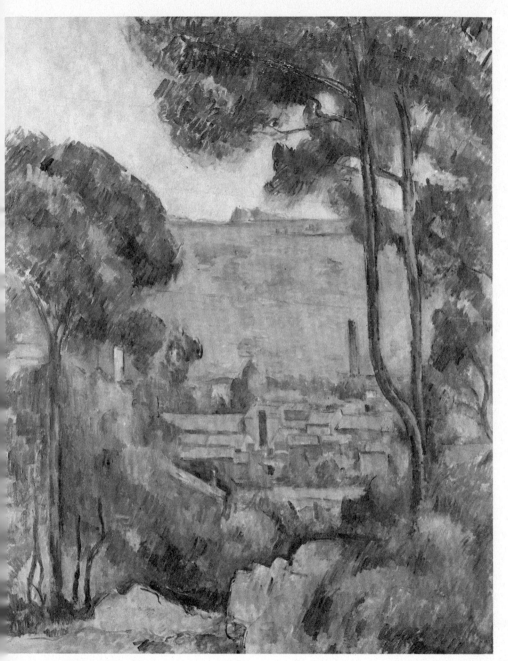

146 Cézanne *L'Estaque* c. 1885

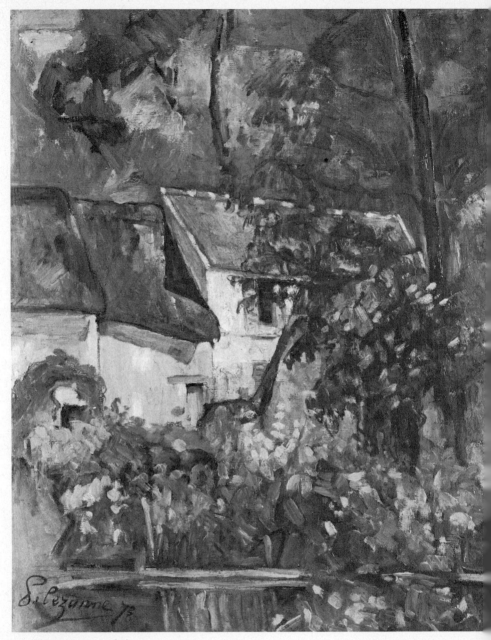

147 Cézanne *House of Père Lacroix, Auvers* 1873

190

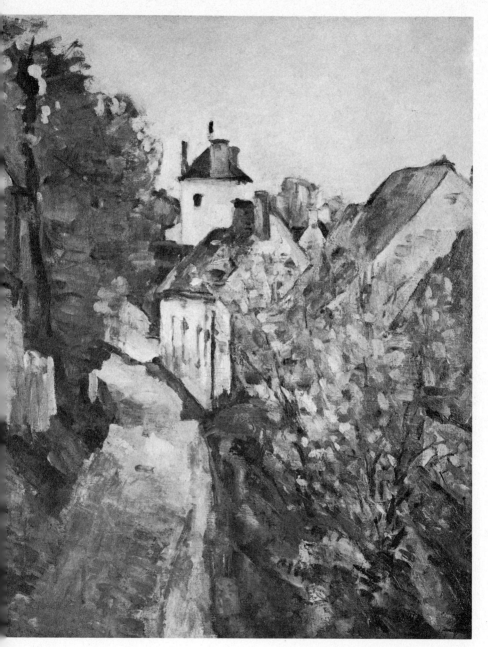

148 Cézanne *House of Dr Gachet, Auvers* 1873

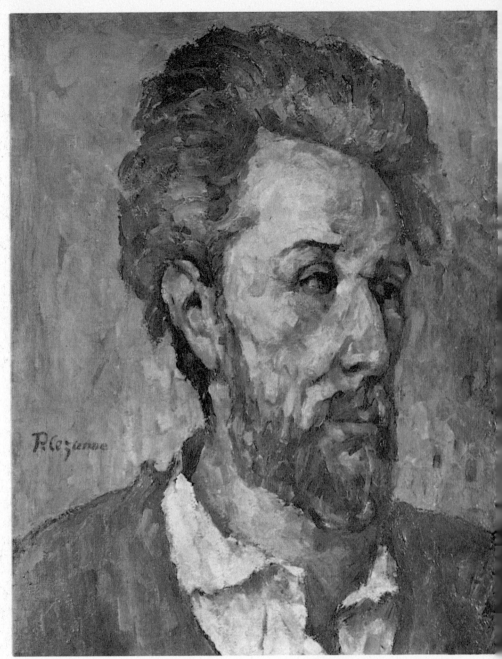

149 Cézanne *Victor Choquet* 1875–7

But the mystery remains, partly because both Cézanne's art and his sayings are full of conflict and paradox. Although he seems consistently anxious to keep the surface of his canvas flat, he was disgusted by the flatness of Gauguin's canvases and wrote to Louis Arenche: 'Nature for us is more depth than surface.' In old age he believed that 'one can never be too submissive to nature', but in the next sentence he declared that one must master one's model. This he often did by distortions and reductions of shape, rendering nearby objects in less detail in order to reduce the sense of a visual pull into the distance. It was typical of his inconsistency to say, 'If I think, everything is lost', and yet also to write that 'a powerful organizing mind is the best aid to sensation.' It is partly this conflict, this sense of violence held in check, counterbalanced by the use of singing colour and the habit of patient contemplation, which explains the secret of Cézanne's greatness.

150 Cézanne *The Seine at Bercy* 1875–80

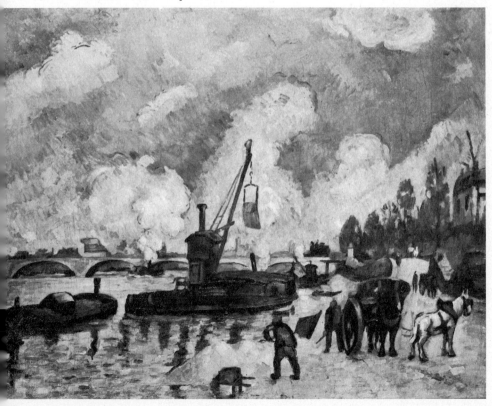

The Impressionist paintings of Gauguin and Van Gogh are less in need of interpretation. Unlike Cézanne, both these painters enjoyed discussing their pictures; they wrote letters describing in detail what they were trying to do, and took part in artistic and literary arguments with the writers of the time. They recognized that, in the rebellion against naturalism, writers and painters faced some of the same problems. Even when they were using Impressionist techniques, Gauguin and Van Gogh included in their pictures many decorative and expressionistic features which stamp them as extremely un-Impressionistic (though, admittedly, it is hard to study these works without being affected by our knowledge of the more revolutionary pictures which soon followed).

Unlike Renoir and Manet, who began their artistic training early and soon became skilled craftsmen, neither Van Gogh nor Gauguin recognized their vocation for many years. For Van Gogh, art became another means to personal salvation, when other ways of doing good (for instance, life as a priest) had been denied him. 'I want to say something comforting in painting as music is comforting,' he wrote. Gauguin was far less concerned with being a good man in any conventional sense; he often gloried in being a cad and an egoist, though this did not prevent him from pursuing a profound artistic quest.

The development of Gauguin and Van Gogh is best considered in the light of a general change in artistic sensibility that was current in the 1880s. The younger generation was beginning to react against what they considered the card-index (*fichier*) mentality of naturalists such as Zola. The realist or naturalist ethos (Degas used both words interchangeably), which had once made Impressionism seem not only possible but exciting, now seemed dull, pedestrian and lacking in mystery. Manet's criticism of Gustave Moreau's symbolist paintings ('He goes in a bad direction; he leads us to the unknown – we who wish everything to be understood.') was diametrically opposed to *avant-garde* ideals. This is clearly demonstrated by Goldwater's study of the increased recognition given to Puvis de Chavannes in the 1880s. Puvis had always been a non-realistic painter, a literary man inspired by visions of antiquity. Berthe Morisot's letters of the 1860s indicate that a few of her friends (including Degas) admired his draughtsmanship and craft, but the themes and general tenor of his art were then considered ridiculous and *vieux jeu*. Now all this was completely changed. Strindberg, who had been in Paris in 1885, wrote about it later to Gauguin, 'In the midst of the last spasms of naturalism one name was pronounced by all with admiration' – meaning Puvis de Chavannes.

Literary painting and attempts to establish links between the various arts had now become fashionable. Van Gogh, Gauguin and many others constantly sought parallels between painting, music and literature, even if the full force of the Wagnerian *Gesamtkunst* was to be felt more strongly in the 1890s. In poetry and the novel, the reaction against positivism, materialism and naturalism was leading to that cult of the irrational, of mystery and the occult which Pissarro connected with bourgeois-political fears and reactions. Many prominent figures adopted the Roman Catholic faith, notably Huysmans, who had once been a disciple of Zola. Theosophy and spiritualism flourished. Eventually, in 1903 Claudel could write to Gide rejoicing in the defeat of all that the nineteenth century had stood for: 'We shall at last breathe in the holy night of blessed ignorance.'

In the above-quoted letter, Strindberg went on to say: 'We did not yet possess the term "symbolism", a very unfortunate name for so old a thing as allegory.' But even if the term had not been widely used before Jean Moréas produced his manifesto in 1886, the elements which made up the symbolist attitude were already present. Mallarmé, Manet's friend and sitter, had been living a retired life in the 1870s, but he now began to attract a group of aesthetes to gatherings in his flat every Tuesday evening. His own credo was quite different from realism or Impressionism; he believed in evocation and suggestion rather than the description of external reality, and strove for the general idea rather than the particularity of Pissarro or Monet. Such anti-Impressionist ideas were reinforced by the influx of new German idealist philosophies, which dethroned the external world and pronounced nature to be merely a projection of man's mind.

Paul Gauguin was the ideal answer to the current prayer for a real 'symbolist' painter. One feels that, like Voltaire's God, if he had not existed it would have been necessary to invent him. The work of his later 'symbolist' period naturally falls outside the scope of any discussion of Impressionism. (The Symbolist banquet in his honour, attended by Eugène Carrière, Odilon Redon and the critic Aurier, took place in 1891, three years after he had violently rejected the Impressionist ideals.) But even at the time when he was still impressed and influenced by Pissarro, a letter written in 1885 to his friend Schuffenecker shows that he was already interested in the possibilities of line and colour as magic or as the abstract equivalent of sensation, and he included in his intimate journals Achille Delaroche's comment on his art: 'Colour which is vibration in the same way as music.'

Indeed, although Gauguin was one of the earliest collectors of Impressionist paintings and one of the first major artists to be formed under the influence of Delacroix and the Impressionists rather than the old masters (as, for example, Manet and Degas had been), he was less deeply and conclusively affected by Impressionism than either Van Gogh or Cézanne. A man so alert to the intellectual currents around him may have felt, even before he had the technical mastery to express himself in paint, that naturalism was an error and that art 'should not be concerned with the sensations of the eye, but should evoke the inner life of man in the mysterious centre of the mind'. But this reasoning anticipates the pictures he painted in 1888 and especially the famous *Vision after the Sermon* (*Ill. 151*).

Paul Gauguin was born in Paris in 1848, but lived with his mother in Peru between 1851 and 1855. He then returned to France, and at the age of seventeen became a sailor and went on voyages to Valparaiso and Rio de Janeiro. In 1871 Gauguin entered the firm of a stockbroker in Paris and made friends there with a fellow employee, Émile Schuffenecker, who persuaded Gauguin to go painting with him on Sundays. In November 1873 Gauguin married a handsome Danish girl, Mette Gad, and was making a comfortable living as a stockbroker. But after meeting Pissarro and other Impressionists in 1875, he became more and more absorbed in painting. In 1883 he finally resigned from his firm in order to devote all his time to art – a heroic decision which committed him to endless struggles and poverty.

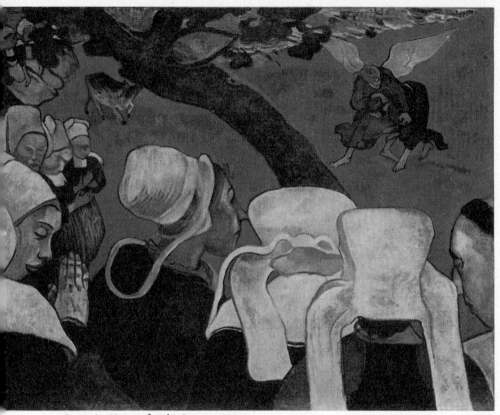

151 Gauguin *Vision after the Sermon* 1888

Gauguin's earliest pictures, done when he was still a 'Sunday painter', are influenced by Corot, Jongkind and Daubigny. These works include the *Landscape at Viroflay* (*Ill. 152*), accepted by the Salon in 1876, and the well-known *Landscape in Normandy* (now in the Fitzwilliam Museum, Cambridge), which was probably painted out of doors shortly before he married Mette.

The whole of Gauguin's career, particularly the authentication and dating of many of his early pictures, has been obscured and be-devilled by the lies of his friends, his wife, his children and Gauguin himself. Mette once declared that when she married him she had no idea that he painted at all. This has been plausibly contradicted by their son Émile: 'I have a drawing he made of my mother in 1873.

197

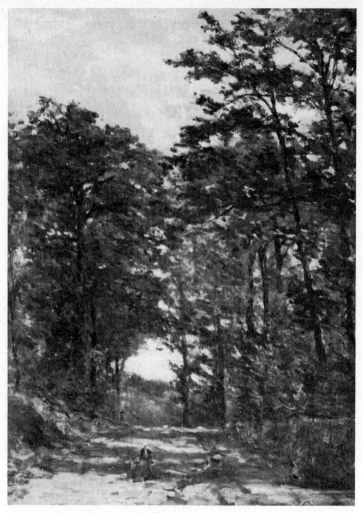

152 Gauguin *Landscape at Viroflay* 1875

. . . Indeed all his life he had dabbled with paints, much to my mother's annoyance when he would use her best linen tablecloth for canvas or her finest petticoat for paint-rags.' But Gauguin may well have thought it prudent to stress his more conventional role as a rising stockbroker to a bride who came from a bureaucratic family and at no time showed any enthusiasm for art.

198

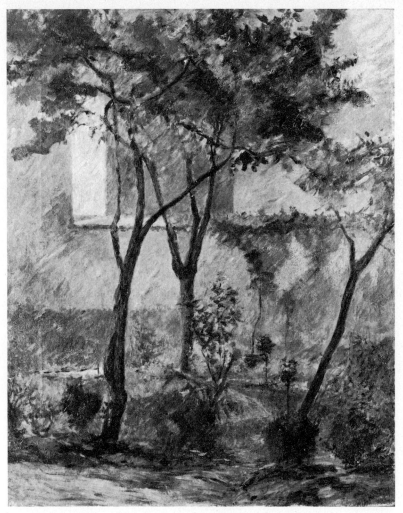

153 Gauguin *Garden of Vaugirard seen from the Rue Carcel* 1879

During 1875 and 1876 Gauguin became more accomplished in
rendering light and space, as in the rather sullen rendering of the
Seine near the Pont d'Iéna, in which tonal values are still more
important than colour. During these years he was attending some
of the more liberal-minded studios, such as the Atelier Colarossi, in
order to practise drawing from models. Soon after getting to know

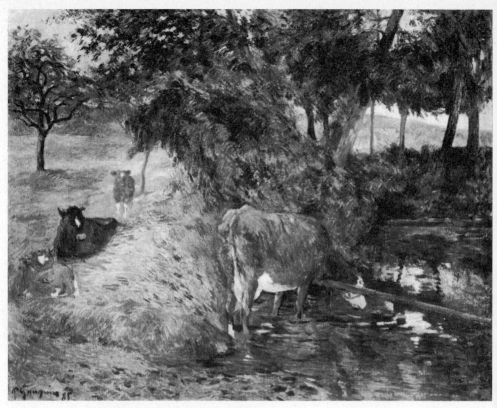

154 Gauguin *Landscape with Cattle* 1885

the Impressionists he began collecting. It is a mark of his taste and originality that he acquired not only works by Manet and Renoir, who were gradually becoming more respectable, but also of Cézanne, who was still the most vituperated and ridiculed painter associated at that time with the group. Indeed, Cézanne's power, strength and concision would have been more sympathetic to Gauguin than the atmospheric delicacies of Monet or Pissarro. Both Cézanne and Gauguin, in their very different ways, were more desperate men, more forceful colourists and less interested in fragmentation than any of the Impressionists proper. A still-life by Cézanne, which Gauguin bought in 1877–8, appears behind the sitter in Gauguin's *Portrait of Marie Henry*, painted in 1890. At one

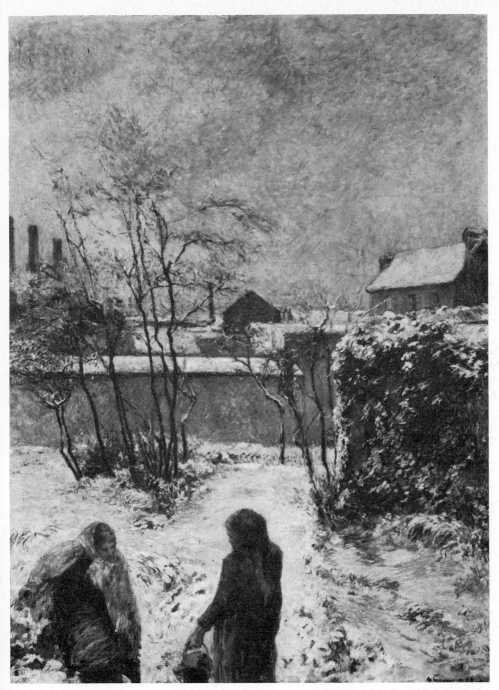

155 Gauguin *Winter, Rue Carcel, Paris* 1883

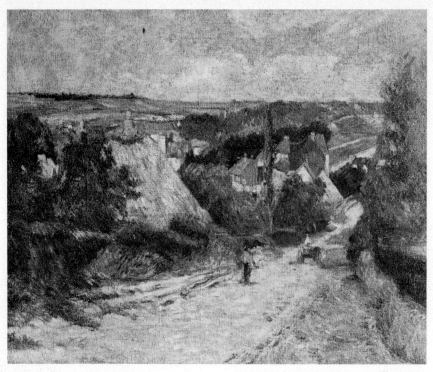

156 Gauguin *Entrance to a Village* 1884

time Schuffenecker tried to buy this still-life in order to help Gauguin, but the latter replied that it was a pearl of exceptional delicacy and that he would rather part with his last shirt.

There is some truth in the exaggerated view that Gauguin was never a wholly Impressionist painter. The Impressionist technique suited Gauguin's more decorative conceptions less than it had suited Cézanne, but Impressionism certainly provided a springboard for the future liberation of his colour, and – still more – a creed, however loose, for Gauguin to fight against later.

It is rarely safe to ignore entirely Gauguin's accounts of his own art, and later in the South Seas he wrote that Pissarro had been his master. From Pissarro he learned the same lesson as Cézanne: to abandon blacks, browns and ochres, and to concentrate on the three primary colours and their main derivatives. He began in the late

1870s to depict angular views, to use broken colours and to choose the same kind of everyday subjects as the Impressionists. Huysmans complained that some of Gauguin's exhibited pictures were 'dilutions of the still hesitant works of Pissarro'. Certainly *Winter, Rue Carcel, Paris* (c. 1883, *Ill. 155*), quite apart from its subject, is reminiscent of the delicate snow-scenes Pissarro and Sisley had painted almost ten years earlier. There is also the *Entrance to a Village* (in the Boston Museum of Fine Arts, *Ill. 156*), which is even more akin to the work of Pissarro, with whom Gauguin spent long holidays in 1879, 1881, 1882 and 1883. At about this time the young Émile Bernard, whom Schuffenecker had met on a road in Brittany, said of a picture by Gauguin: 'Small brush-strokes weave the colour and remind me of Pissarro – and there is not much style.'

157 Gauguin *Landscape, Pont-Aven* 1885–7

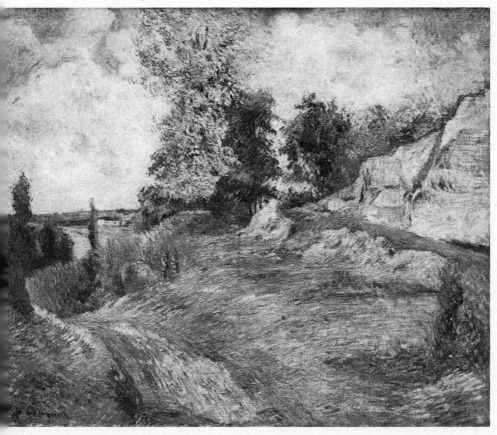

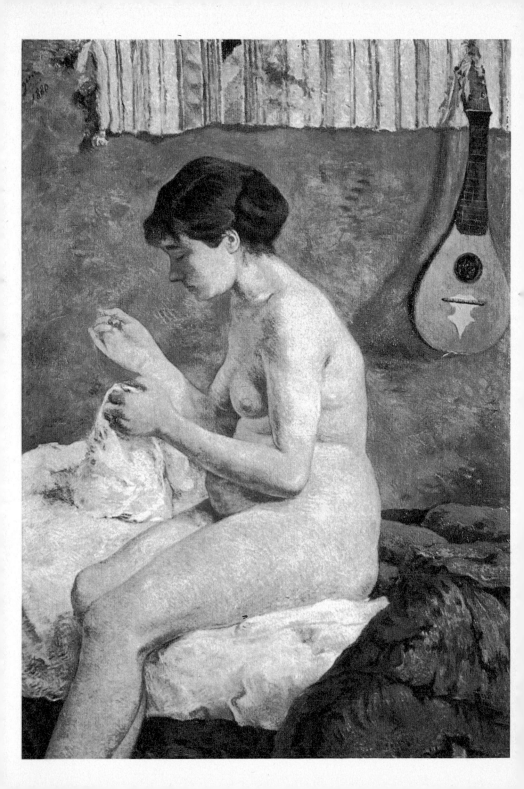

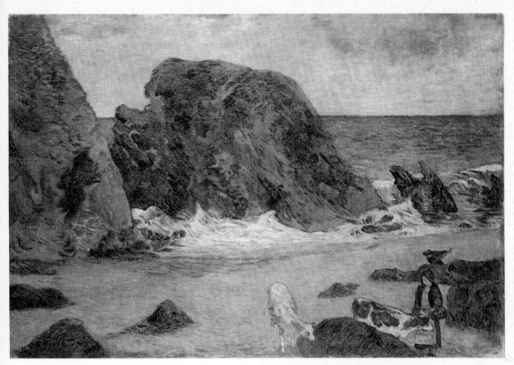

159 Gauguin *Breton Seascape* 1886

Gauguin exhibited at the Impressionist exhibition of 1880, then again in 1881, 1882 and in the final exhibition of 1886. A strong, somewhat Courbet-like nude of his children's nursemaid sewing (*Ill. 158*), shown in 1881, was now praised by Huysmans for its 'vehement note of reality', although many of its colours seem to have been chosen for their decorative quality rather than for verisimilitude. By 1886 Gauguin had certainly met Degas, whom he greatly admired, and the multiple viewpoint of his *Breton Seascape* (*Ill. 159*) and some of the geometrical divisions in such works as *The Sculptor Aubi and his Son* show derivation from the older painter. The *Breton Seascape* is still painted mainly in an Impressionist manner, with divided brush-strokes and considerable attention to light. But the critics of the time perceived correctly that Gauguin's colour tones were mixed rather than divided and that his colour harmonies were close rather than contrasted, as distinct from the Impressionists'

205

method. The difference became most marked after Gauguin had gone in 1887 with a painter friend, Charles Laval, to Martinique, where he was enraptured by the 'primitive' way of life and dazzled by the bright colours. In works like the *Farm in Martinique* and the picture shown here (*Ill. 160*), although there is still some resemblance to Pissarro's colours, the tones tend to coalesce into a single tone – the prelude to his later flat colour arrangements.

This visit to Martinique was the first definite stage in Gauguin's emancipation from Pissarro's tutelage. But even before this he had been speculating in his letters on the emotive value of lines and colours. He was beginning to compose in flat colours rimmed with contour lines and to use arabesques. He was also becoming more critical of Impressionist methods, more capable of blending their technique with his own new discoveries. The contrasts between light and dark areas in his pictures became more decided than those of the Impressionists. Already in 1886, staying at the Pension Gloanec in Pont Aven, Brittany, he had met Émile Bernard, and in the same year he had met Vincent van Gogh in Paris. Both of these new friends were concerned with the new semi-literary ideas and with the application of general laws to art, in a way which the Impressionists were not.

Gauguin's *Vision after the Sermon* (*Ill. 151*), painted in Brittany in 1888 after his return from Martinique, marks the end of his allegiance to Pissarro and Impressionism. Now he had found the technical mastery to express in paint what he may long have felt: that naturalism was, as he said, an abominable error. Gauguin, who was much admired in the Pension Gloanec for his flippancy, physical strength and romantically wild behaviour, now became one of the leaders in the movement away from naturalism (and the representation of the external world) towards the suggestion of dreams and visions by means of allusion, symbol and the expressive rather than naturalistic use of colour and line. In the *Vision after the Sermon* he depicts a moment when the peasants imagine they can see Jacob wrestling with the angel. Gauguin sets the scene against an unreal background of vivid crimson. The picture is painted in large flat areas of colour, not in the small brush-strokes of his Impressionist period. He called his new technique 'synthetism' – an almost complete reversal of all that Impressionism stood for.

In a letter he wrote in 1902 to his friend Georges Daniel de Monfreid, Gauguin said:

> You have known for a long time what it has been my aim to vindicate: the right to dare anything. My capacities (and the pecuniary difficulties in my life have interfered greatly with the carrying out of my task) have not allowed me to achieve a great result, but the mechanism has been set in motion nevertheless. . . . The public owe me nothing since my pictorial *œuvre* is only relatively good, but the painters of today who are benefiting from this new-born freedom do owe me something.

One should recall this very accurate self-judgment before stigmatizing Gauguin as a man blinded by arrogance and self-love. Considered purely as painting, Gauguin's work, compared with that of Cézanne or Degas – or even Renoir and Manet – is, as he said, only relatively good. But his inventive originality was decisive for much of early twentieth-century art. He swept away the naturalist tradition, rejecting the view that pictures are mirror-like reflections of the outside world. Instead he regarded them as conceptual images which would reflect and work upon man's inner or spiritual nature. More than any other modern artist, Gauguin was responsible for the widespread cult of primitivism during the next twenty years, not least by putting this ideal into practice and actually going to spend his life in Tahiti. The German Expressionists and the young Picasso's circle of friends in the early 1900s were significantly intrigued by his legend and example.

The portraits painted by Gauguin and Van Gogh leave no doubt that they were both antipathetic by nature to the spirit of Impressionism. Cézanne, nearer in age and aims to the Impressionists, might wish to paint his sitters with the calm gravity and permanence of apples; and Renoir could produce a portrait of Wagner so lacking in intellectual distinction that the subject complained that he was made to look like a Protestant clergyman. But both Gauguin and Van Gogh were interested in the subjects as human beings, or as the expression of their own ideas about human destiny.

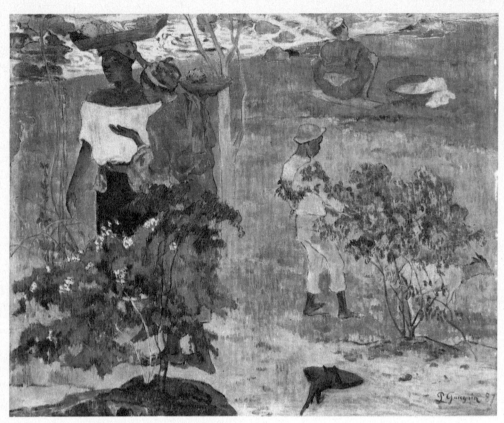

160 Gauguin *Martinique Landscape* 1887

Van Gogh did not come to Paris out of enthusiasm for the Impressionists, as has sometimes been held. He was curious about them, it is true, but had no real knowledge of what they were doing. His motives were different: he needed an exchange of ideas with other young artists and wished to see some traditional pictures. 'I sometimes long very badly to see the Louvre and Luxembourg again, and to study there the technique and colour of Millet, Corot, Delacroix and others.' He was also offended by the advice he had received at the Académie des Beaux-Arts in Antwerp – to spend at least another

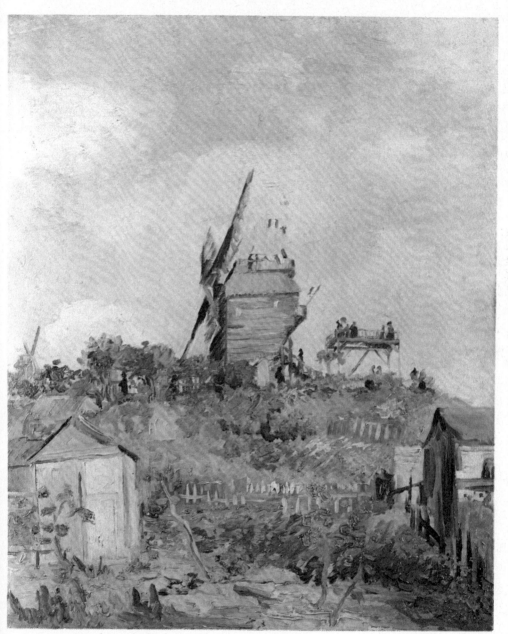

161 Van Gogh *Le Moulin de la Galette, Montmartre* 1886

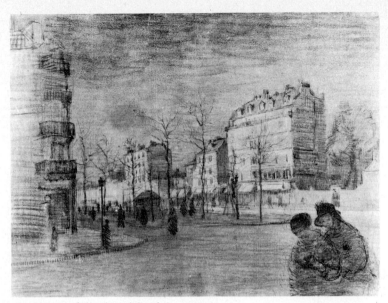

162 Van Gogh *Boulevard de Clichy* 1886-7

year doing nothing but executing drawings from plaster casts. Considering how few years he had to live and what magnificent use he made of them, it is fortunate that he paid no attention to this idiotic counsel.

Van Gogh's violence, his inability to be calm and passive before nature, his concern with drawing, contour, solid objects and human beings, rather than with atmosphere and fragmented brush-strokes, would no doubt always have prevented his becoming an orthodox Impressionist (if such a thing were possible by as late as 1886). Like many other painters who had once benefited from Impressionist technique, he was quick to disown it. In Arles, where he lived during 1888, he said that his art had been fertilized more by Delacroix than by the Impressionists. (While he was in the hospital at St Remy from 1889 to 1890 he copied or transposed several works by Delacroix, including *The Good Samaritan*.)

While still in Antwerp, Van Gogh had begun to use brighter colours (under Rubens' influence) and to be affected by the style of Japanese prints, from which he learned to use swift, exaggerated

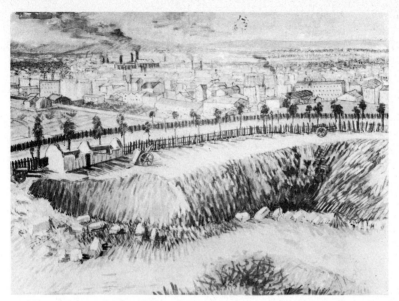

163 Van Gogh *View of an Industrial Town* 1887–8

contour-lines and poster-like effects of flat colour. Soon after his arrival in Paris in 1886 he wrote to the painter Levens, whom he had known in Holland, that the Impressionist method was quite different from their own. He seemed to be far more excited by the exhibition of work by Adolphe Monticelli, the painter who lived near Marseilles, and his many flower pieces executed at that time betray Monticelli's influence. But in Paris, through his brother Theo, he met Pissarro, whose example led him to adopt brilliant, pure colours. He also stopped almost sculpting his figures with broad brushes and heavy masses of chiaroscuro in the manner of Millet and Daumier, and experimented with the smaller, more controlled brush-strokes, the dots and tiny strokes laid on with fine marten-hair brushes, used by his new Impressionist friends. His paintings were now smaller, and much more exactly and delicately formed (compare the *Boulevard de Clichy, Ill. 162,* or *The Bridge at Asnières* with the earlier *Potato Eaters*). Although his brush-strokes in the works executed in Paris were more Impressionist in character than they had been before, they were longer, heavier and more emphatic than those in the paintings of Renoir, Monet and Pissarro. The last-named, who in 1886 was himself changing his style of painting to accord with that of his son's friends Seurat and Signac, was none the less characteristically generous in his appraisal of Van Gogh's gifts. He is later reported to have said that he had felt immediately that Van Gogh would either go mad or surpass them all, 'but I didn't know he would do both'.

During 1887 Van Gogh painted typically Impressionist subjects: street-scenes, restaurants, flowers and men in boats. He combined the shimmer of water or sunlight with a distinctly un-Impressionist definition of outline, as in *The Bridge at Asnières*, or built up the

164 Van Gogh *Fishing in Spring* 1886–7

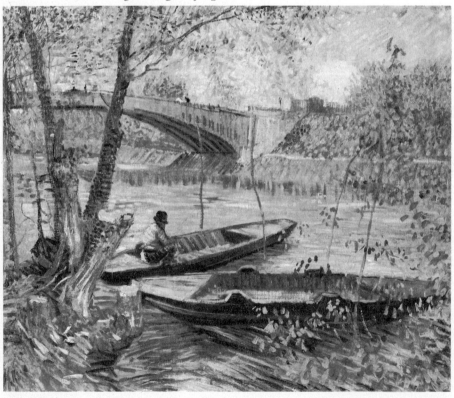

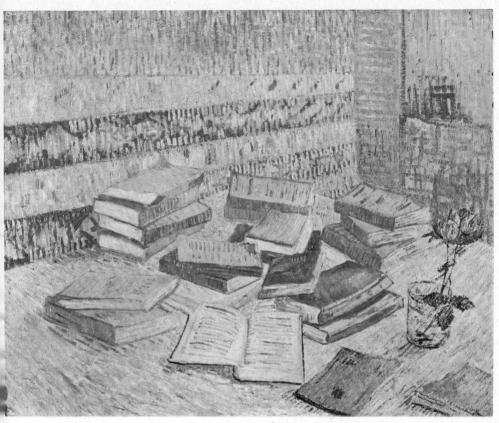

165 Van Gogh *The Yellow Books, Parisian Novels* 1887

composition in planes, as in *The Wheatfield*, which contrasts notably with the amorphous harvests and poppyfields painted by Monet and Renoir in the early 1870s. Through Pissarro he soon came to know and (unlike Gauguin) become friendly with Signac and, to a lesser extent, Seurat. Seurat was in fact the last person he visited before he left Paris for Arles. Some of the later works of his Paris period (for example, *The Interior of a Restaurant*) are painted almost entirely in the small dots and divided complementary colours of the divisionist technique.

Everybody who met Van Gogh at this time, including Guillaumin and the British artist A. S. Hartrick, has noted his intense

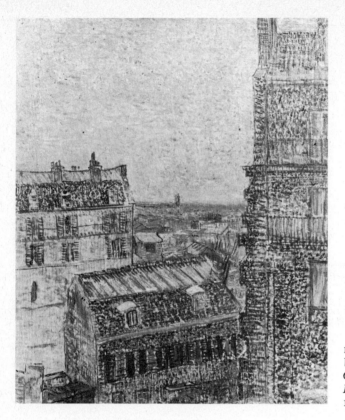

166 Van Gogh
*View from Van
Gogh's Room in the
Rue Lepic, Paris*
1887

over-excitability, which was scarcely to be wondered at in view of the many new stimuli Paris offered him after his lonely years in Holland. In the current conflict between naturalism and symbolism Van Gogh's position, like that of many other artists, was highly ambivalent. In many ways he was an extremely literary man and painter. His picture of *The Yellow Books, Parisian Novels (Ill. 165)* shows the books juxtaposed in a far from haphazard way. Like Seurat, he was addicted to the novels of the Goncourts, Huysmans and Zola – novelists who often combine naturalistic subject-matter with a romantic mood, as Van Gogh himself did. He certainly did not have or attempt to acquire the documentary, card-index approach of a true naturalist. His great strength lay in his passionate identification with the object.

'It sounds rather crude,' he wrote, 'but it is perfectly true that the feeling for reality is more important than the feeling for pictures.' He also wrote (in opposition to Gauguin, who was telling Bernard not to paint from the model), 'I am so intrigued by what really exists that I have not the desire or courage to seek after the ideal as it might result from abstract studies.'

One cannot think of Van Gogh without visualizing those violent tones of pure colour, those distinct brush-strokes, which, particularly in the pictures painted at Auvers in 1890 before he killed himself, are highly personal and yet bear the imprint of his contact with the Impressionists. He often wrote of himself as preparing the way for future painters, and here he did not delude himself. Like Cézanne, he had a decisive effect on the future. Both he and Gauguin brought the tragic sense of life back into painting after the quotidian subject-matter of Impressionism; and Van Gogh, by his very extremism and directness, made all kinds of new painting seem possible. The Fauves, and Matisse and Picasso, owed a great deal to him, but perhaps no more than he himself owed to Impressionism in the vital two years of his development in Paris.

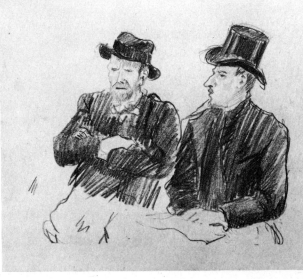

167 Lucien Pissarro
*Vincent van Gogh
and Félix Fénéon*

CHAPTER EIGHT

The later works of Monet, Renoir and Pissarro

In the early 1880s each of the great Impressionists became obsessed with problems of style and went through a crisis of doubt. In each case the causes were different, but the basic problem may have been the very success of the techniques these artists had invented – techniques which opened so many new possibilities of further exploration. The Impressionists may have become afraid (as Picasso was so often to be afraid) of growing merely slick, since they were all artists of considerable virtuosity.

No single explanation can be given for the disquiet of each member of the group. Renoir had always shown leanings towards classicism, and after 1881 these dominated his art. Monet was, in a sense, carrying the principle of naturalism a stage further than Impressionism; he was striving to analyze with exactitude the web of pure colour of which light is composed. At the same time he appeared to reject pure reportage in favour of interpretation and a transposition of observed facts which allowed him greater creative freedom. Pissarro was predominantly influenced by the wish for constant novelty in an age which, inspired by scientific discoveries such as those of Darwin, was still by no means sceptical of the idea of progress.

Jules Laforgue, who seems to have divined the Impressionists' intentions throughout their development, declared that 'the only criterion was newness. In short, that which the instinct of the ages has always exalted when it proclaimed as geniuses, according to the etymology of the word, those and only those who have revealed something new.' When Pissarro learned from his son about the new methods of Seurat and Signac, he evidently could not bear to be left behind in the march of artistic progress, which he tended to equate with the quest for the liberty of mankind. Seurat and Signac themselves, and to some extent the Impressionists, were doubtless affected by the intellectual and literary reaction against naturalism and positivism – a reaction which, in literature, found expression in the Symbolist movement and was still flourishing among the Modernist writers of Barcelona where the young Picasso was living at the turn of the century.

Apart from their individual difficulties, the Impressionists were threatened by adverse cultural and economic conditions. In 1882 the collapse of the Grand Union Bank embarrassed their faithful dealer Durand-Ruel, and two years later there was a further financial crisis. Eventually, these troubles were to be mitigated by the exhibitions in Madison Square, New York, and the improved economic circumstances of the 1890s, but naturally the painters could not foresee this.

It was also irritating for men who had recently been rebels to find that, as Zola pointed out with some malice, the official Salon was already being transformed by their tame and dreary imitators. Zola was now proving a very questionable friend; in 1880 he wrote four articles on 'Naturalism at the Salon', showing that the Impressionists were no longer a group. Worse still, he declared that they were only forerunners, and that 'the man of genius' had yet to arrive. It is ironical that if this view is correct the 'man of genius' was undoubtedly Zola's old friend Cézanne, whom the writer was soon to wound by publication of *L'Œuvre* (1886), the novel in which Zola travestied Impressionism.

It was Pissarro who expressed himself most strongly about new trends in the arts. 'In my opinion,' he wrote, 'the most corrupt form of art is sentimental art, orange blossom art which makes pale women swoon.' This may seem a strange judgment on Gauguin or Van Gogh, but it is somewhat more appropriate to the work of Huysmans in his novels, Émile Bernard or, later, Maurice Denis. Pissarro felt that the change in the artistic climate was connected with economic and political reaction. Neither Renoir nor Monet would have been so much disturbed by this; but they cannot have relished the new idea of envisaging nature as merely a projection of man's mind, nor found congenial a situation in the arts which made it possible for Strindberg to write of 'the last dying throes of naturalism'.

217

The publication of Zola's *L'Œuvre* came as a blow to the Impressionists as well as Cézanne. As a touchy man and as Zola's oldest friend, Cézanne was naturally the most offended by the book; he broke off all relations with Zola after thanking him for the book 'in memory of the days that are gone'. On the whole, the Impressionists agreed that the mad hero was Henri Gervex or conceivably Guillemet, with strong touches of their dead friend Bazille, but Zola had known them all well and each could privately recognize incidents which related to himself. Monet wrote a letter to Zola which was distinctly worried in tone: he had read *L'Œuvre* 'with very great pleasure, discovering old memories on each page. You know, besides, my fanatical admiration for your talent. It has nothing to do with that, but I have been struggling fairly long and I am afraid that in the moment of succeeding, our enemies may make use of your book to deal us a knockout blow.' He was right; enemies did pounce, just as they had once pounced on Duranty's pamphlet of 1876, which damned the Impressionists with faint praise in comparison with Degas.

The year 1886 was altogether a bad one for the Impressionists. R.L.Herbert, in his admirable book on Seurat's drawings, declares that, after reading the many articles by Seurat's friends on *Un Dimanche à La Grande Jatte*, he has no doubt that 'it was a deliberate challenge to Impressionism and that the choice of subject was dictated in part by a wish to re-make one of their favourite scenes.' In Seurat's earlier *Une Baignade* (1883-4), the landscape, like the charming little oil-sketches made by way of preparation (*Ill. 169*), was Impressionist, but the figures were monumental and Puvis-like, even reminiscent of the somewhat solemn grandeur of an artist like Piero della Francesca. Huysmans enquired in *L'Art Moderne*, 'What artist will now render the imposing grandeur of industrial cities? It is true that M.Monet has attempted to paint the railway sheds, but without succeeding in diverging from his uncertain abbreviations.' It was at about this time that Durand-Ruel felt forced by his clients to ask Monet to 'finish' his pictures more – a suggestion which was almost blasphemous to the true Impressionist. Ideals of the calm and permanent, which had originally been used by academic opponents

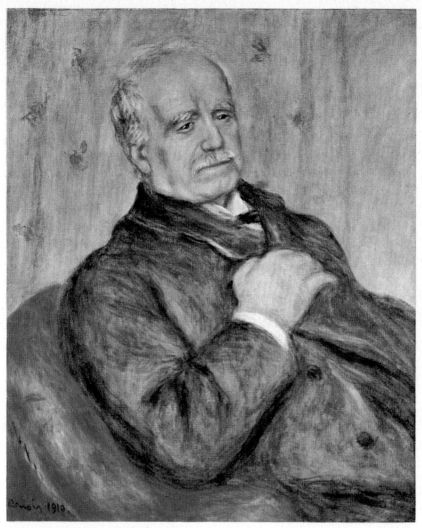

168 Renoir *Paul Durand-Ruel* 1910

to castigate the early Impressionists, were now revived by a younger generation to make the group appear old-fashioned. A frequent criticism, repeated over and over again, was that the Impressionists made their landscapes 'convulse' or 'grimace'. Even Cézanne, who never forswore Impressionism and generally remained loyal to his

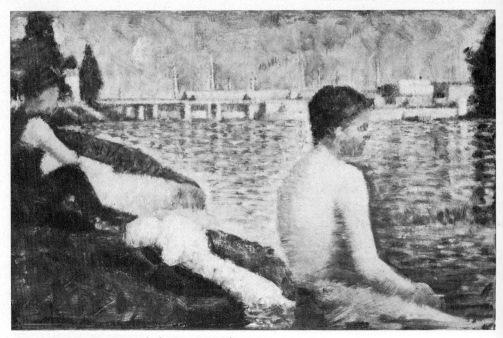

169 Seurat *Study for Une Baignade c.* 1883

friends, adopted this phrase, and in later life often remarked how much he disliked artists who made trees and skies grimace. He abhorred the later art of Van Gogh, perhaps for this reason, and said to him, with more frankness than tact: 'In all sincerity you paint like a madman.'

The doubts which began to affect the great Impressionists in the early 1880s, then, had many external causes and cannot, or need not, be explained entirely by their internal disunity, their comparative lack of contact with one another, and the depressing economic situation. Indeed, their isolation was often self-chosen; at one point Monet asked Durand-Ruel not to tell Renoir where he was going to paint, since he needed to work out his artistic problems alone.

During this phase, when naturalism and Impressionism were under attack, Monet, as the arch-Impressionist, received some of the most virulent abuse. Huysmans, in addition to alluding to Monet's 'uncertain abbreviations', also decried the 'hairdresser's blue' which he and Renoir often used in the 1880s. Zola declared that Monet had given in too much to his facility of production (an odd criticism from such a highly prolific writer): 'Too many informal drafts have left his studio in difficult hours.' The essence of Monet's art was its speed and spontaneity, but this too was considered by the new generation to be less important than the new kind of 'grandes machines' painted by Seurat or Puvis de Chavannes.

The current dislike of Monet's art was no doubt reinforced by his non-literary personality. Van Gogh could hold debates on a high intellectual level with the critic Aurier; Gauguin could paint a self-portrait with allusions to Verlaine's *Poètes maudits* (1884); but the writers at the Café Volpini, the centre of the Symbolist movement, would not have elicited an eloquent contribution from Monet in any discussion of Schopenhauer's view that nature is only an appearance. The leader of Impressionism had had very little use for books or writers from his schooldays onwards. When writing to Zola about *L'Œuvre*, he had, it is true, professed an immense admiration for Zola's talents, but that does not prove he had actually read many of the novels. Gustave Kahn soon began to say that there were parallels between Seurat's hieratic and static paintings and the ideals for which Kahn and his fellow writers were striving: 'This endeavour to extract the absolute . . . we were responsive to the mathematic of his art.' Writers could not be responsive to the mathematic of Monet's very individual, uncompromising and wildly asymmetrical art, no matter how well disposed towards it they might have been. It is far easier for writers and critics to understand paintings which either contain intellectually significant subject-matter or are planned with great care in advance, like some of Ingres' works. But the work of Monet (like that of Cézanne) is based so much on tactics worked out by the painter on the spot that it is very difficult for a critic to explain it to a non-painter, just as good intuitive cooking is hard to analyze in words.

In the early 1880s, soon after his wife's death and the production of his wonderful pictures of thawing ice (*Ill. 170*), Monet's style had begun to change. It is difficult to be sure exactly what he was trying to do, and far more difficult to discuss his later development than that of Renoir or Pissarro. They at least expressed themselves in words on the shortcomings of early Impressionism and the new, more classical or more scientific procedures which they were now trying to adopt. Monet's sense of dissatisfaction, parallel with the emergence of his new style, may have begun even earlier than 1880, but the change in his style developed gradually and was in some ways an intensification of both his reliance on sense-data and the aims he had always had in mind. Even in his early paintings he had possessed a very exact sense of colour structure, and this aspect of

170 Monet *Break-up of the Ice, Lavacourt* 1880

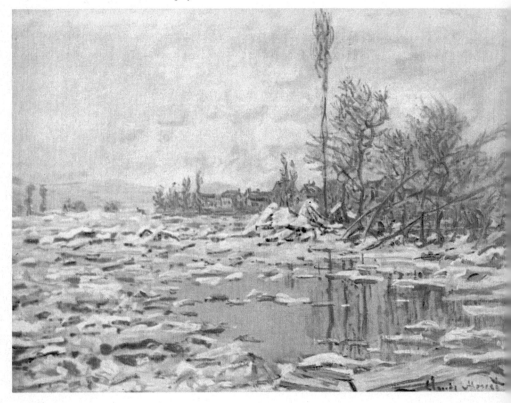

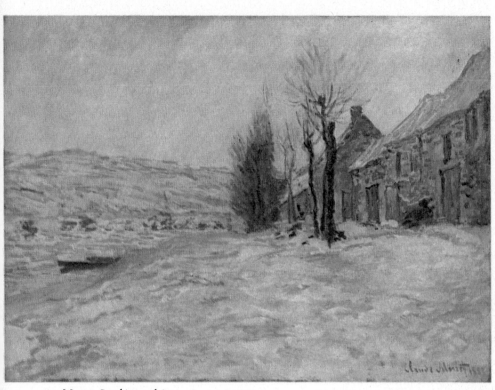

171 Monet *Sunshine and Snow, Lavacourt* 1881

his pictures was to become increasingly elaborate, forcing him to take liberties with natural appearances and sometimes, as in the views of Pourville (*Ill. 172*) and Etretat (1882–5, *Ill. 173*), to resort to simplification and stylization. He may have had some idea of taking the Impressionist method further towards scientific objectivity. The scientific atmosphere of the 1880s was very persuasive, and Monet would have found Seurat's use of the works of colour theorists less uncongenial than he found the *au delà* and decorative ideals of Gauguin's associates.

Monet had no great feeling for the self-sufficiency, what might almost be called the sanctity, of objects, such as can be sensed in so

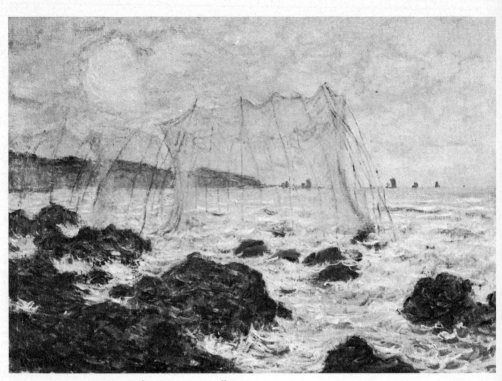

172 Monet *Fishing Nets, Pourville* 1882

many of Van Gogh's drawings. While Monet was capable of drawing, it played a very minor part in his art. He enjoyed flux and all
that was indeterminate and amorphous in nature, though he also had
a fondness for vertical lines, which explains his paintings of poplars
(*Ill. 175*).

Another illustration of his scanty respect for individual objects
is his wish, recorded by the American painter, Mrs Lilla Cabot
Perry, to see the world as a pattern of nameless colour patches
– as might a man born blind who has suddenly regained his sight. In
his late work he generalized his forms even more freely than before,
suppressing details entirely; and he was not in the least hesitant about
consciously re-arranging the natural scene in front of him. He often

224

painted more broadly than before, and the varieties of texture in his work became even more obvious. He travelled a great deal too, presumably to study different kinds of light; and he continued to paint the sea (*Ills. 172, 173*), sometimes with grandeur and always with empathy. Even though, in this late phase, he shifted and changed the views he painted, he never went so far as the Post-Impressionists. He remained in the same tradition as Sainte-Beuve and Degas, preferring the true to the pretty or the pleasing.

After his unsuccessful attempt in the 1860s to paint large figure compositions which might vie with those of Courbet and Manet, references to human beings became increasingly fewer in his work. He was driven more and more to concentrate on what Auden has called 'the friendless and unbrothered stone', although Monet far preferred water, air and snow to stone. It was from about 1881 that he began to use a slotted box containing several canvases of a given size, from which, when he returned to paint a certain subject each day, he chose the one that best suited the light of the moment. He would work on this canvas until the light changed, then replace it with another. Monet explained the reason for this to Mrs Perry in the 1890s. He thought that his first glance at the subject was likely to yield the most faithful impression, and that as much of the canvas as possible should be covered at the first session to determine at once the tonality of the whole. He felt that a painter must stop working immediately the light changed in order to obtain a true impression and not a composite picture. His strong respect for sense-data was characteristic of his generation, and he might well have been sad and angry if any of the *avant-garde* writers of the 1880s and 1890s had been silly enough to tell him that nature was only a projection of his own mind.

Monet's interest in light and colour had always led him to pay comparatively little attention to solidity and structure. In order to maintain a certain order and realism in his pictures, he began to use rhythmical simplifications of rocks, cliffs or poplars. (In the opposite way, when concentrating on the problems of volume involved in the early phase of Cubism, Picasso and Braque were forced to minimize the distracting element of colour.) Monet had actually

225

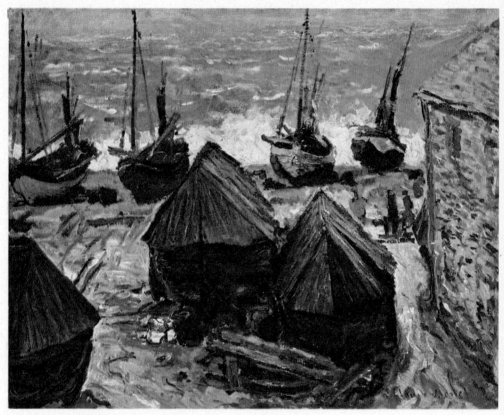

173 Monet *Boats in Winter Quarters at Etretat* 1885

begun to make such simplifications some years before Gauguin, in
1888, embarked on the synthetism that seemed to the critics such an
original development; and the older man's work shocked not only
the public but also his friends. As reported in one of Pissarro's letters,
Degas called it 'the art of a very skilful but short-lived decorator'.
The critics were right not to imply any connection between these
simplifications and those of Gauguin at Pont-Aven, since the two
artists were using them for entirely different ends. Monet was still
concerned with the portrayal, however summary, of external reality,

whereas Gauguin was preoccupied with magic and suggestion, and with evoking states of mind.

Many of Monet's paintings during the 1880s have dramatic subject-matter and fierce, sometimes coarse, colours – for example, some of the works painted at Antibes. In 1888, when he exhibited ten of his Antibes seascapes at the gallery managed by Theo van Gogh, Félix Fénéon wrote in a review of the artist's 'excessive bravura of execution, fecund powers of improvization and vulgar brilliance'. Fénéon admittedly idolized the restraint and the distilled purity and classicism of Seurat, but other critics also disapproved, with some reason, of the splotchy and unpleasing texture which Monet sometimes affected. It should be added, however, that distaste for his work was far more marked in *avant-garde* and literary circles than among ordinary patrons of art, who were just beginning to appreciate first Manet and then Monet. Monet's first real successes date from 1889, when he held a joint exhibition with Rodin. In the 1890s he began to enjoy a comfortable income, and by 1895 his reputation in the United States was greater than that of any other Impressionist.

Monet's 'series' pictures are the very essence of Impressionism. In May 1891 he exhibited fifteen of his haystack series, which show the same subject in a succession of different lights (*Ill. 174*). For this undertaking Monet needed all that physical strength which enabled him to paint all day in the snow, wind or rain, and which led Guy de Maupassant (who sometimes accompanied him) to compare his life to that of a trapper. He had become almost as moody as Cézanne, was often frustrated by rapid changes of light and often destroyed his canvases. In October 1890, while working on the *Haystacks* (which stood on a slope above his farmhouse at Giverny), he wrote to Geffroy: 'I am beginning to work so slowly that I am desperate, but the more I continue, the more I see that a great deal of work is necessary in order to render what I seek: instantaneity, especially the envelope, the same light spreading everywhere, and more than ever am I dissatisfied with the easy things that come in one stroke.' The physical bulk of these haystacks is absorbed by the light encircling them. Kandinsky, who saw one of the haystack pictures in Moscow in 1895, wrote: 'Painting took on a fabulous strength and splendour,

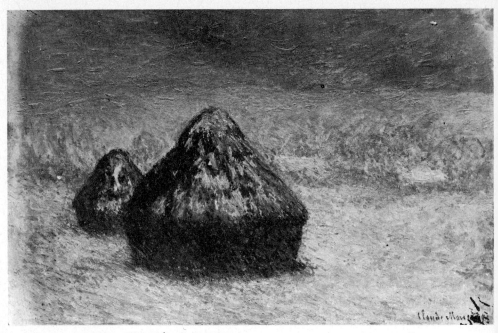

174 Monet *Haystacks, Sunset* 1891

and at the same time, unconsciously, the object was discredited as an indispensable element of the picture.'

In the series *Poplars on the Epte* (1891), Monet turns from the curved forms of the haystacks to verticals treated almost geometrically; this sequence has even more generalized atmospheric colour and fewer local tones. Monet apparently valued very highly the direct and spontaneous sketch now in the Tate Gallery, London (*Ill. 175*). One critic said that the series represented 'a cosmic pantheism, giving the sense of duration, even of eternity'. But Monet himself evidently never gave countenance to this and similar extravagances; up to the year of his death he repeated that his only aim was 'to paint directly from nature, striving to render my impression in the face of the most fugitive effects'.

In the late winter of 1892–3, and again in the following year, Monet painted the façade of Rouen Cathedral from the window of a shop opposite, following the light on the variegated and weathered

228

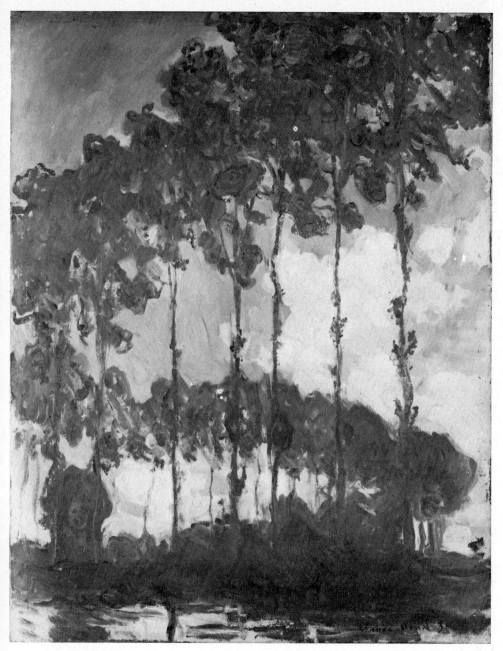

175 Monet *Poplars on the Epte* 1891

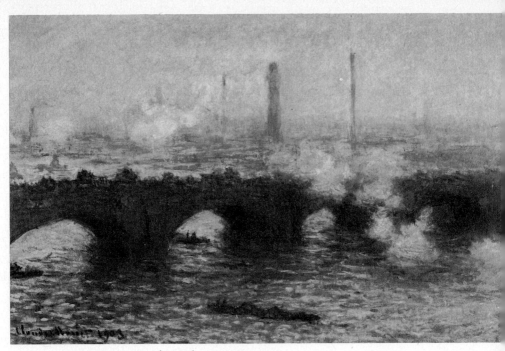

176 Monet *Waterloo Bridge, Grey Day* 1903

façade from morning to evening (*Ill. 177*). When twenty paintings in this series were shown at the Durand-Ruel gallery in 1895, comments were mixed. Some critics were rhapsodically enthusiastic; others, such as Georges Leconte, complained that there was 'not enough sky', 'not enough ground', and George Moore took exception to the lack of allusion to distance.

Even in his early canvases Monet had been inclined to paint what Seitz calls 'the visual curtain rather than conceptual bulk'; there can scarcely ever have been a less Cubist artist than Monet. In his late years he analyzed more and more carefully what he saw and therefore, according to the same writer, he painted sensations as well as appearances. In his last works, 'subject, sensation and pictorial object have all but become identical.' In 1900, when he was sixty years old, Monet characteristically and indefatigably embarked on two great projects: a series representing the Thames (by 1904 there were over a hundred canvases on this theme, *Ill. 176*), and another of his

230

177 Monet *Rouen Cathedral: Full Sunlight* 1894 ▶

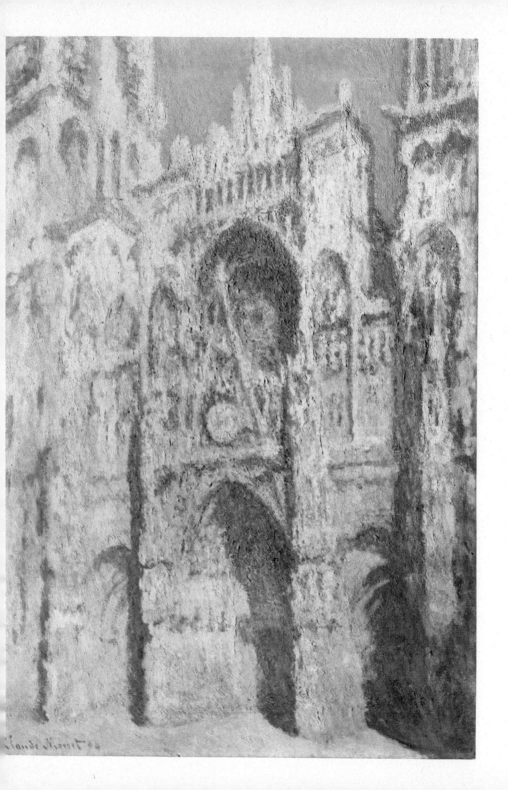

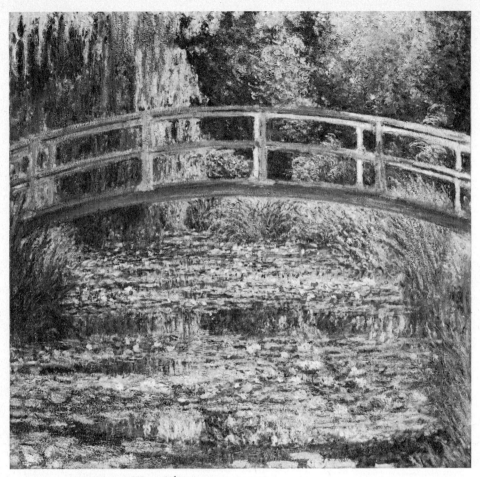

178 Monet *Water Lilies* 1899

water-gardens at Giverny (*Ills. 178, 179*), which he went on elaborating and enlarging until his death in 1926. To execute the Thames scene, each winter from 1899 to 1901 Monet made a journey to London, where his son had gone to study English, and stayed at the Savoy Hotel. From his fifth-storey balcony he could see three bridges and behind them the Gothic huddle of Westminster. In 1918 and again in 1920 he described the fascination of London in winter: 'Without the fog London would not be a beautiful city. It is the fog which

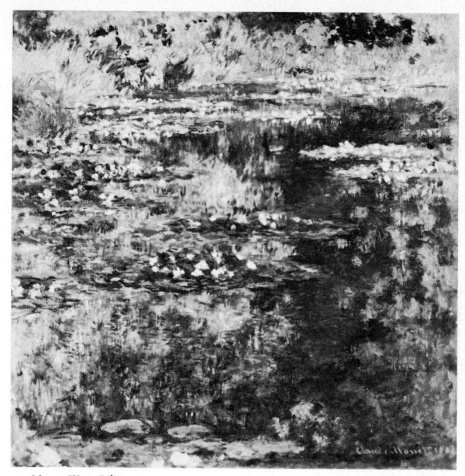

179 Monet *Water Lilies* 1904

gives it its magnificent amplitude . . . it is a mass, an ensemble, and
it is so simple . . . its regular and massive blocks become grandiose
in that mantle. . . . How could the English painters of the nineteenth
century have painted bricks that they did not see . . . that they could
not see?' The accurate and travelled Monet seems to have suffered
from that common French delusion that London is obscured by fog
throughout the greater part of the year – a delusion no doubt
engendered, or at least confirmed, by the novels of Dickens.

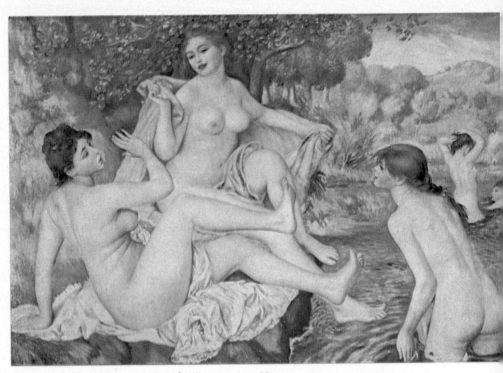

180 Renoir *Les Grandes Baigneuses c.* 1887

During the early 1880s Renoir passed through a time of doubt and
misgiving which has been called his 'sour period'. On a visit to Italy
in 1881, the sight of the frescoes at Pompeii and those of Raphael
made him realize that he was losing too much through the Impressionist abolition of shape and contour. Later he told Vollard:
'Towards 1883 there occurred what seemed to be a break in my
work. I had travelled as far as Impressionism could take me and
I realized the fact that I could neither paint nor draw. In a word, I
had reached an impasse.'

In the works of 1881–3, Renoir used more intense reds and yellows,
probably as a result of journeys to Algiers in 1881 and 1882. His
drawing became more sharply linear and he adopted certain traits
from the eighteenth century: a smooth nacrous surface, relatively

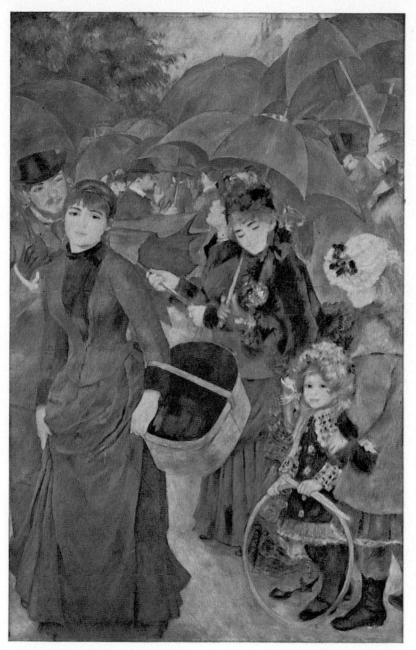

181 Renoir *Les Parapluies c.* 1884

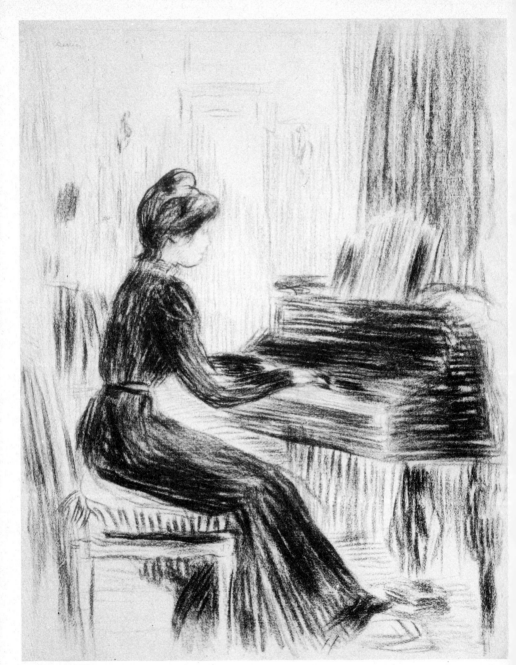

182 Renoir *Mlle Lerolle at the Piano c.* 1892

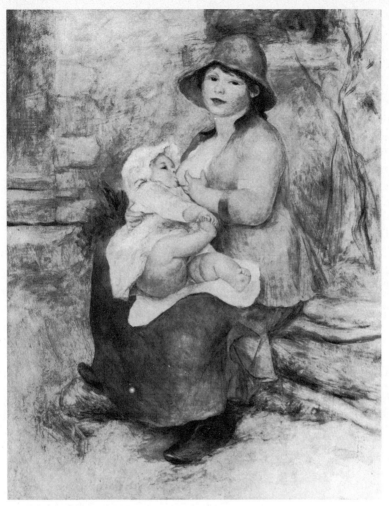

183 Renoir *Maternité* 1885

dry pigments and a method of painting skin (for example, in the blonde bather of 1881) somewhat similar to that of Boucher. A new insistence on the decorative and formal design of a picture appears in a work like *Les Parapluies* (1884, *Ill. 181*), which is in great contrast to the earlier, more casually planned *The Skiff* (c. 1879, *Ill. 118*). Renoir now began to employ more timeless elements (draping instead of contemporary clothes) and more sculptural forms, and to

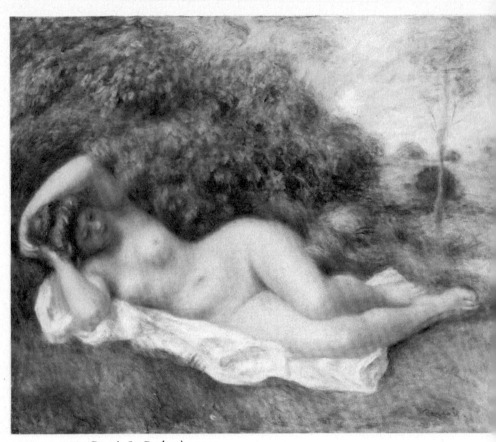

184 Renoir *La Boulangère* 1904

place greater emphasis on the human figure. For the *Grandes Baigneuses* of *c.* 1887 (*Ill. 180*) he adopted the classical method of preparation with many drawings, and even borrowed from a seventeenth-century bas-relief by François Girardin at Versailles. The leaves were no longer the dappled airy leaves of *Le Moulin de la Galette* (*Ill. 116*), but hard and dry like cough lozenges.

Renoir's disenchantment is well expressed, in general terms, in the rough draft of a letter to Durand-Ruel, in which he expresses his

238

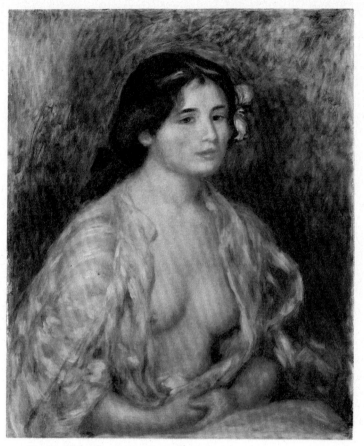

185 Renoir *Gabrielle with an Open Blouse* 1907

refusal to exhibit with the Impressionists in 1884:

> To exhibit with P.G. [Gauguin] and Guillaumin would be as if I were exhibiting with some group or other. Without much further encouragement Pissarro would invite the Russian Lagrof [an Anarchist] and other revolutionaries. The public does not like things which smell of politics, and at my age I do not want to be a revolutionary. To remain along with the Israelite Pissarro is revolution.

The letter which was actually sent, though milder in tone than the draft, gives a sad glimpse of the once insouciant and adventurous Renoir, and of the general limitations of the impersonal aesthetic of Impressionism. Renoir was only in his early forties, and had very recently been struggling against official conservatism in art. But even if by now he had been largely tamed by his fashionable clientele, and was preoccupied both by the need to exhibit his pictures at all costs and by his growing dissatisfaction with his style, his old instinct and intuition had not deserted him. He recognized that a revolution in art (and, indeed, in culture generally) was taking place and that it was concerned with social and political conditions. He saw, too, that it was based on the survival and resurgence of attitudes, both Romantic and classical (for example, in Seurat), which had prevailed before the advent of Impressionism.

Renoir, however, was as much an emotional conservative as Degas. In his attitude towards colour he was less of a naturalist than the other Impressionists; if he chose unnatural violets and blues it was because he liked their decorative effect. His later subjects, such as the *Judgment of Paris* or *River Nymphs*, were often drawn from ancient mythology. One can well understand his popularity in the classical 1920s, and also his continuing friendship with Cézanne, whose outlook was similarly classical and Mediterranean. When he felt himself emerging from the frustrations of the early 1880s he wrote: 'I would, I think, have reached the grandeur and simplicity of the ancient painters.' This grandeur and simplicity are particularly apparent in the splendid late nudes (*Ill. 184*), treated without any Impressionist neglect of contour lines. It is evident too in the many pictures which show the Arcadian family life of the Renoirs: his children and their toys or their beautiful nurse Gabrielle (*Ills. 185, 186*), chosen, like all the painter's servants, because her skin 'took the light'.

Gradually Renoir, like Pissarro, abandoned his experiments of the 1880s and returned to those methods which seemed more in harmony with his nature and instincts. The hard outlines melted and the figures seemed to become at one with their surroundings. His last period, from about 1895, is sometimes called 'red', because of

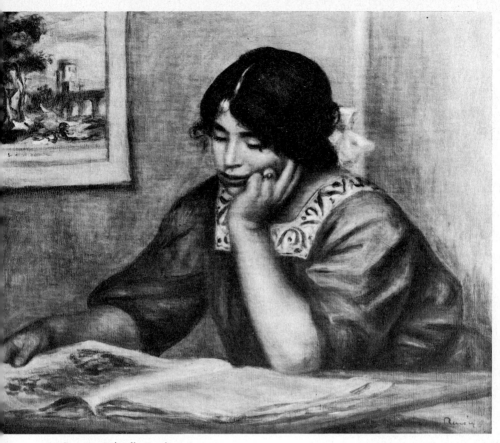

186 Renoir *Gabrielle Reading* 1890

the hotter colours he now used. He often harked back to those transparent, watercolour-like effects he had loved as a porcelain painter, and from which he had been diverted by his admiration for Courbet, Manet and Monet.

Renoir was in many ways the ideal complement to Monet, the man best suited to play Braque to Monet's Picasso in the development of Impressionism. He had charm and serenity to balance Monet's force and self-criticism; he could apply Impressionist techniques to figure paintings, as Monet rarely did after the 1860s. His son's memoirs make one realize that he was certainly the most

241

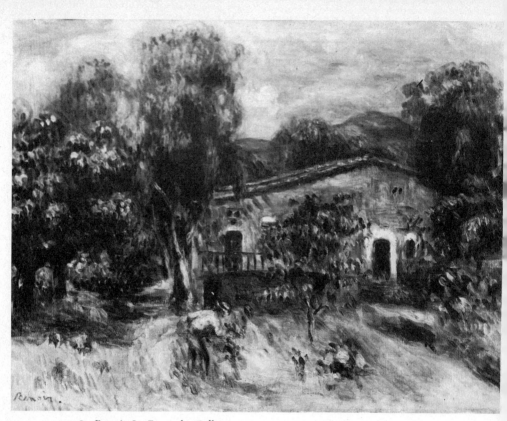

187 Renoir *La Ferme des Collettes* 1910

personally likable and socially adaptable of all the Impressionists. By this ease of manner in company, notably absent from Monet, he probably helped to achieve the recognition of Impressionism by the *bourgeoisie* and the upper classes. After one had joked with this genial painter in the Charpentier or Bérard salons, it must have been increasingly difficult to envisage the Impressionists as dangerous revolutionaries intent on the destruction of society. A banker's wife or publisher's daughter sitting next to Renoir at dinner might have inferred (wrongly) that perhaps even the formidable Monet or the macabre young Cézanne might prove to be convivial and unalarming. In short, by his personality alone, Renoir helped to destroy prejudice against the Impressionists and to sell their pictures.

242

Pissarro was so generous and steadfast as a man, and his influence on Cézanne, Gauguin and Van Gogh was of such vital importance to the future of painting, that there is a danger of underrating the value of his own art. It is true that when some of Pissarro's paintings are compared with Cézanne's renderings of similar themes they appear rambling and lacking in concentration, but how many artists could sustain comparison with the greatest of the moderns? (Pissarro, incidentally, gave this title not to Cézanne but to Degas.)

From the letters he wrote to his son Lucien from 1883 onwards, we learn that Pissarro had as many doubts about his work as Monet and Renoir had about their own. 'I am much disturbed', he wrote, 'by my unpolished and rough execution; I should like to develop a smoother technique which, while retaining the old fierceness, would be rid of those jarring notes which make it difficult to see my canvases clearly except when the light falls from the front.' For a while he found an escape from these difficulties by adopting the new *pointilliste* technique of his son's friends. Seurat, the apostle of a new static and monumental art, was trying to reduce the haphazard empiricism of the Impressionists to a more orderly, less subjective method by invoking the scientific discoveries of Chevreul, Rood and Charles Henry, who had studied the expressive qualities inherent in different types of lines. Unlike most of his friends, Pissarro was fully capable of understanding these treatises, as one can see from the wide-ranging and intelligent comments in his letters. He wrote, for example:

> Surely it is clear that we could not pursue our studies of light with much assurance if we did not have as a guide the discoveries of Chevreul and other scientists. I would not have distinguished between local colour and light if science had not given us the hint; the same holds true for complementary colours, contrasting colours, etc.

In a letter to Durand-Ruel, Pissarro gave the following definition of the aim of the neo-Impressionists:

> To seek a modern synthesis of methods based on science, that is, based on M. Chevreul's theory of colour and on the

243

experiments of Maxwell and the measurements of N.O.Rood. To substitute optical mixture for mixture of pigments. In other words, the breaking-up of tones into their constituents. For optical mixture stirs up more intense luminosities than mixture of pigments does. As far as execution is concerned we regard it as of little importance . . . originality depends only on the character of the drawing and the vision peculiar to each master.

Once Pissarro had begun to adopt the divisionist technique, the split deepened between him and the other Impressionists. They accused him of employing 'chemical' techniques, and he called them 'romantic Impressionists' (to distinguish them from 'scientific Impressionists', the group of Seurat and Signac to which he now adhered). In the end Pissarro came to realize that the replacement of the Impressionist method of intuitive perception by techniques based on scientific and optical laws did not suit his talents. One cannot imagine him painting for long in the even studio light, as Seurat did, instead of in the fluctuating open-air conditions he had always loved. During his *pointilliste* phase he was subjected to widespread vituperation. Even Gauguin turned against his former master and friend, criticizing him for a weak desire to be modern and fashionable. Gauguin did not understand that for Pissarro progress and advance in conformity with science and realism were as much a religion, as much a part of the struggle for the liberation of man, as Gauguin's own fight against narrow bourgeois values and his search for Utopia. The older man's aims were still those of a realist; he considered that Gauguin's eclecticism (for example, the use of elements from Japanese and Byzantine art) was an unfortunate and retrograde tendency.

At the last Impressionist exhibition in 1886 (which included works by Seurat and Signac, admitted through Pissarro's advocacy), the public and critics were unable to distinguish between the works of Seurat, Signac and the two Pissarros. This must have been gratifying to Seurat, who desired a completely impersonal, almost collective art, but it did not lead to favourable reviews.

Pissarro worked according to divisionist methods for about four years, producing such paintings as L'Île Lacroix, Rouen (1888, *Ill. 188*).

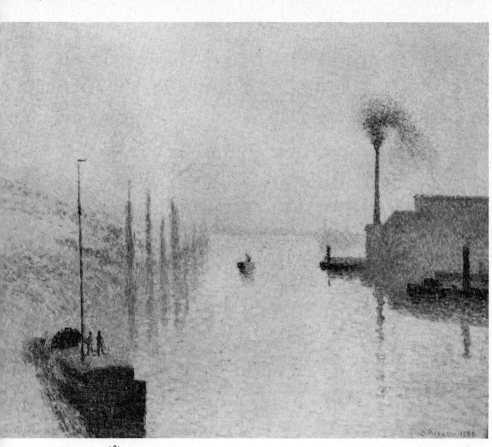

188 Pissarro *L'Île Lacroix, Rouen* 1888

It is significant that he did not go to Rouen that year, so the effect of fog in the picture must have been created in the studio from a sketch or study. But as soon as Pissarro began to find that this technique was hampering his spontaneity, he abandoned it with an empiricism typical of the Impressionists. He told one of Seurat's disciples: 'Having found after many attempts that it was impossible to be true to my sensations and consequently to render life and movement, impossible to be faithful to the effects, so random and so admirable, of nature, impossible to give an individual character to my drawing, I had to give it up.' That was in 1890. During his

245

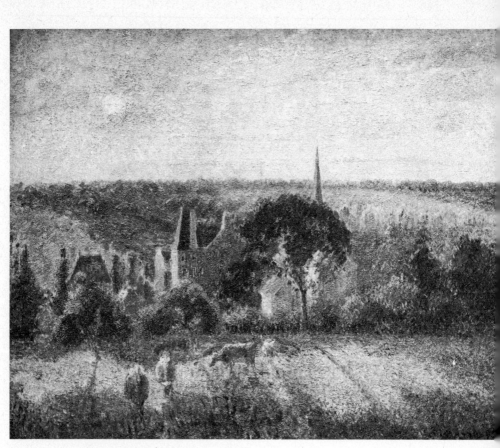

189 Pissarro *Landscape, Eragny* 1895

divisionist period Pissarro's pictures became more unpopular than ever, and his wife grew so desperate about their debts that she nearly drowned herself.

In 1889 Pissarro had begun to suffer from a chronic eye ailment which often prevented him from working out of doors. The year 1892 was more fortunate: Durand-Ruel organized a large and successful exhibition of his works, and the increasing activities of Anarchist movements in Paris also encouraged him. His execution was becoming more subtle and, to judge from the results, the

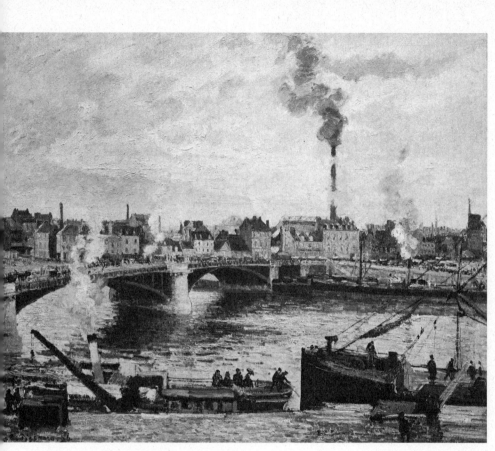

190 Pissarro *The Great Bridge at Rouen* 1896

enforced habit of working behind closed windows was by no means disadvantageous. Durand-Ruel's success in the United States (he opened a branch in New York in 1888) enabled him to support the Impressionists more steadily. Pissarro and his family were able to settle in a large house at Eragny near Gisors. Theo suggested that Van Gogh should come and live with them in 1890, but Pissarro's wife was understandably unwilling, after hearing the story of the cut ear, to have so wild a man at close quarters with her children. Van Gogh went instead to stay with Dr Gachet at Auvers.

247

Pissarro had always been an uneven artist. The last decade of his life (he died in 1903) was perhaps his greatest. His essential feeling for humanity appears in the wonderful populated views of Rouen (1896–8, *Ill. 190*) and Paris (*Ill. 191*). Pictures like the *Place du Théâtre Français* (*Ill. 192*) and the *Place du Vert Galant, Sunny Morning* have no equals among the pictures of his earlier years, though some of the pre-Impressionists and early Impressionist works of the 1860s are magnificent, with their sombre, almost gloomy tonalities.

191 Pissarro *Le Pont des Arts and the Louvre* 1902

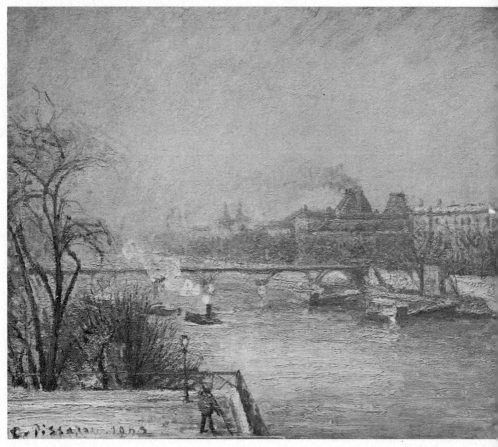

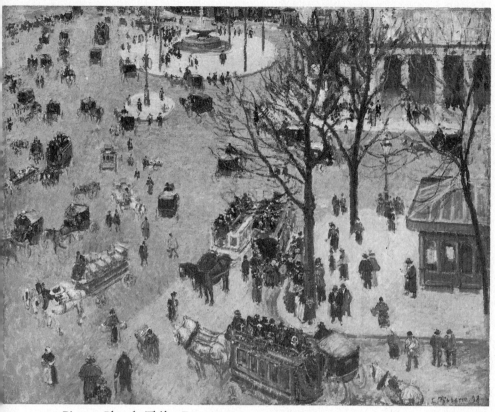

192 Pissarro *Place du Théâtre Français* 1898

It is regrettable that Pissarro never heard two of the greatest tributes ever paid to him. In 1902 Gauguin wrote: 'If we observe the whole of Pissarro's work we find there, despite fluctuations, not only an extreme artistic will, never belied, but also an essentially intuitive, pure-bred air. . . . He looked at everybody, you say! Why not? Everybody looked at him too but denied him. He was one of my masters and I do not deny him.' Even more touching, when Cézanne was invited to exhibit in Aix in 1906, the now much venerated master had himself entered in the catalogue as 'Paul Cézanne, pupil of Pissarro'.

Although it is difficult not to consider Monet's prior right to be called the torch-bearer of Impressionism, one cannot altogether discount Cézanne's testimony: 'Perhaps we all come from Pissarro. As early as 1865 he eliminated black, dark browns and ochres, this is a fact. Paint only with the three primary colours and their immediate derivatives, he told me.' If Cézanne's memory is reliable, Pissarro must be saluted as not only the most generous and steadfast of the Impressionists, but also as their leader.

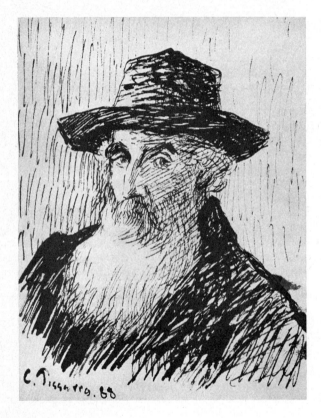

193 Pissarro *Self-portrait* 1888 (Courtesy of the S. P. Avery Collection. The New York Public Library; Astor, Lenox and Tilden Foundations)

CHAPTER NINE

Impressionism outside France. Conclusions

In their hopes for appreciation outside France, the Impressionists placed special faith in England, and it was in that country that they suffered their greatest disappointment. During the early part of the century Géricault, Delacroix, Corot, Daubigny and Fantin-Latour had all been warmly received there. In 1868 Manet returned to Paris from a visit to London excited by the prospect of holding a one-man exhibition there, and even suggested to Degas that he should try to do the same. (In fact, no painting by Manet was acquired by a British collector until 1890, when his art had become a perfectly safe, even banal, choice.) Durand-Ruel first gave the English a chance to see the new development in painting when he opened a gallery at 168 New Bond Street in September 1870. During the next few years he held ten exhibitions there. Although the bulk of his pictures were by such recognized masters as David, Ingres, Delacroix and Corot, he also included Monet's *Trouville*, Pissarro's *Upper Norwood* and Manet's *Fife Major* and *Moonlight, Boulogne-sur-mer*. When Durand-Ruel fell on lean days in Paris in the early 1880s he began to exhibit again in London, where the Impressionists' pictures were soon filling their old role as comic relief and *succès de scandale*. A contributor to *Punch* wrote that he had been urged by a friend to look in because it was so 'horrid funny'. The pictures were sometimes given slightly more serious consideration, but in general the old charge was brought against them that had been levelled against the Barbizons: that too much attention was paid to landscape, and too little to that higher and more worthy subject, the human figure.

Before closing down his first gallery in 1875, Durand-Ruel appears to have sold about seven paintings by Degas to a man who used to be referred to as 'the tailor of Brighton'. He has now been plausibly identified as a Mr Henry Hill, of Marine Parade, Brighton. Another of the first English collectors of Impressionist paintings was Samuel

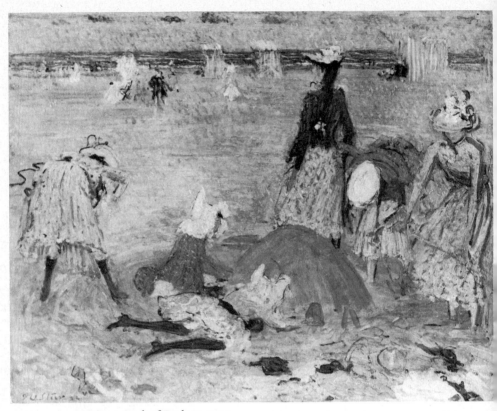

194 Steer *Sands of Boulogne* 1892

Barlow, a botanist and owner of a bleach factory in Lancaster, as well as an art collector. At an early date he acquired four pictures by Pissarro, including the *Village Street* (1871), which was still in his family in the 1960s. The Impressionists had hoped that Whistler might create an atmosphere favourable to their work, but he was far too much of an egoist to see beyond the confines of his own art, which was not realistic so much as suggestive and akin to music. He had a certain regard for Degas' talent, but, apart from that, he did not help the Impressionists until they were less in need of his assistance. From 1898 he encouraged their active participation in the

252

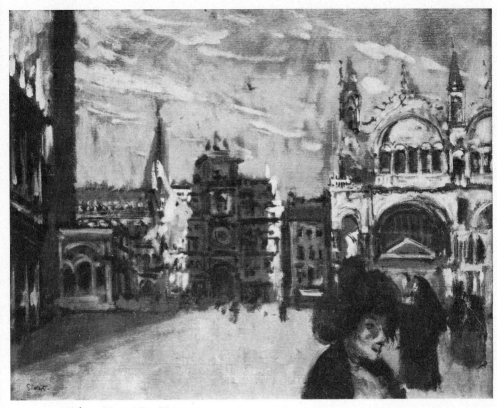

195 Sickert *Piazza San Marco* 1902–3

annual exhibitions of the International Society of Sculptors, Painters and Engravers, of which he was the originator and first president. George Moore, who spent so much time in Paris and was in the artistic swim, did not buy any Impressionist pictures until as late as 1896. Steer (*Ill. 194*) went to the retrospective exhibition of Manet's work held in 1884, but confessed that he had never heard of this artist before. Considering the furore created by Manet in France in the 1860s, this is a striking illustration of British provincialism.

In 1883 Sickert (*Ill. 195*) went to Paris and was introduced to Degas. He was to become one of Degas' great champions. But the

253

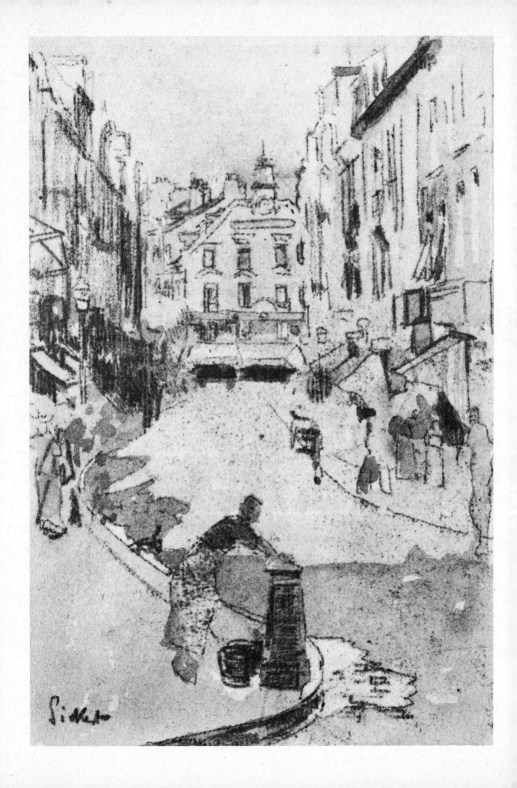

New English Art Club was extraordinarily hidebound in its attitude towards the Impressionists. The taste of the Club could not assimilate any painting more advanced than that of the Barbizon masters. Sir George Clausen, one of its members, wrote: 'One cannot help feeling that some Impressionist work is in spite of its beauty disgusting and violent and that it is questionable if, after all, this method is as true to nature as the older conventions of painting, where the effect is more restful if less brilliant.' Roger Fry, Henry Tonks and their friends had many discussions on 'The old masters and the failure of the Impressionists to absorb their meaning'; Fry soon showed very clearly his preference for the Post-Impressionists. In general, the British greatly preferred Degas and Manet to the landscape artists. They confused the delicacy of the Impressionists with slightness,

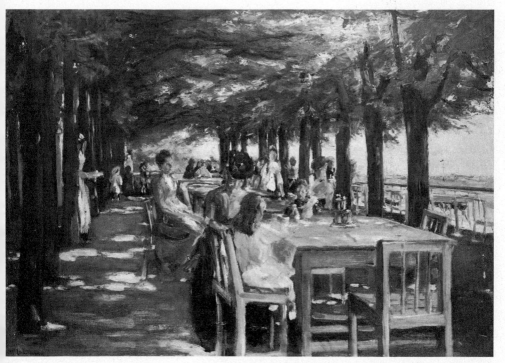

197 Liebermann *Terrace of Restaurant Jacob* 1902

◀ 196 Sickert *Le Puits Salé c.* 1890

and felt that they lacked the higher spiritual values. The old notion that human figures must appear in the highest types of art was hard to eradicate.

Impressionism came late to Germany. It was only after his move to Berlin in 1900 that Lovis Corinth, together with Max Liebermann (*Ill. 197*) and Max Slevogt (*Ill. 199*), became a leader of German Impressionism. Corinth could not have created such works as *Under the Chandelier* (1900) or *Emperors Day in Hamburg* (1911, *Ill. 198*) without the appreciation of light which he learned from the Impressionists. Liebermann had been to Barbizon and painted somewhat

198 Corinth *Emperors Day in Hamburg* 1911

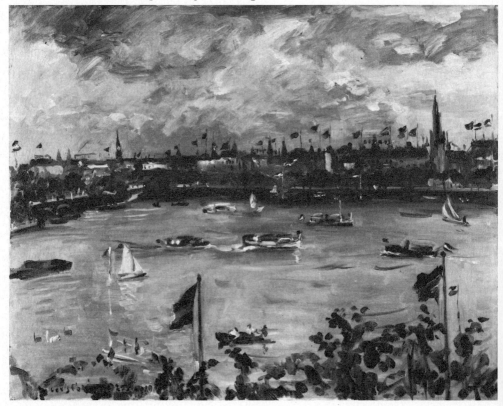

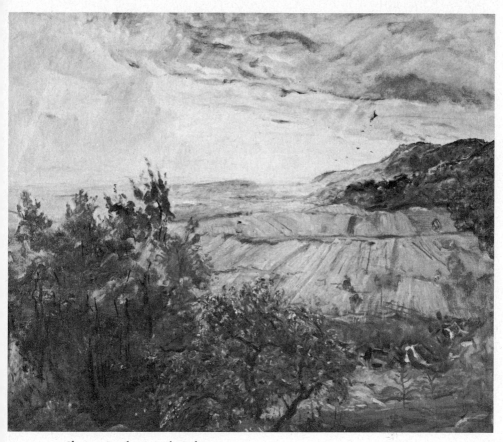

199 Slevogt *Landscape in the Palatinate* 1927

sentimental genre scenes until the 1890s, when he began to adopt the Impressionist manner.

In Spain, particularly in Barcelona, the adoption of Impressionism was the outcome of visits to Paris by such artists as Ramon Casas (*Ill. 201*) and Isidro Nonell (*Ill. 200*). They were later to develop very different idioms of their own, that of Nonell anticipating the hunched figures of Picasso's 'blue period'.

It may seem strange that the Italians, so visually alert and often artistically in advance of other countries, did not adopt Impressionism in any true sense of the word. The Macchiaioli group, so called

257

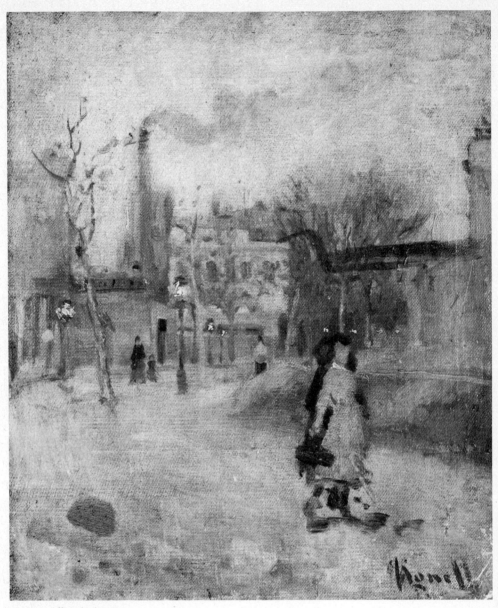

200 Nonell *Suburbio* 1894

258

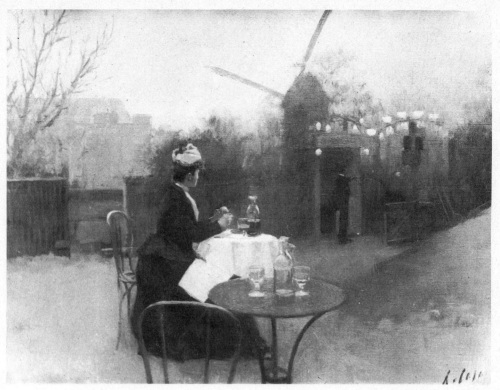

201 Casas *Plein Air*

because they painted in patches and dabs, were friends of Degas. But though they painted in the open air and chose informal subjects, they were working too early to know Impressionist painting and their art is more like that of the Barbizon painters. The lessons of Impressionism, however, were picked up by such painters as Giacomo Balla, Umberto Boccioni and Giovanni Severini at the beginning of the century, and these men, together with the somewhat more naturalistic and literary artists Giovanni Segantini and Angelo Morbelli, all used the technique of divisionism, which would never have existed but for the earlier discoveries of the Impressionists.

In 1885, when he was suffering from financial difficulties in Paris, Durand-Ruel was invited by the American Art Association to organize a large exhibition in New York. He arranged to show

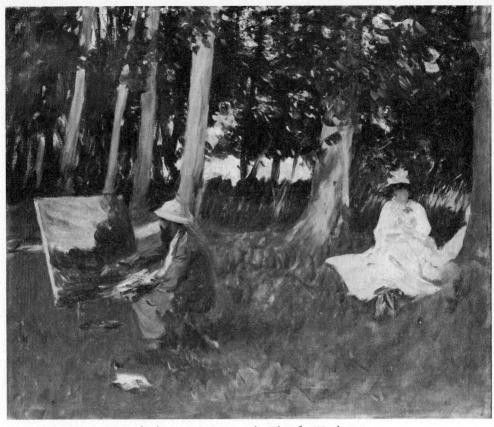

202 Sargent *Claude Monet Painting at the Edge of a Wood* 1888

three hundred of the Impressionists' best canvases as well as Seurat's
Une Baignade. Fortunately the ground had been prepared by Mary
Cassatt, who was rich and socially influential, and by John Singer
Sargent (*Ill. 202*). Durand-Ruel was already known in the United
States as the champion of the now respectable Barbizon school, and
it was rightly assumed that his new protégés might turn out to be
equally important.

Some of the comments on the exhibition showed the familiar
ineptitude: Renoir was the 'degenerated and debased pupil of so
wholesome, honest and well-inspired a man as Gleyre', Degas could
not draw, Seurat was 'seeking distinction by the vulgar expedient of

size'. But seven or eight pictures were soon sold, and the exhibition was extended for another month. The jealousy of other New York dealers, however, was aroused and prohibitive taxation eventually made it necessary for Durand-Ruel to open a permanent branch in the United States.

American artists soon began to experiment with this kind of painting, particularly the careful study of light effects. In 1898 a group called 'Ten American Painters', led by J. H. Twachtman and J. A. Weir, systematically introduced the principles of French Impressionism. Opinion in the United States turned out to be far less obdurate and conservative than had been anticipated; indeed that country was to prove a more favourable *milieu* than England.

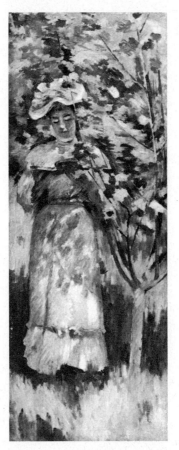

203 Robinson
  Sunlight and Shadows 1896

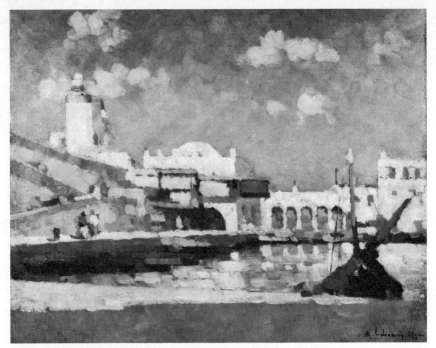

204 Lebourg *Port d'Alger* 1876

205 Loiseau *St Mammes Moret-sur-Loing* c. 1899

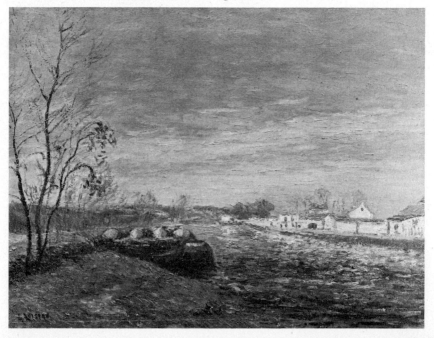

Attempts to sum up the achievements and legacy of Impressionism are doomed to failure. It is even questionable whether its full consequences have yet been worked out. It was said of Gauguin that he had given men a new heaven and a new earth, but this was much more true of the Impressionists, who had made Gauguin's discoveries possible. From one point of view the movement can be seen as an expression of that highly characteristic nineteenth-century feeling for the precise delineation and hoarding of the actual which one finds in different forms in Constable, Tolstoy, Balzac, Zola, the notebooks of Gerard Manley Hopkins and, indeed, in the over-literal, sentimental nightmares produced by the Pre-Raphaelites. The philosophical climate, realistic and pragmatic, was encouraging to this kind of art, just as later the German idealist philosophies created a climate favourable to the more conceptual or introspective attitude of Gauguin and his contemporaries.

The greatest innovation of the Impressionists, and their greatest gift to posterity, lay in the achievement most apparent to their contemporaries: their liberation of pure, bright colours. It was this which enabled their successors, such as Van Gogh or Matisse, to paint with hitherto undreamt-of immediacy and vividness.

Another great quality of the Impressionists was the concision and unity that they achieved in their compositions. Passing from a roomful of Impressionist pictures to a group of earlier French masters of the nineteenth century (even Delacroix and Courbet), one is struck by the comparative fussiness of the older work; too much seems to be going on in one picture. One might praise the Impressionists by transposing the words used of Stendhal: 'How little they labour the point!'

The Impressionists' attitude to their subject-matter was also new. By comparison they were indifferent to it, and held that too great a concern with a theme distracted the artist from the purpose of the painting itself. In any case they were reacting against the portentous classical themes favoured by the academics on the one hand, and the sprawling dramas depicted by the Romantics on the other. The Impressionists and those painters within their orbit were interested in movement rather than in drama or action. When Bazille wrote

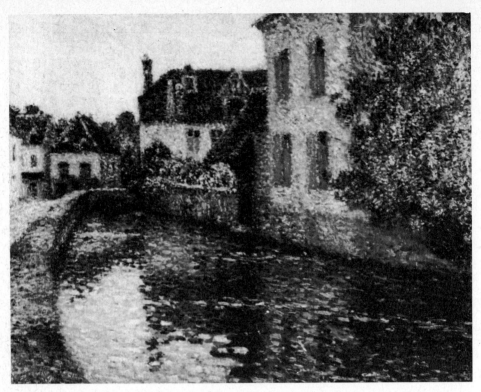

206 Sidaner *Canal at Bruges* (*Gisors Gris, Pignon Gris*) 1914

that the choice of subject-matter was unimportant, he added that he generally chose (though without any dogmatic compulsion) to depict the life of his time. This attitude was a cause of bewilderment to those writers who believed that the Impressionists were trying (rather unsuccessfully, it was thought) to fulfil their own programme of painting contemporary life in an almost documentary way. But none of them was in fact trying to do this, unless one excepts Manet – not a true Impressionist – at the time when he was seeing a great deal of Baudelaire. Whether they painted the contemporary scene or not was a matter of no great importance to the Impressionists; in any case, their concentration on landscape gave their painting a comparatively timeless air. There is a kind of subtle *naïveté* about most Impressionist painting, an accomplished simplicity which

264

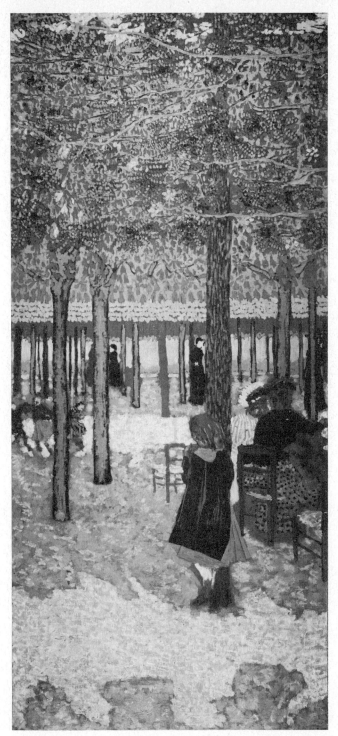

207 Vuillard
Under the Trees
1894

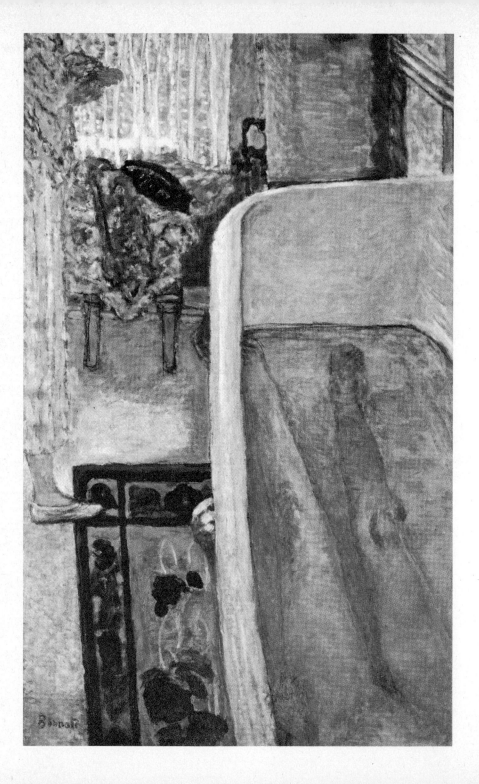

relates it to the writings of Gautier, Flaubert or the Goncourts, and which is very different from the feverish and esoteric literary productions of both the Romantic and Symbolist periods.

It is scarcely surprising that there should be analogies between the literature and the art of this period, since both painters and writers were subject to many of the same pressures – social, economic and philosophical. In the mid-nineteenth century there were often complaints that writers and artists had become too close, and critics professed to find a disease called 'la peinturité' in the painterly language and similes of such books as *Manette Salomon* by the Goncourts. Both painters and writers had the same journey to make away from Romantic subjectivity to the cooler description or reportage which they were to make so peculiarly their own. It is interesting, but not unexpected, to find Cézanne praising precisely those qualities in Zola's work ('the power and unity of characterization, the rhythm of the action') which we find in his own paintings of the late 1870s. Zola's *Un Page d'Amour* is almost as precise a literary equivalent as one could hope to find to the lyricism of a picture by Renoir (and we know, in fact, that Renoir delighted in this novel). Apart from such resemblances, it is worth noting those writers who made it their business to interpret the painting of their day: Baudelaire, Duranty, Duret and Fénéon, among others. Their interpretations, by reacting on the painters themselves, often became positive contributions to new ways of seeing.

Music generally obeys an internal temporal rhythm, far more sealed off from either literature or painting than those arts are from each other. One might consider some of Debussy's early works, such as *La Cathédrale Engloutie*, to be Impressionist were he not so obviously allied to the later Symbolist and Post-Impressionist movements. Edward Lockspeiser has declared that the composer Chabrier, a friend of Manet, was the musician closest in his aims to the Impressionists.

The art of the twentieth century, or for that matter the paintings of Van Gogh and Gauguin, could not have been created, or even envisaged, without the prior discoveries of Impressionism. The fact that by 1900 this idiom no longer seemed to offer a solution for

267

rebellious and aspiring young artists is irrelevant. The continuing influence of Impressionism can be seen in the cases of Bonnard and Vuillard.

Pierre Bonnard (1867–1947) did not begin his career as an Impressionist. In the 1890s, influenced by Gauguin and Japanese prints, his aim was mere decoration. But around 1900 he was groping towards a kind of Impressionism: he paid more attention to nature, to colour and light, and assimilated into his own style some of the technical methods of the Impressionists – the short brush-strokes, lighter tone value and more subtle colour relationships. Like many other great

209 Matisse *The Dinner Table* 1897

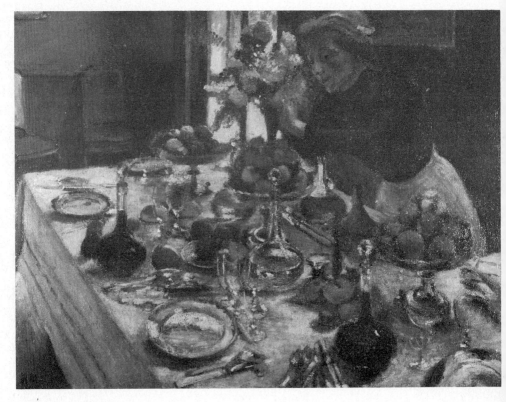

practitioners in the Impressionist idiom, he began to feel that he was sacrificing form and draughtsmanship to light and colour, and after 1914 returned to some extent to his earlier, less naturalistic and more decorative style.

Édouard Vuillard (1868–1940) was influenced more by Degas, Redon and Gauguin than by the Impressionists, but there are indications throughout his life that he had studied the Impressionists and his subject-matter is closely related to theirs. His garden scenes owe much to the early paintings of Monet; *Under the Trees* of 1894 (*Ill. 207*) derives from Monet's *Women in the Garden* of 1867. Vuillard seems to have relished the striped and spotted dresses in Monet's painting, and the use of dappled sunlight as a decorative device. But in general Vuillard's sober and detached art is one of suggestion rather than description and is nearer to the poetry of Mallarmé than the painting of Monet.

The influence extends even to Matisse, whose *The Dinner Table* (*Ill. 209*) shows that an apprenticeship to this school of light could still be advantageous in 1900.

The existence of so many lively and skilful young painters in the Parisian ateliers of the 1860s was a singularly happy accident. Their gifts were diverse; perhaps it is correct to say that there was no such thing as Impressionism, only Impressionists. All these young men had a uniquely direct, delicate yet unsentimental approach to nature. It is significant that the generations before and after their own were far more connected with the stage than the Impressionists were, and far more histrionic in private life. The Impressionists are often spoken of as heirs to Courbet and his realist friends at the Brasserie des Martyrs, but their cult of the natural, the countryside, the immediate and spontaneous may more truly be regarded as a late, but by no means a minor, contribution of Romanticism to subsequent European culture.

Selected Bibliography

ALLEY, Ronald, *Gauguin* (London, 1962)

BAUDELAIRE, Charles, *Salon de 1859 – Art in Paris 1845–1862*, edited by Jonathan Mayne (London, 1965)

BAZIN, Germain, *Corot* (Paris, 1942)

BECKETT, R. B., 'Constable and France' *The Connoisseur* (London, May 1956), pp. 249–55

BOGGS, Jean Sutherland, *Portraits by Degas* (Berkeley and Los Angeles, 1962)

BOWNESS, Alan, 'A Note on "Manet's compositional difficulties"' *Burlington Magazine* (London, May–June 1961), pp. 276–7

CÉZANNE, Paul, *Letters*, edited by John Rewald and translated by Marguerite Kay (London, 1941)

CLARK, Kenneth, *Landscape into Art* (London, 1949)

COCTEAU, Jean, *Le Rappel à l'ordre* (Paris, 1926)

COOPER, Douglas, Introduction to Catalogue of Arts Council Exhibition, 'Monet' (London, 1957)

– *The Courtauld Collection* (London, 1954)

COROT, Camille, *Corot raconté par lui-même et par ses amis* (Geneva, 1946)

DAULTE, François, *Alfred Sisley. Catalogue raisonné de l'œuvre peint* (Lausanne, 1959)

– *Frédéric Bazille et son temps* (Geneva, 1952)

DEGAS, Edgar, *Letters*, edited by Marcel Guérin and translated by Marguerite Kay (Oxford, 1947)

DELACROIX, Eugène, *Journal de Eugène Delacroix*, 3 vols (Paris, 1893–5)

DÉLÉCLUZE, M. E. J., in *Journal des debats* (Paris, 4 April 1828)

DEWHURST, Wynford, *Impressionist Painting. Its Genesis and Development* (London, 1904)

DURANTY, Edmond, *La Nouvelle Peinture. A propos du groupe d'artistes qui expose dans les Galeries Durand-Ruel* (Paris, 1876, 1946)

– *Le Réalisme* (Paris, 1856)

DURET, Théodore, *Histoire des peintres impressionnistes* (Paris, 1922)

EASTON, Malcolm, *Artists and Writers in Paris. The Bohemian Idea 1803–1867* (London, 1964)

FAISON, Samuel Lane, *Edouard Manet, 1832–1883* (New York, 1953)

DE FELS, Marthe, *La Vie de Claude Monet* (Paris, 1929)

FÉNÉON, Félix, 'L'Impressionnisme aux Tuileries' *L'Art moderne* (Bruxelles, 19 September 1886), pp. 300–2

FLAUBERT, Gustave, *Correspondance*, 9 vols (Paris, 1926–33)

FLORISOONE, Michel, 'Renoir et la famille Charpentier' *L'Amour de l'Art* (Paris, February 1938)

FUSELI, Henry, Lecture IV *Lectures on Painting, delivered at the Royal Academy, March 1801* (London, 1801–20)

GAUGUIN, Paul, *The Intimate Journals of Paul Gauguin* translated by Van Wyck Brooks (London, 1930)

GAUTIER, Théophile, in *Moniteur Universel* (Paris, 13 July 1868)

GEFFROY, Gustave, *Claude Monet, sa vie, son temps, son œuvre* (Paris, 1922)

GOLDWATER, Robert, 'Puvis de Chavannes: Some Reasons for a Reputation' *Art Bulletin* (Providence, R.I., March 1946), pp. 33–43

GOLDWATER, Robert, and TREVES, Marco, *Artists on Art. From the XIV to the XX century* (London, 1947)

GOMBRICH, E. H., *Art and Illusion* (London, 1960)

DE GONCOURT, Edmond, *The Goncourt Journals, 1851–1870*, edited and translated by Lewis Galantière (London, 1937)

GOWING, Lawrence, *Renoir* (Paris, 1947)

GREENBERG, Clement, 'Avant-garde Art' *Arts and Letters* No. 4 (Spring, 1965)

GRIFFITHS, Richard, *The Reactionary Revolution* (London, 1966)

HAZLITT, William, *The Complete Works of William Hazlitt*, edited by P. P. Howe, 21 vols (London and Toronto, 1930–4)

HEMMINGS, Frederick William, *Emile Zola* (Oxford, 1953)

HERBERT, Robert Louis, *Barbizon Revisited* (Boston, 1963)

– *Seurat's Drawings* (London, 1965)

HUYSMANS, Joris Karl, *L'Art moderne* (Paris, 1883)

HOMER, W. I., *Seurat and the Science of Painting* (Cambridge, Mass., 1964)

JEANNIOT, Georges, 'Souvenirs sur Degas' *La Revue Universelle* (Paris, 15 October 1933), pp. 280–304

JOHNSON, Lee, *Delacroix* (London, 1963)

KANDINSKY, Wassily, 'Rückblick 1901–1913' *Der Sturm* (Berlin, 1913)

LAFORGUE, Jules, *Oeuvres complètes*, 3 vols (Paris, 1903–17)

LANES, Jerrold, 'Current and Forthcoming Exhibitions: New York' (Camille Pissarro) *Burlington Magazine* (London, May 1965), pp. 275–6

LEHMANN, G., *Sainte-Beuve* (London, 1962)

'Leicester Galleries. Memorial Exhibition of the Works of Camille Pissarro' *Burlington Magazine* (London, June 1920), pp. 310, 315

DE LEIRIS, Alain, 'Manet: "Sur la plage de Boulogne"' *Gazette des Beaux-Arts* (Paris, January 1961), pp. 53–62

LEMOISNE, Paul André, *Degas et son œuvre* (Paris, 1954)

LOCKSPEISER, Edward, in *The Listener* (London, 1966)

MANET, Edouard, *Manet raconté par lui-même et par ses amis*, edited by P. Courthion and P. Cailler (Vésenaz-Geneva, 1954)

MOORE, George, *Reminiscences of the Impressionist Painters* (Dublin, 1906)

NICOLSON, Benedict, (Introduction) *Cézanne. Paintings* (London, 1946)

PERRY, Lilla Cabot, 'Reminiscences of Claude Monet from 1889–1909' *The American Magazine of Art*, vol. 18 (New York, March 1927)

PISSARRO, Camille, *Letters to His Son Lucien*, edited with the assistance of Lucien Pissarro by John Reward; translated by Lionel Abel (London, 1944)

PISSARRO, Ludovic, and VENTURI, Lionello, *Camille Pissarro. Son art – son œuvre*, 2 vols (Paris, 1939)

POULAIN, Gaston, *Bazille et ses amis* (Paris, 1932)

RÉGAMY, Raymond, 'La Formation de Claude Monet' *Gazette des Beaux-Arts* (Paris, February 1927), pp. 65–84

RENOIR, Jean, *Renoir, My Father*, translated by Randolphe and Dorothy Weaver (London, 1962)

REWALD, John, *Camille Pissarro* (London, 1963)

– *Paul Cézanne* (New York, 1948)

– *The History of Impressionism* (New York, 1962)

RICHARDSON, John, (Introduction) *Edouard Manet. Paintings and drawings* (London, 1958)

RIVIÈRE, Georges, 'Les intransigeants de la peinture' *L'Esprit Moderne* (Paris, 13 April 1876)

ROSENTHAL, Léon, *Manet aquafortiste et lithographe* (Paris, 1925)

RUSKIN, John, *Modern Painters*, 5 vols (London, 1920)

SANDBLAD, Nils, *Manet. Three studies in artistic conception*, translated by Walter Nash (Lund, 1954)

SCHAPIRO, Meyer, 'Joseph C. Sloane, French Painting between the Past and the Present' (Book review) *The Art Bulletin* (Providence, R.I., June 1954), pp. 163–4

– *Paul Cézanne* (London, New York, 1952)

– *Vincent Van Gogh 1853–1890* (London, 1951)

SCHARF, Aaron, *Photography and Painting in the Nineteenth Century* (University of London Thesis, 1963)

SEITZ, William Chapin, *Claude Monet* (London, 1960)

– *Claude Monet. Seasons and Moments*, Exhibition Catalogue, Museum of Modern Art (New York and Los Angeles County Museum, 1960)

SLOANE, Joseph Curtis, *French Painting between the Past and Present* (Princeton, 1951)

STOKES, Adrian, *Monet, 1840–1926* (London, 1958)

TABARANT, Adolphe, *Pissarro*, translated by J. Lewis May (London, 1925)

TABOUREUX, E., 'Claude Monet' *La Vie Moderne* (Paris, 12 June 1880)

TAYLOR, Basil, *The Impressionists and their World* (London, 1953)

THIÉBAULT-SISSON, F., 'Claude Monet: An Interview' *Le Temps* (Paris, 27 November 1900)

VAN GOGH, Vincent, *The Complete Letters of Vincent Van Gogh*, translated by J. van Goch-Bonger and C. de Dood, 3 vols (London, 1958)

VENTURI, Lionello, *Archives de L'Impressionnisme* (Paris and New York, 1939)

– *Cézanne. Son art – son œuvre*, 2 vols (Paris, 1936)

VOLLARD, Ambroise, *En écoutant Cézanne, Degas, Renoir* (Paris, 1938)

– *La vie et l'œuvre de Pierre-Auguste Renoir* (Paris, 1919)

WOLFF, Albert, in *Le Figaro* (Paris, 3 April 1876)

ZOLA, Emile, 'Le Naturalisme au Salon' *Le Voltaire* (Paris, 18–22 June 1886)

– 'Mon Salon' (1866) reprinted in *Mes Haines* (Paris, 1866)

List of Illustrations

1 Pierre Henri de Valenciennes, 1750–1819: *Tivoli* oil on canvas $12\frac{1}{4}'' \times 18''$ (31×46 cm). Courtesy, Museum of Fine Arts, Boston (Abbott Lawrence Fund)

2 Paul Cézanne, 1839–1906: *Apotheosis of Delacroix* c. 1894 oil on canvas $10\frac{5}{8}'' \times 13\frac{3}{4}''$ (27×35 cm). Collection J.-V. Pellerin, Paris

3 Théodore Rousseau, 1812–1867; *Marshy Landscape* 1842 oil on paper laid on canvas $8\frac{3}{4}'' \times 11\frac{1}{2}''$ (22×28 cm). From a private collection

4 John Constable, 1776–1837: *Study of Sky and Trees* 1821 oil on paper $9\frac{3}{4}'' \times 12''$ ($24{\cdot}8 \times 30{\cdot}5$ cm). Victoria and Albert Museum, London (Crown Copyright)

5 Frédéric Bazille, 1841–1870: *Réunion de famille* 1876 oil on canvas $59\frac{7}{8}'' \times 90\frac{1}{2}''$ (152×230 cm). Louvre, Paris

6 Claude Monet, 1840–1926: *Boulevard des Capucines* 1873 oil on canvas $31\frac{1}{2}'' \times 23\frac{5}{8}''$ (79×60 cm). Collection Mrs Marshall Field III, New York

7 Paul Cézanne, 1839–1906: *Self-Portrait* 1858–61 oil on canvas $17\frac{3}{8}'' \times 14\frac{5}{8}''$ (44×37 cm). Private collection

8 Nicolas Poussin, 1594–1665: *The Gathering of the Ashes of Phocion* 1648 oil on canvas $45\frac{5}{8}'' \times 69\frac{1}{4}''$ (121×176 cm). Collection The Rt. Hon. The Earl of Derby, M.C., photo National Gallery, London

9 John Constable, 1776–1837: *Study for The Haywain* 1821 oil on canvas $54'' \times 74''$ ($13{\cdot}7 \times 18{\cdot}8$ cm). Victoria and Albert Museum, London (Crown Copyright)

10 Eugène Delacroix, 1798–1863: *Massacre at Chios* 1824 oil on canvas $167\frac{1}{8}'' \times 138\frac{5}{8}''$ (422×352 cm). Louvre, Paris

11 Paul Huet, 1803–1869: *Stormy Sea* 1826 panel $11\frac{3}{8}'' \times 15''$ (29×38 cm). Collection M. and Mme Perret-Carnot, photo Courtauld Institute of Art

12 Camille Corot, 1796–1875: *Fontainebleau, le charretier et les bucherons* c. 1835 oil on canvas $15'' \times 20\frac{3}{4}''$ (38×53 cm). Private collection, London

13 Camille Corot, 1796–1875: *Forest of Fontainebleau* 1846 oil on canvas $35\frac{5}{8}'' \times 50\frac{3}{4}''$ ($90{\cdot}5 \times 129{\cdot}5$ cm). Courtesy, Museum of Fine Arts, Boston (gift of Mrs Samuel Dennis Warren)

14 Eugène Delacroix, 1798–1863: *Study for Femmes d'Alger* 1833–4 pastel $11\frac{3}{8}'' \times 16\frac{1}{2}''$ (29×42 cm). Louvre, Paris

15 Camille Corot, 1796–1875: *Le Pont de Narni* 1826 paper on canvas $13\frac{3}{8}'' \times 18\frac{7}{8}''$ (34×48 cm). Louvre, Paris, photo Bulloz

16 Camille Corot, 1796–1875: *View near Volterra* 1834 oil on canvas $27\frac{5}{8}'' \times 37''$ (70×94 cm). Louvre, Paris

17 Camille Corot, 1796–1875; *L'Hôtel Cabassus à Ville d'Avray* 1834–40 oil on canvas $11'' \times 15\frac{3}{4}''$ (28×40 cm). Louvre, Paris

18 Camille Corot, 1796–1875: *Harbour of La Rochelle* 1852 oil on canvas $19\frac{7}{8}'' \times 28\frac{1}{4}''$ (50×71 cm). Yale University Art Gallery (Bequest of Stephen Carlton Clark, B.A., 1903)

19 Gustave Courbet, 1819–1877: *The Sleeping Spinner* 1853 oil on canvas $37\frac{7}{8}'' \times 45\frac{1}{4}''$ (91×115 cm). Musée Fabre, Montpellier

20 Auguste Renoir, 1841–1919: *At the Inn of Mother Anthony* 1866 oil on canvas $76\frac{3}{4}'' \times 51\frac{1}{4}''$ (195×130 cm). National Museum, Stockholm

21 Eugène Boudin, 1824–1898: *Jetty at Trouville* 1865 panel $13\frac{3}{8}'' \times 22\frac{7}{8}''$ (34×58 cm). Collection of Mr and Mrs Paul Mellon

22 Johann Barthold Jongkind, 1819–1891: *Sortie du Port de Honfleur* 1865 oil on canvas $22'' \times 31''$ (56×79 cm). Private collection, Paris

23 Johann Barthold Jongkind, 1819–1891: *The Beach at Sainte-Adresse* 1863 watercolour $11\frac{3}{4}'' \times 20\frac{7}{8}''$ (30×53 cm). Louvre, Paris, photo Archives Photographiques

24 Camille Pissarro, 1830–1903: *Cocotiers au bord de la Mer, St Thomas* 1856 oil on canvas $10\frac{5}{8}'' \times 13\frac{3}{4}''$ (27×35 cm). Collection of Mr and Mrs Paul Mellon

25 Camille Pissarro, 1830–1903: *Corner of a Village* 1863 oil on panel $15\frac{3}{4}'' \times 20\frac{1}{2}''$ (40×52 cm). Collection: O'Hana Gallery, London

26 Camille Pissarro, 1830–1903: *Banks of the Marne in Winter* 1866 oil on canvas $36'' \times 59''$ (92×150 cm). The Lefèvre Gallery, London

27 Camille Pissarro, 1830–1903: *La Roche Guyon* 1866–7 oil on canvas $19\frac{5}{8}'' \times 24''$ (50×61 cm). Nationalgalerie, Staatliche Museen, Berlin

28 Gustave Courbet, 1819–1877: *Le vieux pont* oil on canvas $22\frac{5}{8}'' \times 28\frac{3}{4}''$ (60×73 cm). Musée des Beaux-Arts, Algiers, photo Giraudon

29 Camille Pissarro, 1830–1903: *View of Pontoise, Quai de Pothuis* 1868 oil on canvas $20\frac{1}{2}'' \times 37\frac{7}{8}''$ (52×81 cm). Kunsthalle, Mannheim

30 Armand Guillaumin, 1841–1927: *The Bridge of Louis Philippe, Paris* 1875 oil on canvas $18'' \times 23\frac{3}{4}''$ (46×60 cm). National Gallery of Art, Washington, D.C. (Chester Dale Collection, Loan)

31 M. C. G. Gleyre, 1808–1874: *La Charmeuse* 1868 oil on canvas $32\frac{1}{2}'' \times 19\frac{7}{8}''$ ($82{\cdot}5 \times 50{\cdot}5$ cm). Öffentliche Kunstsammlung, Basel

32 Auguste Renoir, 1841–1919: *La Baigneuse au Griffon* 1870 oil on canvas $72\frac{1}{2}'' \times 45\frac{1}{2}''$ (184×114 cm). Museu de Arte, São Paulo

33 Auguste Renoir, 1841–1919: *Diane Chasseresse* 1867 oil on canvas $77'' \times 51\frac{1}{4}''$ (196×130 cm). National Gallery of Art, Washington, D.C. (Chester Dale Collection, Loan)

34 Auguste Renoir, 1841–1919: *Alfred Sisley and his Wife* c. 1868 oil on canvas $42\frac{1}{4}'' \times 30''$ (105×75 cm). Wallraf-Richartz Museum, Cologne, photo Rheinisches Bildarchiv

35 Auguste Renoir, 1841–1919: *The Skaters in the Bois de Boulogne* 1868 oil on canvas $28\frac{7}{8}'' \times 36\frac{1}{8}''$ (72×90 cm). Private collection, Switzerland

36 Claude Monet, 1840–1926: *La Grenouillère* 1869 oil on canvas $29\frac{3}{8}'' \times 39\frac{1}{4}''$ (75×99 cm). Metropolitan Museum of Art, New York (Bequest of Mrs H. O. Havemeyer 1929, The H. O. Havemeyer Collection)

37 Auguste Renoir, 1841–1919: *La Grenouillère* 1869 oil on canvas $19\frac{1}{2}'' \times 22\frac{1}{2}''$ (50×57 cm). Private collection, Milwaukee, Wis.

38 Auguste Renoir, 1841–1919: *La Grenouillère* c. 1869 oil on canvas $26'' \times 31\frac{7}{8}''$ (66×81 cm). National Museum, Stockholm

39 Alfred Sisley, 1839–1899: *Vue de Montmartre prise de la Cité des Fleurs* 1869 oil on canvas $27\frac{1}{2}'' \times 46''$ (70×117 cm). Musée de Peinture, Grenoble

40 Alfred Sisley, 1839–1899: *Canal St Martin, Paris* 1870 oil on canvas $19\frac{5}{8}'' \times 25\frac{5}{8}''$ (50×65 cm). Louvre, Paris

41 Alfred Sisley, 1839–1899: *Barges on Canal St Martin, Paris* 1870 oil on canvas $21\frac{5}{8}'' \times 29\frac{1}{8}''$ (55×74 cm). Stiftung Oskar Reinhart, Winterthur

42 Claude Monet, 1840–1926: *Rough Sea, Etretat* 1883 oil on canvas $31\frac{7}{8}'' \times 39\frac{3}{8}''$ (81×100 cm). Musée des Beaux-Arts, Lyons

43 Claude Monet, 1840–1926: *Japanese Footbridge* 1922 oil on canvas $35'' \times 36\frac{3}{4}''$ (91×93 cm). Collection of Mr and Mrs Walter Bareiss

44 Claude Monet, 1840–1926: *Mario Ochard* 1856–8 pencil $12\frac{5}{8}'' \times 9\frac{3}{4}''$ (32×24 cm). Courtesy, The Art Institute of Chicago (Mr and Mrs Carter H. Harrison Collection)

45 Constant Troyon, 1810–1865: *Le Matin* 1855 oil on canvas $10\frac{1}{4}'' \times 15\frac{3}{4}''$ (26×40 cm). Louvre, Paris, photo Giraudon

46 Claude Monet, 1840–1926: *The Breakwater at Honfleur* 1846 oil on canvas $16'' \times 29''$ (41×74 cm). From a private collection

47 Claude Monet, 1840–1926: *The Beach at Sainte-Adresse* 1867 oil on canvas $22\frac{1}{4}'' \times 32\frac{1}{4}''$ (56×82 cm). Art Institute of Chicago (Mr and Mrs L. L. Coburn Collection)

48 Gustave Courbet, 1819–1877: *Bonjour Monsieur Courbet* 1854 oil on canvas $50\frac{3}{4}'' \times 58\frac{5}{8}''$ (129×149 cm). Musée Fabre, Montpellier, photo Giraudon

49 Auguste Renoir, 1841–1919: *Portrait of Bazille* 1867 oil on canvas $41\frac{3}{4}'' \times 29\frac{1}{2}''$ (106×74 cm). Louvre, Paris

50 Frédéric Bazille, 1841–1870: *Portrait of Renoir* 1867 oil on canvas $24\frac{1}{2}'' \times 20''$ (62×51 cm). Musée des Beaux-Arts, Algiers, photo Giraudon

51 Edouard Manet, 1832–1883: *Musique aux Tuileries* 1862 oil on canvas $30'' \times 46\frac{1}{2}''$ (76×118 cm). Trustees of the National Gallery, London

52 Charles-François Daubigny, 1817–1878: *Evening* oil on canvas $23\frac{3}{4}'' \times 35\frac{1}{2}''$ (60×90 cm). Metropolitan Museum of Art N.Y. (Bequest of Robert Graham Dunn, 1911)

53 Claude Monet, 1840–1926: *Farmyard in Normandy c.* 1864 oil on canvas $25\frac{5}{8}'' \times 31\frac{1}{2}''$ (65×80 cm). Louvre, Paris, photo Archives Photographiques

54 Edouard Manet, 1832–1883: *Study for Déjeuner sur l'Herbe* 1865–6 watercolour and pencil $9\frac{1}{2}'' \times 15\frac{3}{4}''$ ($34 \times 40{\cdot}5$ cm). Collection Bruno Cassirer, Oxford

55 Claude Monet, 1840–1926: *Déjeuner sur l'Herbe (sketch)* 1866 oil on canvas $51\frac{1}{4}'' \times 73''$ (130×185 cm). Pushkin Museum, Moscow, photo Durand-Ruel

56 Berthe Morisot, 1841–1895: *La Lecture* 1869–70 oil on canvas $39\frac{5}{8}'' \times 31\frac{7}{8}''$ (100×81 cm). National Gallery of Art, Washington, D.C. (Chester Dale Collection)

57 Berthe Morisot, 1841–1895: *Eugène and Julie Manet* 1886 pastel $18'' \times 23\frac{1}{2}''$ (46×60 cm).

58 Berthe Morisot, 1841–1895: *Harbour of Lorient with the artist's sister Edma* 1869 oil on canvas $17'' \times 28\frac{3}{4}''$ (43×73 cm). Collection of Mrs Mellon Bruce

59 Claude Monet, 1840–1926: *Quai du Louvre, Paris* 1866–7 oil on canvas $25\frac{5}{8}'' \times 36\frac{5}{8}''$ (65×93 cm). Gemeentemuseum, The Hague

60 Auguste Renoir, 1841–1919: *Pont des Arts* 1867 oil on canvas $24\frac{1}{2}'' \times 40\frac{1}{4}''$ (62×102 cm). Private Collection, New York, photo Knoedler

61 Claude Monet, 1840–1926: *The River* 1868 oil on canvas $32'' \times 39\frac{1}{2}''$ (87×100 cm). Courtesy, The Art Institute of Chicago (Potter Palmer Collection)

62 Edouard Manet, 1832–1883: *Café Interior (Café Guerbois?)* 1869 pen and ink $11\frac{5}{8}'' \times 15\frac{1}{2}''$ (29×39 cm). Fogg Art Museum, Harvard University, Cambridge, Massachusetts (Bequest of Meta and Paul J. Sachs)

63 Jean-François Millet, 1814–1875: *L'arrivée au Barbizon* 1847 pencil. Collection Mme Landesque-Millet, from *Millet raconté par lui-même* by Moreau-Nélaton, published by H. Laurens

64 Camille Pissarro, 1830–1903: *Peasant Woman with a Donkey* 1890 oil on canvas $21'' \times 24''$ (51×61 cm). Collection: O'Hana Gallery, London

65 J. L. Gérôme, 1824–1904: *Sword Dance* Present whereabouts unknown

66 Edgar Degas, 1834–1917: *Les malheurs de la Ville d'Orléans* 1865 paper on canvas $33\frac{1}{2}'' \times 57\frac{7}{8}''$ (85×147 cm). Louvre, Paris

67 Théodore Fantin-Latour, 1836–1904: *Homage to Delacroix* 1864 oil on canvas $62\frac{5}{8}'' \times 96\frac{7}{8}''$ (159×251 cm). Louvre, Paris

68 Théodore Fantin-Latour, 1836–1904: *A Studio in the Batignolles Quarter* 1870 oil on canvas 68½″×82″ (204×270 cm). Louvre, Paris

69 Frédéric Bazille, 1841–1870: *The Artist's Studio, Rue de la Condamine* 1870 oil on canvas 38⅞″×47″ (98×128 cm). Louvre, Paris

70 Claude Monet, 1840–1926: *On the Beach, Trouville* 1870 oil on canvas 15″×18¼″ (38×46·5 cm). Trustees of the Tate Gallery, London

71 Claud Monet, 1840–1926: *The Beach at Trouville, Hôtel des Roches-Noires* 1870 35⅜″×27⅝″ (90×70 cm). Collection M. Jacques Laroche. Paris

72 Claude Monet, 1840–1926: *Westminster Bridge* 1871 oil on canvas 18½″×28½″ (47×72·5 cm). Collection Lord Astor of Hever

73 Claude Monet, 1840–1926: *Hyde Park* 1871 oil on canvas 15¾″×28⅞″ (40×73 cm). Museum of Art, Rhode Island School of Design, Providence, R.I.

74 Camille Pissarro, 1830–1903: *Lower Norwood, London* 1870 oil on canvas 13¾″×18¼″ (35×41 cm). Trustees of the National Gallery, London

75 Camille Pissarro, 1830–1903: *Crystal Palace* 1871 oil on canvas 18″×28¼″ (41×71 cm). Estate of Henry J. Fisher

76 Camille Pissarro, 1830–1903: *Upper Norwood, London* 1871 17¾″×21⅝″ (45×55 cm). Neue Pinakothek, Munich

77 Camille Pissarro, 1830–1903: *Dulwich College* 1871 oil on canvas 19½″×24″ (50×61 cm). From the MacAulay Collection, Winnipeg, Canada

78 Camille Pissarro, 1830–1903: *Entrance to the Village of Voisins* 1872 oil on canvas 18¾″×22″ (45×55 cm). Louvre, Paris

79 Claude Monet, 1840–1926: *Unloading Coal, Argenteuil* 1872 oil on canvas 21⅝″×25″ (55×66 cm). Collection Durand-Ruel, Paris

80 Camille Pissarro, 1830–1903: *The Road, Louveciennes* 1870 oil on canvas 23⅝″×28¾″ (60×73 cm). Louvre, Paris

81 Auguste Renoir, 1841–1919: *Pont Neuf* 1872 oil on canvas 29¼″×36½″ (74×93 cm). Collection Benziger, photo Knoedler

82 Frédéric Bazille, 1841–1870: *Walls of Aigues-Mortes* 1867 oil on canvas 18⅛″×21⅝″ (46×55 cm). Musée Fabre, Montpellier

83 Camille Pissarro, 1830–1903: *Diligence at Louveciennes* 1870 oil on canvas 9⅞″×13⅜″ (25×34 cm). Louvre, Paris

84 Camille Pissarro, 1830–1903: *The Haystack, Pontoise* 1873 oil on canvas 18⅛″×21⅝″ (46×55 cm). Collection Durand-Ruel, Paris

85 Claude Monet, 1840–1926: *Impression: Sunrise* 1872 oil on canvas 19½″×24½″ (50×62 cm). Musée Marmottan, Paris

86 Edgar Degas, 1834–1917: *Carriage at the Races* 1870–3 oil on canvas 14⅛″×21⅝″ (36×55 cm). Courtesy, Museum of Fine Arts, Boston (Arthur Gordon Tompkins Residuary Fund)

87 Berthe Morisot, 1841–1895: *Hide and Seek* 1872–3 18″×21½″ (46×55 cm). Collection of Mr and Mrs John Hay Whitney

88 Edgar Degas, 1834–1917: *The Dancing Class* 1874 oil on canvas 33½″×29½″ (85×75 cm). Louvre, Paris

89 Edgar Degas, 1834–1917: *Nursemaid in the Luxembourg Gardens* 1871-2 oil on canvas 12″×16⅛″ (65×92 cm). Musée Fabre, Montpellier

90 Edgar Degas, 1834–1917: *The Pedicure* 1873 paper on canvas 24½″×18½″ (61×46 cm). Louvre, Paris

91 Edgar Degas, 1834–1917: *The Cotton Exchange, New Orleans* 1873 oil on canvas 29⅛″×36⅛″ (71×92 cm). Musée des Beaux-Arts, Pau, photo Giraudon

92 Edouard Manet, 1832–1883: *The Barricade* 1871 lithograph $18\frac{5}{8}'' \times 13\frac{3}{8}''$ (47×34 cm). The New York Public Library, Prints Division, Astor, Lenox and Tilden Foundations (S. P. Avery Collection)

93 Edgar Degas, 1834–1917: *Semiramis Founding a Town* 1861 oil on canvas $59\frac{3}{8}'' \times 102\frac{1}{4}''$ (151×258 cm). Louvre, Paris

94 Edouard Manet, 1832–1883: *The Execution of Maximilian* 1867 oil on canvas $99\frac{1}{4}'' \times 120\frac{1}{8}''$ (252×305 cm). Kunsthalle, Mannheim

95 Edgar Degas, 1834–1917: *Mme Gobillard-Morisot* 1869 oil on canvas $21\frac{3}{8}'' \times 25\frac{5}{8}''$ (54×65 cm). The Metropolitan Museum of Art, New York (Bequest of Mrs H. O. Havemeyer, 1929, The H. O. Havemeyer Collection)

96 Edouard Manet, 1832–1883: *Mme Manet at the Piano* c. 1867 oil on canvas $15'' \times 18\frac{1}{8}''$ (38×46 cm). Louvre, Paris

97 Edouard Manet, 1832–1883: *Portrait of Emile Zola* 1868 oil on canvas $57\frac{1}{8}'' \times 44\frac{7}{8}''$ (145×114 cm). Louvre, Paris, photo Bulloz

98 Edgar Degas, 1834–1917: *Mme Camus with a Japanese Screen* 1870 oil on canvas $28\frac{3}{4}'' \times 36\frac{1}{4}''$ (73×92 cm). National Gallery of Art, Washington, D.C. (Chester Dale Collection)

99 Edouard Manet, 1832–1883: *Queue in front of the Butcher's Shop* 1871 etching $6\frac{5}{8}'' \times 5\frac{3}{4}''$ (1·69×1·45 cm). Courtesy, The Baltimore Museum of Art (George A. Lucas Collection on indefinite loan from the Maryland Institute)

100 Edouard Manet, 1832–1883: *The Game of Croquet* 1873 oil on canvas $28\frac{3}{8}'' \times 41\frac{3}{4}''$ (72·5×106 cm). Städelsches Kunstinstitut, Frankfurt, photo Blauel

101 Edouard Manet, 1832–1883: *River at Argenteuil* 1874 oil on canvas $24\frac{1}{2}'' \times 40\frac{1}{2}''$ (62·3×103 cm). Collection Christabel, Lady Aberconway, London

102 Edouard Manet, 1832–1883: *The Grand Canal, Venice* 1875 oil on canvas $22\frac{1}{2}'' \times 18\frac{7}{8}''$ (57×43 cm). Property of the Crocker Family, San Francisco

103 Edouard Manet, 1832–1883: *On the Beach at Boulogne* 1869 oil on canvas $12\frac{3}{4}'' \times 25\frac{3}{4}''$ (33×65 cm). Collection of Mr and Mrs Paul Mellon

104 Edgar Degas, 1834–1917: *At the Seaside* c. 1876 paper mounted on canvas $18\frac{1}{2}'' \times 32\frac{1}{2}''$ (47×82·5 cm). Trustees of the National Gallery, London

105 Edouard Manet, 1832–1883: *The Departure of the Folkestone Boat* 1869 oil on canvas $23\frac{1}{2}'' \times 28\frac{5}{8}''$ (60×73 cm). Philadelphia Museum of Art (Mr and Mrs Carroll S. Tyson Collection)

106 Edouard Manet, 1832–1883: *Lady with the Fans* 1873–4 oil on canvas $44\frac{1}{2}'' \times 69\frac{1}{4}''$ (113×176 cm). Louvre, Paris

107 Edouard Manet, 1832–1883: *The Road Menders in the Rue de Berne* 1877–8 oil on canvas $25'' \times 31\frac{1}{2}''$ (64×80 cm). Collection Lord Butler

108 Edgar Degas, 1834–1917: *Place de la Concorde* c. 1875 oil on canvas $31\frac{3}{4}'' \times 47\frac{3}{8}''$ (81×121 cm). Formerly Gerstenberg Collection, Berlin

109 Edgar Degas, 1834–1917: *Melancholy* c. 1874 oil on canvas $7\frac{1}{2}'' \times 9\frac{5}{8}''$ (19×24 cm). The Phillips Collection, Washington, D.C.

110 Edgar Degas, 1834–1917: *Mary Cassatt at the Louvre* c. 1880 pastel $27'' \times 20\frac{1}{4}''$ (69×51 cm). Henry P. McIlhenny Collection, Philadelphia

111 Mary Cassatt, 1845–1926: *The Cup of Tea* oil on canvas $36\frac{3}{8}'' \times 25\frac{?}{4}''$ (93×65 cm). The Metropolitan Museum of Art, New York (Anonymous Gift 1922)

112 Mary Cassatt, 1845–1926: *In the Omnibus* 1891 colour print with dry point, soft ground and aquatint $14\frac{1}{4}'' \times 10\frac{1}{2}''$ (36×27 cm). Courtesy, The Art Institute of Chicago (Martin A. Ryerson Collection)

113 Mary Cassatt, 1845–1926: *Feeding the Ducks* 1895 colour etching $11\frac{5}{8}'' \times 15\frac{3}{4}''$ (30 × 37 cm). The Metropolitan Museum of Art, New York (Bequest of H. O. Havemeyer, 1929)

114 Auguste Renoir, 1841–1919: *Edmond Renoir by the Mediterranean* 1881 crayon and ink $15'' \times 11\frac{1}{4}''$ (38 × 29 cm). Private collection, New York

115 Auguste Renoir, 1841–1919: *La Balançoire* 1876 oil on canvas $36\frac{1}{4}'' \times 28\frac{3}{4}''$ (92 × 73 cm). Louvre, Paris

116 Auguste Renoir, 1841–1919: *Le Moulin de la Galette* 1876 oil on canvas $51\frac{1}{2}'' \times 69''$ (131 × 175 cm). Louvre, Paris

117 Auguste Renoir, 1841–1919: *Mme Charpentier and her Children* 1878 oil on canvas $60\frac{1}{2}'' \times 74\frac{7}{8}''$ (154 × 190 cm). The Metropolitan Museum of Art, New York (Wolfe Fund 1907)

118 Auguste Renoir, 1841–1919: *The Skiff* c. 1879 oil on canvas $28'' \times 36\frac{1}{4}''$ (71 × 92 cm). Collection Christabel, Lady Aberconway, London, photo Courtauld Institute of Art

119 Auguste Renoir, 1841–1919: *La Loge* 1874 oil on canvas $31\frac{1}{2}'' \times 23\frac{7}{8}''$ (80 × 64 cm). Courtauld Institute Galleries, University of London

120 Auguste Renoir, 1841–1919: *Country Road* 1873 oil on canvas $17\frac{1}{4}'' \times 23\frac{1}{2}''$ (44 × 60 cm). From the collection of the Earl of Inchcape

121 Auguste Renoir, 1841–1919: *Monet Working in His Garden* 1873 oil on canvas $19\frac{3}{4}'' \times 24\frac{3}{8}''$ (50 × 62 cm). Courtesy, Wadsworth Atheneum, Hartford (Anne Parrish Titzell Bequest 1957)

122 Auguste Renoir, 1841–1919: *Mme Monet and Her Son in Their Garden at Argenteuil* 1874 oil on canvas $17'' \times 28\frac{3}{4}''$ (43 × 73 cm). Collection of Mrs Mellon Bruce

123 Claude Monet, 1840–1926: *Le Pont de l'Europe, Gare St-Lazare* 1877 oil on canvas $25\frac{5}{8}'' \times 31\frac{7}{8}''$ (65 × 81 cm). Musée Marmottan, Paris

124 Claude Monet, 1840–1926: *Gare St-Lazare* 1877 oil on canvas $32\frac{1}{4}'' \times 39\frac{3}{4}''$ (87 × 101 cm). The Fogg Art Museum, Harvard University, Cambridge, Mass. (Maurice Wertheim Collection)

125 Claude Monet, 1840–1926: *Winter in Vétheuil* 1878–81 oil on canvas $23\frac{1}{2}'' \times 39\frac{1}{2}''$ (60 × 101 cm). Albright-Knox Art Gallery, Buffalo, New York

126 Claude Monet, 1840–1926: *Vétheuil* 1884 oil on canvas $23\frac{5}{8}'' \times 39\frac{1}{4}''$ (60 × 100 cm). The Metropolitan Museum of Art, New York (Bequest of William Church Osborn 1951)

127 Claude Monet, 1840–1926: *Rue Montorgueil Decked out with Flags* 1878 oil on canvas $21\frac{1}{4}'' \times 13''$ (62 × 33 cm). Musée des Beaux-Arts, Rouen

128 Claude Monet, 1840–1926: *The Harbour, Le Havre* 1873 oil on canvas $29'' \times 39''$ (73·5 × 99 cm). Private collection

129 Camille Pissarro, 1830–1903: *Path through the Fields* 1879 oil on canvas $21\frac{1}{4}'' \times 25\frac{5}{8}''$ (54 × 65 cm). Louvre, Paris

130 Camille Pissarro, 1830–1903: *Harvest at Montfoucault* 1876 oil on canvas $25\frac{1}{2}'' \times 36\frac{1}{4}''$ (65 × 92 cm). Louvre, Paris

131 Camille Pissarro, 1830–1903: *Misty Morning at Creil* 1873 oil on canvas $5\frac{7}{8}'' \times 8\frac{5}{8}''$ (15 × 22 cm). Collection R. Peto

132 Camille Pissarro, 1830–1903: *Potato Harvest* 1886 etching $10\frac{7}{8}'' \times 8\frac{5}{8}''$ (28 × 22 cm). New York Public Library, Prints Division (S. P. Avery Collection)

133 Camille Pissarro, 1830–1903: *Woman with a Wheelbarrow* 1880 etching $12\frac{5}{8}'' \times 9''$ (32 × 23 cm). Courtesy, Trustees of the British Museum, London

134 Camille Pissarro, 1830–1903: *The Seine at Marly* 1871 oil on canvas $17\frac{1}{4}'' \times 23\frac{1}{2}''$ (44 × 60 cm). Collection R. Peto

135 Alfred Sisley, 1839–1899: *Floods at Port-Marly* 1876 oil on canvas $23\frac{5}{8}'' \times 32''$ (60 × 81 cm). Louvre, Paris

136 Alfred Sisley, 1839–1899: *Wooden Bridge at Argenteuil* 1872 oil on canvas $15'' \times 13\frac{5}{8}''$ (38×60 cm). Louvre, Paris

137 Alfred Sisley, 1839–1899: *Bridge at Hampton Court* 1874 oil on canvas $18\frac{1}{8}'' \times 24''$ (46×61 cm). Wallraf-Richartz Museum, Cologne, photo Rheinisches Bildarchiv

138 Alfred Sisley, 1839–1899: *Snow at Veneux-Nadon* 1879–82 oil on canvas $21\frac{1}{4}'' \times 28\frac{3}{4}''$ (54×73 cm). Louvre, Paris

139 Alfred Sisley, 1839–1899: *Misty Morning* 1874 oil on canvas $19\frac{5}{8}'' \times 24''$ (50×61 cm). Louvre, Paris

140 Paul Cézanne, 1839–1906: *The Rape* 1867 oil on canvas $35\frac{1}{4}'' \times 46''$ (90×117 cm). From the collection of the late Lord Keynes

141 Paul Cézanne, 1839–1906: *The Black Clock* 1870 oil on canvas $21\frac{3}{4}'' \times 29\frac{1}{4}''$ (55×74 cm). Stavros Niarchos Collection

142 Paul Cézanne, 1839–1906: *A Modern Olympia* 1872–3 oil on canvas $18\frac{1}{2}'' \times 22''$ (46×55 cm). Louvre, Paris

143 Paul Cézanne, 1839–1906: *Les Chaumières à Auvers* 1873 oil on canvas $27\frac{5}{8}'' \times 22\frac{1}{2}''$ ($70{\cdot}2 \times 57{\cdot}2$ cm). Collection Daniel Maggin

144 Paul Cézanne, 1839–1906: *Street in Pontoise, Winter* 1873 oil on canvas $15\frac{1}{4}'' \times 18\frac{1}{2}''$ (39×47 cm). Collection Bernheim-Jeune

145 Paul Cézanne, 1839–1906: *View of Louveciennes* 1872–3 oil on canvas $28\frac{3}{4}'' \times 36\frac{1}{4}''$ (73×92 cm). Private collection

146 Paul Cézanne, 1839–1906: *L'Estaque c.* 1885 oil on canvas $28'' \times 22\frac{3}{4}''$ ($71 \times 57{\cdot}7$ cm). Collection Lord Butler

147 Paul Cézanne, 1839–1906: *House of Père Lacroix, Auvers* 1873 oil on canvas $24\frac{1}{4}'' \times 20''$ (62×51 cm). National Gallery of Art, Washington, D.C. (Chester Dale Collection)

148 Paul Cézanne, 1839–1906: *House of Dr Gachet, Auvers* 1873 oil on canvas $24\frac{1}{4}'' \times 20\frac{1}{4}''$ (62×51 cm). Collection of Mr and Mrs James W. Fosburgh

149 Paul Cézanne, 1839–1906: *Victor Chocquet* 1875–7 oil on canvas $18\frac{1}{8}'' \times 14\frac{1}{8}''$ (46×36 cm). Private Collection

150 Paul Cézanne, 1839–1906: *The Seine at Bercy* 1875–80 oil on canvas $23\frac{1}{4}'' \times 28\frac{1}{2}''$ ($59 \times 72{\cdot}5$ cm). Kunsthalle, Hamburg

151 Paul Gauguin, 1848–1903: *Vision after the Sermon* 1888 oil on canvas $28\frac{3}{4}'' \times 36\frac{1}{4}''$ (73×92 cm). National Gallery of Scotland, Edinburgh

152 Paul Gauguin, 1848–1903: *Landscape at Viroflay* 1875 oil on canvas $18'' \times 13''$ (46×33 cm). Kaplan Gallery, London, S.W.1

153 Paul Gauguin, 1848–1903: *Garden of Vaugirard Seen from the Rue Carcel* 1879 oil on canvas $22'' \times 18''$ ($56 \times 45{\cdot}75$ cm). Property of Mr and Mrs Paul Kantor

154 Paul Gauguin, 1848–1903: *Landscape with Cattle* 1885 oil on canvas $22'' \times 15\frac{3}{4}''$ ($56{\cdot}5 \times 40$ cm). Museum Boymans-van Beuningen, Rotterdam

155 Paul Gauguin, 1848–1903: *Winter, Rue Carcel, Paris* 1883 oil on canvas $46\frac{1}{8}'' \times 35\frac{3}{8}''$ (117×90 cm). Private Collection

156 Paul Gauguin, 1848–1903: *Entrance to a Village* 1884 oil on canvas $23\frac{1}{2}'' \times 28\frac{3}{4}''$ ($59{\cdot}5 \times 73$ cm). Courtesy, Museum of Fine Arts, Boston (Bequest of John T. Spaulding)

157 Paul Gauguin, 1848–1903: *Landscape, Pont-Aven* 1885–7 oil on canvas $23\frac{1}{2}'' \times 28\frac{1}{2}''$ (60×72 cm). National Gallery of Canada, Ottawa (acquired with a gift from H. S. Southam)

158 Paul Gauguin, 1848–1903: *Nursemaid* 1880 oil on canvas $44\frac{7}{8}'' \times 31\frac{1}{8}''$ (114×79 cm). Ny Carlsberg Glyptotek, Copenhagen

159 Paul Gauguin, 1848–1903: *Breton Seascape* 1886 oil on canvas $30'' \times 43\frac{3}{4}''$ (76×111 cm). Wildenstein & Co. Ltd, London

160 Paul Gauguin, 1848–1903: *Martinique Landscape* 1887 oil on canvas $9\frac{1}{2}'' \times 11\frac{3}{4}''$ (24×30 cm). Collection Mr and Mrs Robert E. Eisner, New York

161 Vincent van Gogh, 1853–1890: *Le Moulin de la Galette, Montmartre* 1886 oil on canvas $18'' \times 15''$ (46×38 cm). Glasgow Art Gallery and Museum

162 Vincent van Gogh, 1853–1890: *Boulevard de Clichy* 1886–7 pen and coloured chalks $14\frac{3}{4}'' \times 20\frac{1}{2}''$ (37×52 cm). Ir V. W. van Gogh Collection

163 Vincent van Gogh, 1853–1890: *View of an Industrial Town* 1887–8 watercolour $15\frac{3}{8}'' \times 21\frac{1}{4}''$ (39×54 cm). Gemeente Musea van Amsterdam

164 Vincent van Gogh, 1853–1890: *Fishing in Spring* 1886–7 oil on canvas $19\frac{1}{4}'' \times 22\frac{7}{8}''$ (49×58 cm). Courtesy, The Art Institute of Chicago (Gift of Charles Deering McCormick, Brooks McCormick and Roger McCormick)

165 Vincent van Gogh, 1853–1890: *The Yellow Books, Parisian Novels* 1887 oil on canvas $27\frac{5}{8}'' \times 35\frac{3}{8}''$ (70×90 cm). Private Collection, Zurich

166 Vincent van Gogh, 1853–1890: *View from Van Gogh's Room, Rue Lepic, Paris* 1887 oil on canvas $18\frac{1}{4}'' \times 15''$ (46×38 cm). Ir V. W. van Gogh Collection

167 Lucien Pissarro, 1863–1944: *Vincent van Gogh and Félix Fénéon in Conversation* black chalk on paper $7\frac{7}{8}'' \times 8\frac{3}{4}''$ (18×22·5 cm). Ashmolean Museum, Oxford, Department of Western Art

168 Auguste Renoir, 1841–1919: *Paul Durand-Ruel* 1910 oil on canvas $25\frac{3}{4}'' \times 21\frac{1}{2}''$ (65×55 cm). Collection Durand-Ruel

169 Georges Seurat, 1859–1891: *Study for Une Baignade c.* 1883 oil on panel $10\frac{3}{8}'' \times 6\frac{3}{4}''$ (26×17 cm). William Rockhill Nelson Gallery of Art, Kansas (Nelson Fund)

170 Claude Monet, 1840–1926: *Break-up of the Ice, Lavacourt* 1880 oil on canvas $26\frac{3}{4}'' \times 35\frac{1}{2}''$ (68×90 cm). C. S. Gulbenkian Collection

171 Claude Monet, 1840–1926: *Sunshine and Snow, Lavacourt* 1881 oil on canvas $23\frac{1}{2}'' \times 31\frac{3}{4}''$ (59·5×81 cm). Trustees of the National Gallery, London

172 Claude Monet, 1840–1926: *Fishing Nets, Pourville* 1882 oil on canvas $23\frac{5}{8}'' \times 31\frac{7}{8}''$ (60×81 cm). Gemeentemuseum, The Hague

173 Claude Monet, 1840–1926: *Boats in Winter Quarters, Etretat* 1885 oil on canvas $29\frac{1}{4}'' \times 36\frac{1}{2}''$ (74×93 cm). The Art Institute of Chicago (Potter Palmer Collection)

174 Claude Monet, 1840–1926: *Haystacks, Sunset* 1891 oil on canvas $25\frac{5}{8}'' \times 39\frac{3}{8}''$ (65×100 cm). Collection Durand-Ruel, Paris, photo Durand-Ruel

175 Claude Monet, 1840–1926: *Poplars on the Epte* 1891 oil on canvas $35'' \times 28\frac{1}{2}''$ (89×72 cm). Trustees of the Tate Gallery, London

176 Claude Monet, 1840–1926: *Waterloo Bridge, Grey Day* 1903 oil on canvas $25\frac{5}{8}'' \times 39\frac{3}{8}''$ (65×100 cm). National Gallery of Art, Washington, D.C. (Chester Dale Collection)

177 Claude Monet, 1840–1926: *Rouen Cathedral: Full Sunlight* 1894 oil on canvas $42\frac{1}{2}'' \times 28\frac{3}{4}''$ (107×73 cm). Louvre, Paris

178 Claude Monet, 1840–1926: *Water Lilies* 1899 oil on canvas $35'' \times 36\frac{1}{4}''$ (89×92 cm). Trustees of the National Gallery, London

179 Claude Monet, 1840–1926: *Water Lilies* 1904 oil on canvas $35\frac{3}{8}'' \times 36\frac{1}{4}''$ (90×92 cm). Louvre, Paris, photo Giraudon

180 Auguste Renoir, 1841–1919: *Les Grandes Baigneuses c.* 1887 oil on canvas $45\frac{3}{4}'' \times 67''$ (116×170 cm). Philadelphia Museum of Art (Mr and Mrs Carroll S. Tyson Collection)

181 Auguste Renoir, 1841–1919: *Les Parapluies c.* 1884 oil on canvas $71'' \times 45\frac{1}{4}''$ (180×115 cm). Trustees of the National Gallery, London

182 Auguste Renoir, 1841–1919: *Mlle Lerolle at the Piano* c. 1892 drawing $25\frac{5}{8}'' \times 19''$ (61·5 × 47·5 cm). Collection Durand-Ruel, photo Durand-Ruel

183 Auguste Renoir, 1841–1919: *Maternité* 1885 oil on canvas $29\frac{1}{2}'' \times 23\frac{1}{4}''$ (75 × 59 cm). Collection Philippe Gangnat

184 Auguste Renoir, 1841–1919: *La Boulangère* 1904 oil on canvas $21\frac{5}{8}'' \times 25\frac{3}{4}''$ (55 × 65 cm). Stavros Niarchos Collection

185 Auguste Renoir, 1841–1919: *Gabrielle with an Open Blouse* 1907 oil on canvas $25\frac{5}{8}'' \times 20\frac{7}{8}''$ (65 × 53 cm). Collection Durand-Ruel

186 Auguste Renoir, 1841–1919: *Gabrielle Reading* 1890 oil on canvas $21\frac{1}{4}'' \times 25\frac{5}{8}''$ (54 × 65 cm). Collection Durand-Ruel, photo Durand-Ruel

187 Auguste Renoir, 1841–1919: *La Ferme des Collettes* 1910 oil on canvas $16\frac{1}{4}'' \times 21\frac{1}{2}''$ (41 × 54·5 cm). Collection Philippe Gangnat

188 Camille Pissarro, 1830–1903: *L'Île Lacroix, Rouen* 1888 oil on canvas $21\frac{1}{4}'' \times 25\frac{5}{8}''$ (54 × 65 cm). John G. Johnson Collection, Philadelphia

189 Camille Pissarro, 1830–1903: *Landscape, Eragny* 1895 oil on canvas $23\frac{5}{8}'' \times 28\frac{3}{4}''$ (60 × 73 cm). Louvre, Paris

190 Camille Pissarro, 1830–1903: *The Great Bridge at Rouen* 1896 oil on canvas $29'' \times 36''$ (74 × 91 cm). Museum of Art, Carnegie Institute, Pittsburgh

191 Camille Pissarro, 1830–1903: *Le Pont des Arts and the Louvre* 1902 oil on canvas $21\frac{1}{2}'' \times 25\frac{1}{2}''$ (55 × 65 cm). Schoneman Galleries, New York

192 Camille Pissarro, 1830–1903: *Place du Théâtre Français* 1898 oil on canvas $28\frac{1}{2}'' \times 36\frac{1}{2}''$ (72 × 93 cm). County Museum of Art, Los Angeles (Mr and Mrs George Gard de Sylva Collection)

193 Camille Pissarro, 1830–1903: *Self-Portrait* 1888 pen and ink on paper $6\frac{9}{10}'' \times 5\frac{1}{8}''$ (17 × 13 cm). Courtesy of the S. P. Avery Collection, The New York Public Library (Astor, Lenox and Tilden Foundations)

194 Philip Wilson Steer, 1860–1942: *Sands of Boulogne* 1892 oil on canvas $23\frac{5}{8}'' \times 29\frac{7}{8}''$ (60 × 76 cm). Trustees of the Tate Gallery, London

195 Walter R. Sickert, 1860–1942: *Piazza San Marco* 1902–3 oil on canvas $6\frac{1}{4}'' \times 7\frac{7}{8}''$ (16 × 20 cm). Laing Art Gallery, Newcastle upon Tyne

196 Walter R. Sickert, 1860–1942: *Le Puits Salé* c. 1890 pencil and watercolour $7'' \times 4\frac{3}{4}''$ (18 × 12 cm). Collection Martin Halperin

197 Max Liebermann, 1847–1935: *Terrace of Restaurant Jacob* 1902 pastel $98\frac{3}{8}'' \times 192\frac{7}{8}''$ (250 × 490 cm). Kunsthalle, Hamburg

198 Lovis Corinth, 1858–1925: *Emperors Day in Hamburg* 1911 oil on canvas $28\frac{5}{8}'' \times 36''$ (70 × 90·5 cm). Wallraf-Richartz Museum, Cologne

199 Max Slevogt, 1868–1932: *Landscape in the Palatinate* 1927 oil on canvas $34\frac{5}{8}'' \times 41\frac{3}{8}''$ (88 × 105 cm). Nationalgalerie, Staatliche Museen, Berlin

200 Isidro Nonell, 1873–1911: *Suburbio* 1894 oil on canvas $12\frac{1}{4}'' \times 14\frac{1}{8}''$ (31 × 36 cm). Collection T. Valenti

201 Ramon Casas, 1866–1932: *Plein Air* Museo de Arte Moderna, Barcelona

202 John Singer Sargent, 1856–1925: *Claude Monet Painting at the Edge of a Wood* 1888 oil on canvas $21'' \times 25\frac{1}{2}''$ (53 × 65 cm). Trustees of the Tate Gallery, London

203 Theodore Robinson, 1852–1896: *Sunlight and Shadows* 1896 oil on canvas $56\frac{1}{4}'' \times 21\frac{1}{2}''$ (143 × 55 cm). Collection Florence Lewison Gallery, New York

204 Albert Lebourg, 1849–1928: *Le Port d'Alger* 1876 oil on canvas $15'' \times 18''$ (38 × 46 cm). Kaplan Gallery, London, S.W.1

205 Gustave Loiseau, 1865–1935: *St Mammes Moret-sur-Loing* c. 1899 oil on canvas $22'' \times 29''$ (56 × 74 cm). Private Collection, Edinburgh

206 H. le Sidaner, 1862–1939: *Gisors Gris, Pignon Gris* 1914 oil on canvas 26"× 32" (66×82 cm). Kaplan Gallery, London, S.W.1

207 Edouard Vuillard, 1868–1940: *Under the Trees* 1894 tempera on canvas 84½" ×38⅜" (215×98 cm). The Cleveland Museum of Art, Gift of Hanna Fund

208 Pierre Bonnard, 1867–1947: *Nude in a Bathtub* 1935 oil on canvas 40½"×25⅝" (103×64 cm). Collection R. T., France

209 Henri Matisse, 1869–1954: *The Dinner Table* oil on canvas 39¼"×51½" (100×131 cm). Stavros Niarchos Collection

Index

Numbers in italic refer to illustrations

Académie Suisse, 38, 40, 66, 180
Arrowsmith, John, 22
Astruc, Zacharie, 76

Balla, Giacomo, 259
Barbizon painters, 9, 15, 19, 23, 26, 30–1, 255, 259
Barlow, Samuel, 251–2
Baudelaire, Charles, 7, 12, 18, 19, 34, 40, 73, 91, 118, 120, 124, 127, 133, 137, 182, 264
Bazille, Frédéric, 16, 47, 52, 68, 69, 71–2, 78, 85, 86, 89, 93, 95, 109, 112, 218, 263–4; *The Artist's Studio, Rue de la Condamine*, 8, 95, *95*; *Portrait of Renoir*, *71*; *Réunion de Famille*, 16, *16*; *La Robe Rose*, 81; *Terrasse de Méric*, 16; *The Walls of Aigues-Mortes*, *109*
Bérard, Paul, 158–9, 242
Bernard, Émile, 203, 206, 215, 217
Bertin, Victor, 19
Blanc, Charles, 12, 31
Boccioni, Umberto, 259
Boggs, Jean, 144–5
Bonington, Richard Parkes, 25
Bonnard, Pierre, 267–8; *Nude in a Bathtub*, *266*
Bonnat, Léon, 132
Boudin, Eugène, 9, 31, 34, 35, 64–5, 67, 96, 113; *Jetty at Trouville*, *34*
Bowness, Alan, 137
Braque, Georges, 225
Brasserie, Andler, 89, 124
Bruyas, Alfred, 68–9, 78
Buchser, Frank, 79

Café Guerbois, 52, 88, *89*
Caillebotte, Gustave, 140, 165
Carrière, Eugène, 196
Casas, Ramon, 257; *Plein Air*, 259
Cassatt, Mary, 146, 148, 150, 260; *The Cup of Tea*, *148*; *Feeding the Ducks*, *150*; *In the Omnibus*, *149*

Castagnary, Jules-Antoine, 40, 54, 67
Cézanne, Paul, 12, 32, 37, 61, 72, 88, 110, 111, 113, 179–84, 186, 188, 193, 200, 217, 218, 219, 240, 249–50, 267; *Apotheosis of Delacroix*, *11*, *12*; *Autopsy*, 181; *The Black Clock*, 181–2, *183*; *Les Chaumières à Auvers*, *185*; *L'Estaque*, 188, *189*; *House of Dr Gachet, Auvers*, *191*; *House of Père Lacroix, Auvers*, *190*; *Maison du Pendu*, 116, 186; *Melting Snow at L'Estaque*, 182; *Melting Snow in Fontainebleau*, 16; *A Modern Olympia*, *184*; *The Picnic*, 181; *Self-portrait*, 16, *18*; *Street in Pontoise, Winter*, 186, *187*; *Tannhäuser Overture*, 183; *The Rape*, 181, *181*; *The Seine at Bercy*, 193; *Victor Choquet*, *192*; *View of Louveciennes*, 186, *187*
Charpentier, Georges, 158, 242
Charpentier, Mme, 158, *155*
Chevreul, Eugène, 14–15, 243–4
Choquet, Victor, 153, *192*
Clark, Kenneth, 60, 100, 151
Claude Lorrain, 20
Clausen, Sir George, 255
Coldstream, William, 62
Constable, John, 9, 10, 20–3, 25, 30, 100–1, 104; *The Bridge on the Stour*, 22; *The Haywain*, 21, 22; *Study for The Haywain*, *21*; *Study of Sky and Trees*, 10, *13*
Corinth, Lovis, 256; *Emperors Day in Hamburg*, 256, *256*; *Under the Chandelier*, 256
Corot, Jean-Baptiste-Camille, 7, 8, 9, 15, 19, 25, 27–8, 30, 31, 38, 81, 113, 175, 197, 208, 251; *Fontainebleau, le charretier et les bucherons*, *24*; *Forest of Fontainebleau*, 24, 25; *Harbour of La Rochelle*, 29, 30; *L'Hôtel Cabassus à Ville d'Avray*, *29*; *Le Pont de Narni*, 27; *View near Volterra*, 28, 30

Cotman, John Sell, 25
Courbet, Gustave, 7, 9, 26, 31–2, 42–4,
    52, 53, 66, 77, 78–80, 91, 124, 175;
    After Dinner at Ornans, 32; *Baigneuses*,
    79; *Bonjour Monsieur Courbet*, 69, *69*,
    186; *Demoiselles au bord de la Seine*, 52,
    79; *The Sleeping Spinner*, 32, *32*; *Le
    vieux pont*, *43*, 44
Couture, Thomas, 64, 120, 136; *Romains
    de la Décadence*, 136

Daubigny, Charles-François, 23, 25, 30,
    31, 39, 52, 65, 77, 81, 100, 140, 197,
    251; *Evening*, *76*, 77
Daulte, F. 72
Daumier, Honoré, 81, 118, 136
Decamps, Alexandre Gabriel, 39
Degas, Edgar, 47, 60, 72, 84, 88, 108,
    111, 113, 118, 120–9, 131–2, 140,
    144–6, 148, 153, 176, 205, 226, 251,
    252, 255, 260; *At the Seaside*, *138*, 140;
    Carriage at the Races, 116, *116*; *Col-
    lector of Prints*, 132; *The Cotton Ex-
    change, New Orleans*, 122, *123*; *The
    Dancing Class*, *119*; *Mme Camus with
    a Japanese Screen*, *131*; *Mme Gobillard-
    Morisot*, *128*, 132; *Les Malheurs de
    la Ville d'Orléans*, 93, *93*; *Mary Cassatt
    at the Louvre*, *147*; *Melancholy*, *109*;
    Nursemaid in the Luxembourg Gardens,
    121; *The Pedicure*, 122, *122*, 153;
    Place de la Concorde, 145, *145*; *Semi-
    ramis Founding a Town*, *126*, 128
Delacroix, Eugène, 7, 8, 12, 14, 21–2, 25,
    26, 31, 72, 79, 153, 182, 196, 208, 210,
    251; *Femmes d'Alger*, 27, 72, *108*; *The
    Jewish Wedding*, 108; *The Justice of
    Trajan*, 72; *The Massacre at Chios*,
    21–2, *22*; *Study for Femmes d'Alger*, *26*
Délécluze, 21
Denis, Maurice, 217
Dewhurst, Wynford, 101
Durand-Ruel, Paul, 100, 104, 112, 217,
    218, *219*, 220, 230, 246–7, 251, 259,
    260, 261
Duranty, Edmond, 46, 88–9, 91, 92, 118,
    153, 170–1
Duret, Théodore, 111–12

Easton, Malcolm, 8

Faison, S. Lane, 132

Fantin-Latour, Henri, 83, 92–3, 113,
    251; *Homage to Delacroix*, 8, 93, *94*;
    *Julia, Daughter of Augustus, Returning
    from a Night's Debauch*, 93; *A Studio in
    the Batignolles Quarter*, 93, *94*
Fauves, 215
Fénéon, Félix, 61, *215*, 227
Flaubert, Gustave, 7, 20, 124
Fromentin, Eugène, 39
Fry, Roger, 62, 136, 144, 255

Galérie Martinet, 73, 118
Gauguin, Émile, 197
Gauguin, Mette (née Gad), 196–7
Gauguin, Paul, 129, 167, 180, 186, 193,
    194–200, 202–3, 205–7, 215, 221,
    226–7, 239, 244, 249; *Breton Seascape*,
    205, *205*; *Entrance to a Village*, *202*,
    203; *Farm in Martinique*, *206*; *Garden
    of Vaugirard seen from the Rue Carcel*,
    199; *Landscape at Viroflay*, 197, *198*;
    Landscape in Normandy, 197; *Land-
    scape, Pont-Aven*, *203*; *Landscape with
    Cattle*, *200*; *Martinique Landscape*, *208*;
    Nursemaid, *204*, 205; *Portrait of Marie
    Henry*, 200; *Still-life with a Mandolin*,
    186; *The Sculptor Aubi and his Son*,
    205; *Vision after the Sermon*, 196, *197*,
    206; *Winter, Rue Carcel, Paris*, 201,
    203
Gautier, Théophile, 11–12, 30, 124, 161
George, Waldemar, 144
Gérôme, Jean-Léon, 92; *Sword Dance*,
    92, *92*
Girtin, Thomas, 25
Gleyre, Marc-Gabriel-Charles, 32, 40,
    46, 47–8, 57, 68, 69, 73; *La Charmeuse*,
    48
Goldwater, Robert, 194
Gombrich, E. H. 9
Goncourt brothers, 7, 36, 118, 124, 214,
    267
Gonzalès, Eva, 84
Gowing, Lawrence, 46
Goya, Francisco de, 126, 136; *Woman on
    the Balcony*, 84
Grappe, Georges, 61
Greenberg, Clement, 139
Guichard, J.-B. 81
Guillaumin, Armand, 46, 180, 213, 239;
    The Bridge of Louis Philippe, Paris, *45*
Guillemet, Antoine, 27, 182, 218

Hamerton, P. G. 104
Hartrick, A. S. 213
Helmholtz, Hermann, 15
Henry, Charles, 243
Herbert, R. L. 218
Hoschedé, Ernest, 112, 165
Hoschedé, Mme, 165
Huet, Paul, 23; *Distant View of Rouen*, 23; *Stormy Sea*, 23, *23*
Hugo, Victor, 120
Huysmans, J. K. 195, 203, 205, 214, 217, 218, 221

Impressionist exhibitions: (1874) 112–13, 116–17; (1876) 160; (1877) 170; (1879) 148, 159, 165; (1880) 159, 205; (1881) 159, 205; (1882) 205; (1886) 205, 244
Ingres, Jean-Auguste-Dominique, 12, 26, 221
Isabey, J. B. 35

Jacque, Charles-Émile, 25
Japanese art, 90–1, 100, 107, 136, 210–11, 244
Johnson, Lee, 14, 26
Jongkind, Johann-Barthold, 9, 35–6, 67, 68, 197; *The Beach at Sainte-Adresse*, 36, *36*; *Sortie du Port de Honfleur*, 35

Kahn, Gustave, 221
Kandinsky, Wassily, 227

Laforgue, Jules, 177–8, 216
Landscape painting, 18–22, 25, 43, 124, 173, 184–5
Lanes, Jerrold, 37, 169–70
Lebourg, Albert, *Pont d'Alger*, 262
Lecadre, Mme, 65, 68
Le Cœur, Charles, 108
Le Cœur, Jules, 52
Legros, Alphonse, 113
Leiris, Alain de, 140
Lépine, Stanislas, 113
Liebermann, Max, 256; *Terrace of Restaurant Jacob*, 255
Loiseau, Gustave, *St Mammes Moret-sur-Loing*, 262
Louis-Napoleon, 73, 100

Macchiaioli, 65, 257–8
Mallarmé, Stéphane, 120, 150, 195

Manet, Édouard, 9, 19, 52, 53, 73, 76, 78, 80–1, 83, 84, 88, 90, 93, 95, 108–9, 113, 118, 120–9, 131–3, 136–7, 139–41, 144, 175, 182, 194, 200, 251, 253, 255, 264; *The Balcony*, 83; *The Barricade*, *125*, 126, 140; *Bon-Bock*, 112, 140; *Café Guerbois*, *89*; *Civil War*, 140; *Déjeuner sur l'Herbe*, 73, 124, 181; *Study for Déjeuner sur l'Herbe*, *79*; *The Departure of the Folkestone Boat*, 139, *139*; *The Execution of Maximilian*, 126, 127; *Fife Major*, 251; *The Game of Croquet*, *134*; *The Grand Canal, Venice*, 135, 141; *The Kersearge and Alabama*, 121; *Lady with the Fans*, 141, *141*; *Lola de Valence*, 73; *Lunch in the Studio*, 137; *Mme Manet at the Piano*, *129*, 132; *Moonlight, Boulogne-surmer*, 251; *Musique aux Tuileries*, 73, 74–5, 118, 123; *Nana*, 153; *Olympia*, 131; *On the Beach at Boulogne*, *138*, 140; *Portrait of Emile Zola*, *130*, 132; *Queue in front of the Butcher's Shop*, *133*, 137; *River at Argenteuil*, *134*; *The Road Menders in the Rue de Berne*, 141, *142–3*; *Rue Mosnier with Flags*, 165; *Spanish Dancers*, 73
Manet, Eugène, 84
Marx, Roger, 36
Matisse, Henri, 144, 215, 263, 269; *The Dinner Table*, *268*, 269
Maxwell, James Clerk, 15, 243–4
Meissonier, Ernest, 140
Melbye, Antoine, 38
Melbye, Fritz, 38
Michallon, Claude, 8
Millet, Jean-François, 30, 31, 64, 77, 208; *L'Arrivée au Barbizon*, *90*, 91
Monet, Camille (née Doncieux), 81, 85, 96, 100, 165
Monet, Claude, 7, 8, 10, 11, 14, 31, 34, 35–6, 37, 40, 47, 48, 53, 54–7, 61–9, 71–2, 76–9, 80–1, 85–6, 88, 93, 95, 96, 100–1, 104–5, 112–13, 140–1, 151, 153, 160–1, 164–5, 167, 182, 216, 218, 220–8, 230, 232–3; *Beach at Sainte-Adresse*, 67, 68; *Boats in Winter Quarters at Etretat*, 223, *226*; *Boulevard des Capucines*, 16, *17*, 117; *Break-up of the Ice, Lavacourt*, 221, *222*; *Breakwater at Honfleur*, 36, *46*, 68; *Déjeuner sur l'Herbe*, 78, 80; *Evening Meal*, 77;

Farmyard in Normandy, 77, *77*; *Fishing Nets, Pourville*, 223, *224*; *Gare St-Lazare*, 161, *162–3*, 164; *Haystacks, Sunset*, 227, *228*; *Hyde Park*, 100, *101*; *Impressionism, Sunrise*, 113, *114–15*; *Japanese Footbridge*, 63; *Jardin de l'Infante*, 86; *La Grenouillère*, 54, *54*; *Mario Ochard*, *64*; *On the Beach, Trouville*, 96, *96*; *Poplars on the Epte*, 224, 228, *229*; *Le Pont de l'Europe, Gare St-Lazare*, 161; *Quai du Louvre, Paris*, 85, 86; *Road in the Forest with Wood Gatherers*, 76; *Rouen Cathedral: Full Sunlight*, 229–30, *231*; *Rough Sea, Etretat*, 61, *62*; *Rue Montorgueil Decked out with Flags*, 165, *166*; *Study for Déjeuner sur l'Herbe*, *80*; *Sunshine and Snow, Lavacourt*, 223; *The Beach at Trouville, Hôtel des Roches-Noires*, 96, *97*; *The Harbour, Le Havre*, 167; *The River*, 87, *87*; *Unloading Coal*, 105, *106*; *Vétheuil*, 165; *Water Lilies*, 231–2, *232*, *233*; *Waterloo Bridge, Grey Day*, 230, *230*; *Westminster Bridge*, *98–9*, 100; *Winter in Vétheuil*, 164; *Women in the Garden*, 269

Monticelli, Adolphe, 211
Moore, George, 88, 230, 253
Morbelli, Angelo, 259
Moréas, Jean, 195
Moreau, Gustave, 132, 194
Morisot, Berthe, 30, 81, 83–4, 108–9, 113, 136, 137, 140, 150; *Eugène and Julie Manet*, 83; *Harbour of Lorient*, 84, *84*; *Hide-and-Seek*, 116, *117*; *La Lecture*, *82*, 84
Morisot, Edma, 81, *82*, *84*, 84
Morstatt, Marion de, 184

Neo-Impressionism, 105
Nicolson, Benedict, 104, 188
Nieuwerkerke, Count, 31
Nittis, Giuseppe de, 113
Nonell, Isidro, 257; *Suburbio*, 258

Open-air painting, 7, 8, 30, 41, 64–5, 78–9, 81, 101, 124, 184

Perry, Mrs Lilla Cabot, 224, 225
Photography, 15–16, 18
Picasso, Pablo, 137, 215, 217, 225, 257

Pissarro, Camille, 7, 8, 10, 12, 15, 30, 32, 37–46, 85, 88, 91, 100, 101, 104, 110–12, 113, 150, 153, 167, 169–72, 176, 180, 182, 184, 196, 202–3, 211, 212, 216, 217, 239, 243–50; *Banks of the Marne in Winter*, 41, *41*, 44–5, *Cocotiers au Bord de la Mer, St Thomas*, 38–9, *39*; *Corner of a Village*, 40, 41; *Crystal Palace*, 102, 104; *Diligence at Louveciennes*, 110, *110*; *Dulwich College*, *103*; *Entrance to the Village of Voisins*, 104, *105*, 111; *The Gardens of the Hermitage, Pontoise*, *43*; *The Great Bridge at Rouen*, 247; *Harvest at Montfoucault*, *168*; *The Haystack, Pointoise*, *111*, 112; *L'Ile Lacroix, Rouen*, 244, *245*; *Landscape, Eragny*, *246*; *La Roche-Guyon*, 42, *42*; *Lower Norwood, London*, *102*; *Misty Morning at Creil*, *169*; *Path through the Fields*, *168*; *Peasant Woman with a Donkey*, *91*; *Place du Théâtre Français*, 248, *249*; *Place du Vert Galant, Sunny Morning*, 248; *Le Pont de Chemin de Fer, Pontoise*, 169; *Le Pont des Art and the Louvre*, *248*; *Potato Harvest*, *170*; *The Road, Louveciennes*, *106*; *The Seine at Marly*, *172*; *Self-portrait*, *250*; *Upper Norwood*, *103*, 251; *View of Pontoise, Quai du Pothuis*, 44, *44*; *Village Street*, 252; *Woman with a Wheelbarrow*, *171*

Pissarro, Julie (née Vellay), 44, 100
Pissarro, Lucien, 101, 176, 243; *Vincent van Gogh and Félix Fénéon*, 215
Pollock, Jackson, 63
Post-Impressionism, 139, 150, 179, 226–7, 255
Poussin, Nicolas, 19–20; *Gathering of the Ashes of Phocion*, 19, *20*
Prudhon, J.-B. 124
Puvis de Chavannes, Pierre-Cécile, 84, 194–5, 221

Redon, Odilon, 196
Regnier, Jacques Auguste, 23
Renoir, Auguste, 32, 46–8, 52–6, 71, 72, 85, 86, 88, 89, 93, 95, 96, 107–8, 113, 117, 132, 140–1, 151–3, 156, 158–61, 200, 216, 234, 237–42, 260; *Alfred Sisley and his Wife*, 51, *52*; *At the Inn of Mother Anthony*, 32, *32*, 48; *La Baigneuse au Griffon*, 48, *49*, 52, 107; *La*

Balançoire, *154*, *156*; *La Boulangère*,
238; *Boy with a Cat*, 52; *Champs-
Elysées*, 108; *The Children's Afternoon
at Wargemont*, 158; *Country Road*,
158; *The Cup of Coffee*, *159*; *Diane
Chasseresse*, 48, *50*, 52; *Edmond Renoir
by the Mediterranean*, 152, 153; *Femme
d'Alger*, 48, 107; *La Ferme des Collettes*, *242*; *Gabrielle Reading*, 240,
241; *Gabrielle with an Open Blouse*,
239, 240; *Grandes Baigneuses*, *234*,
238; *Harvesters*, 116; *Judgment of Paris*,
240; *La Grenouillère*, 54–5, 55, *56*;
Leaving the Conservatoire, 237; *La
Loge*, 116, 15̀7; *Lise à l'Ombrelle*, 52;
Mme Charpentier and her Children,
155, 158; *Mme Monet and her Son in
their Garden at Argenteuil*, 160; *Mlle
Lerolle at the Piano*, 236; *Maternité*,
237; *Monet Working in his Garden*,
159; *Le Moulin de la Galette*, 155, 156,
238; *The Painter Le Cœur in Fontaine-
bleau Forest*, 32; *Les Parapluies*, 235,
237; *Paul Durand-Ruel*, *219*; *Pont des
Arts, Paris*, 86, *86*, 108; *Pont Neuf*, *107*,
108; *Portrait of Bazille*, 70; *Quai de
Conti*, 108; *River Nymphs*, 240; *The
Skaters in the Bois de Boulogne*, 53, *53*;
The Skiff, *156*
Renoir, Edmond, 113, *152*
Rewald, John, 41, 89–90, 144
Richardson, John, 83, 140
Riopelle, Jean-Paul, 63
Rivière, Georges, 170
Robert, Hubert, 19
Robinson, Theodore, *Sunlight and
Shadows*, *261*
Rodin, Auguste, 62, 227
Romanticism, 8, 9–10, 120, 122, 180
Rood, Ogden N., 15, 243–4
Rosenthal, Leon, 137
Rousseau, Jean, 44–5
Rousseau, Jean-Jacques, 9
Rousseau, Théodore, 10, 23, 25, 30, 31;
Marshy Landscape, 10, *13*; *Valley of
Tiffauge*, 10–11
Ruskin, John, 11

Sainte-Beuve, 7, 12
Salon des Refusés, 73, 112
Salon, 19, 85, 92, 112–13, 118, 127,
136–7, 144, 217; (1824) 21; (1859) 38,
40; (1861) 44; (1863) 44, 73, 76; (1864)
42, 81; (1865) 42, 81, 131; (1866) 41,
81; (1867) 85; (1870) 48, 84, 107;
(1873) 112; (1875) 146; (1876) 197;
(1877) 146
Sandblad, N. G. 123
Sargent, John Singer, 260; *Claude Monet
Painting at the Edge of a Wood*, *260*
Schapiro, Meyer, 121, 188
Scharf, Aaron, 15–16
Schuffenecker, Emile, 146, 202, 203
Segantine, Giovanni, 259
Seitz, W. C. 86–7, 100, 230
Seurat, Georges, 12, 15, 66, 111, 144, 167,
172, 212, 213, 216, 218, 221, 223, 227,
240, 243, 244, 260; *Study for Une
Baignade*, *220*; *Un Dimanche à la
Grande Jatte*, 167, 218; *Une Baignade*,
218
Severini, Giovanni, 136, 259
Sickert, Walter, 253; *Le Puits Salé*, *254*;
Piazza San Marco, *253*
Sidaner, H. le, *Canal at Bruges*, *264*
Signac, Paul, 7, 14, 212, 213, 216, 244
Signol, Émile, 47–8, 73
Sisley, Alfred, 47, 57, 60, 85, 89, 132,
151, 173, 175–7; *Barges on the Canal
St Martin*, 60, *60*; *Bridge at Hampton
Court*, 174, 177; *Canal St Martin, Paris*,
58–9; *Floods at Port-Marly*, 60, *173*,
175; *Misty Morning*, *177*; *Snow at
Veneux-Nadon*, *175*; *Vue de Mont-
marte prise de la Cité des Fleurs*, 57, *57*;
Wooden Bridge at Argenteuil, *174*
Slevogt, Max, 256; *Landscape in the
Palatinate*, *257*
Steer, Wilson, 253; *Sands of Boulogne*,
252
Stokes, Adrian, 61
Strindberg, August, 195, 217
Symbolism, 194–6, 217, 221, 267

Taylor, Basil, 15
'Ten American Painters', 261
Thoré-Burger, Théophile, 25, 121
Tissot, James, 113, 141
Tonks, Henry, 63, 255
Toulmouche, Auguste, 68
Toulouse-Lautrec, Henri de, 129
Tréhot, Lise, 52, *49*, *50*
Troyon, Constant, 23, 31, 64, 65; *Le
Matin*, 65–6, *65*

Turner, J. M. W. 11, 100–1, 104
Twachtman, J. H. 261

Valadon, Suzanne, 129
Valenciennes, Pierre-Henri de, 8, 19; *Tivoli, 9*
Van Gogh, Vincent, 37, 180, 194–5, 206, 207–8, 210–15, 220, 221, 247, 263; *Boulevard de Clichy, 210, 211; The Bridge at Asnières, 211, 212; Fishing in Spring, 212; Interior of a Restaurant, 213; Le Moulin de la Galette, Montmarte, 209; Potato Eaters, 211; View from Van Gogh's Room in the Rue Lepic, Paris, 214; View of an Industrial Town, 211; The Wheatfield,*

213; *The Yellow Books, Parisian Novels, 213, 214*
Velasquez, 124, 137, 146
Venturi, Lionello, 41
Villot, Frédéric, 21
Vollard, Ambroise, 61, 108, 234
Vuillard, Édouard, 267–8, 269; *Under the Trees, 265, 269*

Weir, J. A. 261
Whistler, James, 100, 252
Wolff, Albert, 153

Zola, Émile, 45, 68, 81, 92, 93, 95, 120, 124, *130,* 176, 180, 184, 194, 214, 217, 218, 221, 267